D1096923

FLIGHT

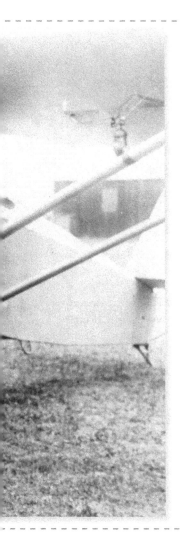

FLIGHT

A Memoir of Loss and Discovery
by an Aviator's Daughter

RASA GUSTAITIS

© 2021 by Rasa Gustaitis

Published by RasaTime Publishing

All rights reserved, including the right to reproduce this book or portions thereof in any form. For information, contact Rasa Gustaitis: rasa@rasatime.com.

Epigraph from *Divisadero*, by Michael Ondaatje. Alfred A. Knopf, New York, 2007, p. 136. Used with permission.

Poem on p. 287, from *Tagore's Last Poems*, by Rabindranath Tagore, transcreated from the Bengali by P. Lal and Shyamasree Devi. Writers Workshop, Calcutta, India, 1972. Used with permission.

Design by Elina Cohen
Maps by David Lindroth

Photos courtesy of their owners. Pages 46, 50, 51, 64, 244, 249, 280, and 288 (bottom): Lithuania's Aviation Museum; Pages 244, 249, 280 and 286 (bottom): Jonas Deltuva; Page 193: Andrej Zdravič; Pages 275–276 and 280: Stasys Daugėla; Page 282: Petras Lozda. All other photographs are from the author's family album.

Library of Congress Control Number: 2021916076

FIRST PAPERBACK EDITION

ISBN: 978 1 7377051 0 9

Printed in the Unites States of America

TO THE MEMORY OF MY MOTHER, BRONĖ GUSTAITIENĖ,
AND MY FATHER, ANTANAS GUSTAITIS

For we live with those retrievals from childhood that coalesce and echo throughout our lives, the way shattered pieces of glass in a kaleidoscope reappear in new forms and are songlike in their refrains and rhymes, making up a single monologue. We live permanently in the recurrence of our own stories, whatever story we tell.

—MICHAEL ONDAATJE

CONTENTS

LATVIA

*BALTIC
SEA*
• Palanga

ŽEMAITIJA

A U K Š T A I T I J A

LITHUANIA

Raseiniai •

Nemunas

Švenioji

RUSSIA
(KALININGRAD)

Šešupė

SUVALKIJA

Kaunas

Neris R.

Nemunas

Sasnava •
Raišupis •
Marijampole •
• Obeline

Vilnius ☆

• Šeštokai

Alytus •

POLAND

BELARUS

0 _____ 40 miles
0 _____ 40 kilometers

(Present-day political boundaries)

ABOUT LITHUANIAN NAMES

The ending of a woman's last name is different from that of the man in the Lithuanian language. It changes according to whether the woman is married or unmarried. The wife of a man named Aleksandravičius is named Aleksandravičienė, and a daughter is Aleksandravičiūtė. The wife of Gustaitis is Gustaitienė, and a daughter is Gustaitytė. A man's last name does not change with marital status. To avoid confusion, many Lithuanians settled abroad have adopted the male form of the last name.

First names have affectionate forms. Elena could be Elytė or Elenutė. Rasa changes to Raselė or Rasutė. Jūratė might be Jūrutė. Bronislava may be Bronė, and Bronytė. Danutė is fondly Danutėlė. Aldona is Aldutė.

Antanas becomes Antanėlis, Jonas is Jonukas, which translates literally to "little Jonas," but "little" is affectionate, more like "dear." Viktoras becomes Viktorėlis. Vytautas, however, is sometimes called Vytas as well as Vytukas. Many other variations exist.

In these pages, Rasa Varkalienė appears as Raselė, to avoid any confusion with the author. Usha would be Ušelė, and Jaden, lovingly, Jadenukas.

With nouns proper and otherwise, suffixes often do the work performed in English by pronouns and prepositions. Lithuanian is an efficient language, as well as being rich and playful.

During my more than fifty years as a working journalist I knew that a time might come when I would want to write a personal story about my father, who disappeared in one of Josef Stalin's prisons in 1941. Before the Red Army invaded our country, he had been the chief of Lithuania's air force. As a daughter and a writer, I felt an obligation to tell that story. Someday.

But what compelled me through the years was always in the present. As a reporter for the *Washington Post* and the *New York Herald Tribune* during the early 1960s, I had close-up glimpses of some of the most historically significant events of our times. Later, in articles for magazines and other publications, I wrote about movements toward a more harmonious future, about far-seeing thinkers and artists. In books, I explored how technology was changing our perception of ourselves and the world. I wrote about struggles for water and other natural resources, and edited a quarterly magazine about the California coast, *California Coast & Ocean*.

Being a journalist allows you to live life as a perennial student.

It enables you to explore whatever interests you, and write about it. I loved my work. Delving into my personal past was not part of it. Eventually, however, the right time arrived. This is not the story about my father I intended to write—it's the memoir that evolved for me to tell.

—*R. G.*
San Francisco, April 2, 2021

1

....

THE END OF THE TIME BEFORE

The moment the world began to collapse around me is precisely recorded in my mind. I can feel it and hear it and see it even now, more than eight decades later.

I was swinging in the rope hammock in the birch grove outside the back door of our home in Kaunas, the second-largest city in Lithuania, near the Baltic Sea. Brushing the tall grass with one bare foot, I was enjoying the soft tickle. Above the treetops, white cumulus clouds were sailing in the pale blue sky, in the shape of sheep, horses, and animals never seen before. In a chair at the foot of the hammock sat my grandmother, Baba, knitting.

It was mandatory nap time, Mama's orders, or at least rest time after a morning of running around with a couple of neighbor kids. Mama was strict on things she thought were good for me and Jūratė, my older sister, and gentle Baba, who spent more time with me than Mama did, carried out her decrees. Mama was beautiful, elegant, and in charge. Baba was plain, rounded, and warm. When she laughed, her belly shook. That was funny and nice when I sat in her lap. I loved to see and feel her laugh.

Rasa, before the Red Army's invasion

In a while, Baba would go into the house and come out with a glass of carrot juice for me, and also the dreaded spoonful of cod liver oil, with a piece of black bread sprinkled with salt to kill the vile taste. Sometimes I tried to avoid it by running away, but whenever I came back she would be waiting for me, ready. It was best to just open my mouth as the spoon approached and be done with it.

Maybe today I could persuade her to make me some *kogil-mogil* before we went for our afternoon walk. This traditional Lithuanian treat is made of egg yolks beaten with sugar, with some of the whites folded in, and sometimes a bit of cocoa. Then Jūratė would be home from school, and I'd try to hang around while she had a lesson from Phyllis, the English governess who lived with us. I was learning English too, just by listening.

In a couple of weeks Jūratė's school vacation would begin, and then we'd go to Palanga, a resort town on the Baltic Sea, and spend two months there. Phyllis would come with us for a while, then return to Birmingham to visit her family during August. My father,

Brigadier General Antanas Gustaitis, would take us to Palanga and then come back, to work, usually returning to visit us from Saturday afternoon to Sunday. He designed and built airplanes and also was the chief of Lithuania's air force.

I'D HAD ENOUGH of cloud animals and thoughts of the seashore and my right foot was tingling.

"Grandma, maybe it's enough? Can I get up?"

"All right," she said. And then the day was shattered by a man's loud voice at our doorway: "The Russians have already crossed the border!"

Baba drew in her breath and crossed herself.

"*Bozhe moi*," she said softly. My God.

I looked up at her face and saw fear. In Lithuanian, the word for border is the same as the word for wall. So I understood that some Russians had come across some wall and that this was bad—very bad.

A morning with our grandmother in Palanga

My grandma and I hurried to join the cluster of neighbors who had gathered to listen to the man's news. I was six years old and this was the moment when my peaceful and comfortable childhood ended. It was June 15, 1940.

FROM THAT DAY on, the rhythm of our days was disrupted as a vague uneasy feeling pervaded the house. My father was often gone before breakfast and missing at the midday meal. Mama was also often away, and when she returned, she and Baba would huddle and whisper intensely, sometimes speaking in Russian or Polish so I didn't understand.

One day I walked into Phyllis's room to find her packing brightly patterned blouses into a suitcase.

"Where are you going?" I asked.

"To Australia," she said. "I'm sorry to leave you, but your parents said I must. When everything returns to normal, I'll be back."

Antanas Gustaitis with his ANBO VIII

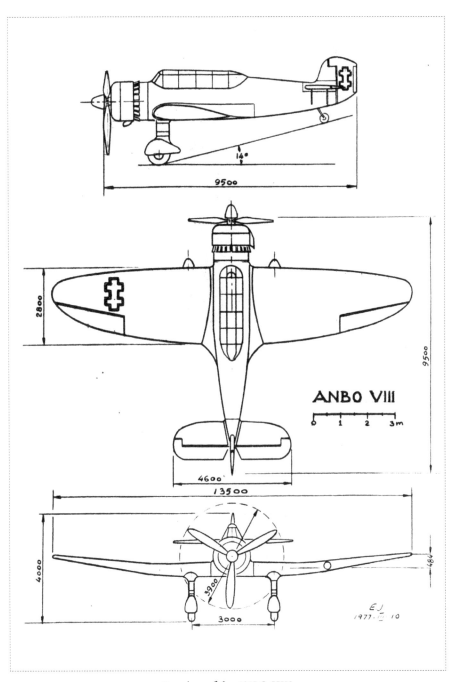

14°

9500

2800

9500

ANBO VIII

0   1   2   3m

4600

13500

4000

484

3900

3000

E.J.
1977. VII 10

Drawings of the ANBO VIII

Last photo with our father, Summer 1940

I began to cry. The last time Phyllis went away, home for vacation while I was quarantined with scarlet fever, I missed her terribly. When she returned I was still confined and my skin was peeling. She stood in the garden outside my window, and I leaned out to talk with her. But I couldn't. During the weeks she was gone I had forgotten all my English.

Now Phyllis took me in her arms. Her body was hard and stiff, not soft like Baba's, but she held me tenderly, her cheek against mine, and I felt the tears on her face mix with my own.

MANY YEARS LATER, when she was living in Chicago, Mama wrote forty-one pages in a school notebook with a dappled black-and-white cardboard cover, the kind used for years in American schools. Jūratė and I had urged her to write a memoir we could pass on to our children. Mama wrote in her strong hand, in unadorned prose. The first line on the first page is "My Life," although her account contains almost nothing after 1947, when we arrived in America. In this notebook I read, "The Russian invasion was imminent, people were fleeing, but Antanas would not be persuaded to go."

Lithuania's president, Antanas Smetona, had already fled, and other government and military leaders had scattered to countries in Western Europe and the Americas. My father, however, refused to leave his country, despite my mother's entreaties.

I begged him, for the sake of the children, but to no avail.

"The intelligentsia have a duty to stay with the people at a time of danger, to suffer with them and help," he replied. "I'm not a political man, and might not be bothered."

By the time he understood how mistaken he was, it was too late.

AS A CHILD, sheltered within my family, I was oblivious to the horrors that were engulfing Eastern Europe. On September 1, 1939, Germany had invaded Poland under the terms of the Molotov-Ribbentrop Pact of nonaggression, signed seven days earlier by the Soviet and German foreign ministers. Two secret protocols divided Eastern Europe into Soviet and Nazi spheres of influence. In a third protocol, signed a few days later, most of Lithuania was allotted to the Soviets.

Soon, thousands of Jews were fleeing to my country from Poland in hopes of continuing through Russia to Shanghai. More than 2,100 survived thanks to Chiune Sugihara, the Japanese consul in Kaunas, according to the United States Holocaust Museum. Without permission from his government, Sugihara wrote visas for transit through Japan for all who crowded desperately at the consulate's door, delaying his departure as long as he was able to.

Meanwhile, other Eastern Europeans were fleeing south across Nazi-occupied Poland, vague visions of Switzerland or the Americas in their minds, but with little idea of where real safety might be found.

Soon our family would be among them.

THE SOVIET UNION took over the Baltic countries—Lithuania, Latvia, and Estonia—through a sham process meant to give the illusion of democratic choice. Transitional "people's parliaments" were formed under Soviet supervision. Then elections were held in which voters were presented with a single slate; no opposition candidates were allowed. The "parliaments" met with one item on the agenda: a request for admission to the Soviet Union. The Supreme Soviet obliged. On August 3, 1940, the Soviet Union annexed the Baltic States as Soviet Socialist Republics.

From the time before the Soviet takeover, what remains in my mind is a series of moments, like film clips that I can call up at will.

During breakfast, my father, whom I called Tėtė, often invited me to sit on his lap and tell him my dreams. This particular morning I had no dream to tell, so began to invent one.

"I'm alone, it's getting dark . . ." I began. But then, flushed with shame, sure that Tėtė could tell I was lying, I dashed back to my seat at the table.

My father usually left home after breakfast, to go to the airplane factory at the airfield, where he supervised the construction of the planes he designed. He returned for the midday meal, then withdrew into his study. Mama made sure he was not disturbed.

Sometimes I heard him strumming his mandolin. Mama explained that meant he was thinking.

Another memory: It's a winter day. I'm kneeling on a chair, elbows on the windowsill, looking out at the snow and reciting the word *žvirblis* (sparrow). The word sounds like the chatter of a sparrow, so I say it again and again while watching a few sparrows hop around on the bare branches of the birch tree outside. A storm window has been installed behind the regular window for the cold months. Between the two panes is a space wider than a man's hand, packed at the bottom with a thick layer of cotton wool, in which Baba and I have planted the brown-headed, white-stemmed mushrooms we crafted from horse chestnuts in autumn. I blow on the glass, and in the resulting fogged blob draw a pine tree with my right index finger.

Going out into the snow meant putting on many layers of scratchy clothes, including two pairs of stockings, first cotton, then wool; a heavy coat with mittens attached to a string that was threaded through the coat sleeves; and a woolen cap with earpieces tied together under the chin. Also a muff against which I could warm my face when my nostrils and the tip of my nose began to freeze. Boots, of course, with warm lining.

Once I was bundled up sufficiently to meet Baba's or Mama's approval, I could go sledding or ice skating, build snowmen, or—when an ice crust had formed atop the snow after a thaw—walk on top of the snowbanks. Going out was not optional: Mama was a strong believer in the importance of fresh air.

In March or thereabouts we would start hearing the ice crack on the river Nemunas. If it did not start moving quickly, it would be blasted with explosives to prevent a jam-up and flooding. And then, soon, the snowbanks along roads would get muddy and rivulets would flow through footprints and wheel tracks.

One day Phyllis took me out for a walk to the nearby creek to search for *žibutės* (*Anemone hepatica*), the little blue flowers that emerge in early spring while there is still snow on the ground. We found a cluster of them next to a melting snowbank, a dazzling sight after months of white, gray, and winter brown.

➤ ➤ ➤

SOMETIME IN LATE June, after Jūratė's school year had ended, the family packed up and rode in my father's big black Mercedes to Palanga, where we rented a couple of rooms in a green guesthouse with a wide veranda. Tėtė would go back to Kaunas after a few days, returning later for short visits, while Baba, Mama, my elder sister, and I would stay till the end of August. We ate our meals at long tables with the two or three other families staying at the guesthouse. These meals sometimes lasted too long, but otherwise life in Palanga was very pleasant.

Every morning we would walk to the beach, where waves washed the fine white sand, and by late morning a child couldn't step barefoot onto the upper beach without burning her soles. We would return for the noon meal, then stroll, usually with friends vacationing in the same guesthouse, through a pine forest to the top of a hill known as Birutė's Mountain, and spread blankets under the pines. I would be told to take a nap, and usually did, listening to the sound of the wind in the trees and the surf below. Those are still two of my favorite sounds in the world.

On my sixth birthday, on May 19, 1940, some children came to our house for a party. One of them, Ugnė, whom I had not met before, brought me a big, white stuffed bear. Sometime after, Mama took me to visit the girl at her family's home, a big house surrounded by a garden. Ugnė Karvelis would become my best friend.

WAS MY EARLY childhood as idyllic as I remember? We cannot recall the past. We construct memories in the present, and those memories change as our outlook changes. But certainly our peaceful life ended after the Red Army took over our country.

We did not go to the seashore in June 1940.

One morning—perhaps in July—my grandmother woke me early and told me to dress quickly and eat my breakfast.

"We are leaving for your aunt and uncle's farm in Raišupis," she said. "I'm going to pack now."

"Right now? Why right now? For how long?"

Baba did not answer.

"I'm not hungry, I'll help you pack."

"You go eat," she ordered sternly. My grandmother was almost never stern.

Normally, I would have jumped for joy at the prospect of visiting my aunt and uncle at their farm in Raišupis, a village south of Kaunas. But we never went on the spur of the moment. Something was wrong.

The boiled egg and buttered bread were dry in my mouth, but I forced them down with the help of warm cocoa so I could follow Baba to the room we shared. She was stuffing some of my clothing into the black leather traveling bag we always took with us to the seashore. Her hands were trembling as she snapped the bag shut.

"Let's go," she said. Mama and Tėtė were already outside, standing beside the black car usually driven by the chauffeur. Tėtė got into the driver's seat; Mama slipped in beside him. Baba, Jūratė, and I climbed into the back seat. I soon fell asleep and woke only after the car had turned onto the dirt road to the farm.

Everything looked reassuringly familiar. Cows and horses were grazing in the pasture behind the hay barn; chickens were pecking the ground outside the granary. In front of the house, several giant sunflowers loomed above the picket fence surrounding the garden. Everything was as I remembered.

My father pulled the car up near the kitchen door. Both Auntie and Uncle came out to greet us. "You are probably hungry," Auntie said in her slow country voice. "Please, come in."

In the kitchen, on the long table next to the window that faced the orchard, Auntie had laid out the noon meal for family and help. A loaf of dark rye bread, cucumbers and tomatoes, white farmer cheese. Beet soup and a pot of potatoes simmered on the stove. Auntie took five more plates from the cupboard and set them out for us. Apparently we had not been expected.

After the meal, Mama suggested we take a walk into the woods, for it was a beautiful sunny day. Baba stayed at the house, while my parents, Jūratė, and I headed out, past the hay barn and along the path through the pasture toward the forest. I lagged behind, stopping to look for four-leaf clovers. We were nearing the birches at the edge of the woods when I heard Mama say something in a hushed voice to Tėtė without turning her head: "We are being followed."

I turned to look. Two men in dark jackets and dark pants were coming up the path toward us. They did not look like country people.

"Time to turn back," my father said.

As we did, so did the men. They walked briskly to the road leading into the farmyard, crossed it, and continued toward the neighboring farm.

Back at the house we found Aunt and Uncle very upset.

"Our neighbor was here," said Auntie. "There's a black car parked behind her barn. Two men. They came soon after you arrived."

Mama told us that she and Tėtė had to return to Kaunas, but that Baba, Jūratė, and I would stay for a week or two. Apprehension began to grow into a big cotton ball inside my belly.

During the ensuing days, the world returned to normal as I helped Auntie feed the chickens and pigs and watched her cook, milk the cows, and spin some flax. I hoped I could come back in winter, when the loom was set up in the kitchen and she wove the threads into cloth.

When Baba, Jūratė, and I returned to Kaunas, it was by train. I watched the mist hovering above lakes and meadows, so lovely through the window. In the city, however, the leaves of the maple trees lining the streets were gray with dust. And coming home brought back that uneasy feeling. The sun was pouring through the tall windows, warming the parquet floors, but home felt empty. Not only was Phyllis gone but I soon learned that some of my playmates, including Ugnė, had left the country.

My parents were preoccupied. Baba seemed to be spending most of her time praying, running the rosary beads through her fingers. Tėtė often sat by a window that looked out at the ANBO VIII, his latest plane and the one he was most proud of. He had only recently taken it up on its test flight. The Russians had pushed it out of its hangar and left it in the rain.

One autumn day Mama was taken to the hospital and came back with my baby sister Elena, born September 21. A great deal of fuss was made over her, but I thought she was just a scrawny thing with a pear-shaped head. My parents kept her in their bedroom for some time, and then I had to move to Jūratė's room because the baby took my place in the room I had shared with Baba.

Winter came, and snow. One afternoon my father came home and immediately disappeared into his study. Shortly after, the doorbell rang. I ran to answer, but Mama hurried in from the living room, shook her head, and held a finger to her lips. The doorbell rang again. We didn't move. At the third ring Mama opened the door, and I pressed myself into the dark corner behind the coatrack. Two men in Russian military uniforms stepped inside.

"*Zdrastvujtya,*" Mama said. Hello!

They had come to see Tėtė. Mama indicated they should wait and went to tell him. By the grim look on her face as she passed I knew these visitors were not welcome. I stood frozen, hoping they would not take off their coats and come toward me to hang them up. They didn't. She showed them in. I watched the study door close behind them, then stepped out of my hiding place.

"Mama, who are they?"

"One of them is a commissar. They want to talk with Tėtė."

"Why didn't they talk with him at his office?"

"I don't know. They came here."

The men left, but they came again. And twice more.

"They're trying to persuade your father to work for them," Mama said.

In her memoir, Mama wrote,

He had told them he was willing, but only in his own country. They told him that there would be no airplane construction in Lithuania, only small repair facilities where he would not be able to make use of his knowledge. After that last visit the commissar said, ironically, that it was impossible for them to understand why he was refusing, when he was being offered terms that their own best engineers were not given. His tone was such that Antanas finally understood that now he would be deported by force.

According to Mama, at the beginning of the Soviet occupation my father seemed to believe that cooperation with the Russians might be possible, and that the Lithuanian air force could remain intact. Such hopes proved naïve. The aviators were forbidden to fly. Officers were ordered to remove their epaulets. My father was charged with the task of liquidating the air force he had built. He carried out the assignment, trying to leave the fleet in good shape. When he learned that some Russians had vandalized a series of airplanes simply to remove the clocks, he lamented, "What a waste."

After the commissar's third visit, my father yielded to my mother's entreaties and agreed to leave the country. He had had good offers of work from Sweden and some other countries, but had turned them down. He and Mama had inquired at the American consulate, but were told that the quota for Lithuania was already exhausted. The consul told her it would be possible for us to go to the Philippines, but that because of the climate there, most Europeans survived only five years.

She later wrote,

One of the few diplomats who had not yet been called back to his country was the Argentinian consul, Barsanti, a nice man whose wife was Lithuanian. He told us he could provide visas for the whole family and a good job for Antanas, but only on condition that we pick up the documents outside of Lithuania, in Germany or another country.

A way to get to Germany existed: Baltic residents with German roots were being repatriated. We had no German ancestors, but the whole family, except for me, spoke some German. We could pass. My father, however, wanted to avoid any possible entanglements with the Nazis.

My parents agreed to cross the border separately to German-occupied Poland, and then meet and proceed together to Berlin to pick up the visas for Argentina. My father would go in secret, alone, with the help of certain people who would guide him across the border. Mama would get the rest of us through as German nationals. My mother wrote that, on March 2, 1941,

We appeared before the Russian-German commission that was preparing the last transport of German nationals. I said that my grandmother had been a Prussian German from Tilsit. The Russian asked me immediately, "Where is your husband?"

"He went away," I said. "I don't know where. He did not want to travel with us to Germany."

"All right," the German said, "everything is in order."

Mama wrote of her last hours with her beloved husband.

Quite late in the evening he kissed the sleeping children, standing a little longer beside little Elytė, as if wondering whether she would survive the hardships of the uncertain future. It had been agreed

that he would spend the last night with a trusted ally and early in the morning would travel to the border, across which he would be led by a farmer. Where and how, he did not tell me, because he had promised he would not, and I did not question him.

We agreed to walk together to the house where he would be staying. If someone saw us, they would suspect nothing because we often took walks. We walked to the small separate house where the ally lived. They talked briefly, then Antanas escorted me back. The night was dark—it was about 11 p.m. For safety's sake, we decided to go across fields. The frozen earth had already thawed, and our feet sank deep into the ground. The farther we walked, the harder it was. I grew so tired that I could barely drag my feet forward. Antanas, worried, urged me on.

"It's not far now. We'll soon be there."

In the vicinity of home he embraced me for the last time and said rather calmly, "We will see each other day after tomorrow, across the border."

Then he quickly walked away down the road. I watched him receding, but he did not turn back.

That was the last time she saw him.

2

....

MY MOTHER'S TRAJECTORY

Some people who knew my mother in Lithuania only as the elegant wife of General Gustaitis were surprised at how well she had managed alone, with three children and her elderly mother, during the war and its aftermath. But Mama's character had been honed by hardship.

My mama

Our family album rests on a shelf in my home today, within easy reach in case of fire or earthquake. It's wrapped in a Lithuanian linen towel and tied with a handwoven sash in the colors of the Lithuanian national flag—yellow for the sun, green for the land, red for the blood shed for the country.

Bronė with her parents

I lift the first delicate interleaf and, once again, study the formal portrait of my mother as a young girl with her parents. It's a studio photograph from the early 1900s, taken in Vilnius. I can almost hear the photographer say, *Hold still—Don't move now,* as he dips his head under the cloth behind the camera.

Jokūbas Alexandravičius, my grandfather, occupies an armchair as though it were a throne, erect but at ease, eyes looking straight at the camera. His substantial white beard is neither wild like Leo Tolstoy's nor delicate like that of Nicholas II, the reigning czar. It's a solid beard, shaped and evenly trimmed, enhancing his strong features. Ten metal buttons in two vertical rows embellish his double-breasted jacket; gold braid decorates its shoulders and cuffs. This is a serious, self-confident man with a commanding presence.

To my grandfather's left stands a woman much younger than he, my grandmother, Julija, with her head held high, spine straight, in a stiff pose obviously arranged by the photographer. Her hair is pulled back severely; her wide-set eyes look blank. Her roundish face is not especially beautiful, but she is slim and shapely in a long dress with a pintucked bodice cinched at the waist by an ornate metal buckle.

Their child, my mother, Bronislava (Bronė), stands in front of her parents in a sailor-suit frock, a small cross hanging on a chain around her neck and a white peony in her loosely joined hands. She looks to be about nine years old, with delicate features and a remote look in her dark eyes. Her hair is also pulled back, like her mother's, but not as tightly. She looks a bit wan, as if she might be recovering from an illness. I've gazed at this photograph many times, trying in vain to read something more in it about my mother and her parents.

All I know about the life of my grandmother Julija Muravska before she met Jokūbas Alexandravičius is that she was born in Byelorussia (Belarus), one of a tenant farmer's five children, and came to Riga at age fifteen in search of a better life.

About my maternal grandfather I know more. He was born in Žemaitija (Samogitia), in northwestern Lithuania, one of three children in a family of minor nobility. The year of his birth, 1848, is remembered in history for the bold new ideas and movements that swept western Europe—democracy, socialism, nationalism. The German philosophers Karl Marx and Friedrich Engels published the *Communist Manifesto* in London that year. Industrial workers were striking for better wages and humane working conditions. In the Russian Empire, of which Lithuania was a part, however, the feudal monarchy and serfdom still prevailed. Peasants were bound to land owned by the gentry. When land was sold, the serfs, or "souls," went with the property.

My grandfather's family had the good fortune to own a small farm in the Žemaitija region, near the estate of the cosmopolitan and politically influential Duke Oginskis, whose family had, for generations, supported music, literature, and the education of Lithuanian children. A daughter of Duke Oginskis ran a small elementary school on the estate for neighbor children. Her father sponsored those of her pupils who showed promise for further study, sending them to secondary schools in neighboring countries. At this time, schools in Lithuania were reserved primarily for children of Russian officials. Thanks to the duke and his daughter, however, Jokūbas and his older brother Jonas continued their education at a *gymnasium* (academic secondary school) in Riga, the capital of Latvia and the biggest city on the eastern shore of the Baltic Sea.

Here the boys found themselves in a wider world. They met young people who had been to Paris and come back with revolutionary ideas, who spoke scornfully of the czar, saying he indulged in idle luxury, surrounded by his nobles, servants, and military guards, ignoring the vast numbers of his subjects living in misery.

In 1863, when Jokūbas was fifteen years old, uprisings broke out in the empire, primarily in areas that had once been part of the Polish-Lithuanian Commonwealth—Poland, Lithuania, Byelorussia. The immediate cause of rebellion was the announcement of a sweeping military conscription that targeted suspected malcontents. Many of those called failed to report, taking off for the forests instead.

Even before the conscription, both the common people and gentry were angry at Czar Alexander II because, when he at long last abolished serfdom, he failed to allot land to those who tilled it, decreeing, instead, that former serfs would be entitled, eventually, to buy land they worked from the owners. This was bitter news to both the former serfs and the landowners. The peasants knew that few of them would ever have enough money to buy land. The landowners resented the prospect of having to sell their property. So, despite purported reforms, the lives of most peasants hadn't changed after the abolition of serfdom, and in some cases became even worse when landowners drove their "souls" off their property to avoid having to sell them land.

Jokūbas was on summer vacation with his parents in 1863, when a protest took place near his home, and he joined it.

In her notebook, Mama wrote, "Everyone went—old people and half-grown boys, country people with scythes and whatever weapons they had. Lithuanian nobles were the leaders."

Cossacks arrived on horseback and, acting as enforcers for the empire, broke up the crowd with whips. Jokūbas and other young people fled into the forest as the horsemen ransacked homes in search of them.

"They all might well have starved in the forest, had it not been for the good daughter of the Duke Oginskis, who brought them food at night," my mother wrote, recalling what her father had told her.

Eventually, Jokūbas returned to Riga, graduated from the gymnasium, and found a position in the state controller's office. During the next fifteen years he rose through the ranks in the imperial civil service. He longed to return to his homeland, but the czarist government rarely allowed civil servants to work in their own countries. His homesickness grew after the untimely loss of his older brother, who contracted tuberculosis while in medical school and died.

One summer, while visiting his parents, Jokūbas learned that his first teacher and benefactress, the daughter of Duke Oginskis, was still single.

"He owed his life to her," my mother wrote. "In gratitude, he decided to marry her, although she was much older than he was."

The couple lived together in Riga for a couple of years, but Jokūbas's wife was lonely. She didn't adapt well to city life, and when they went to visit her family in Žemaitija, she often stayed on after her husband returned to his job. Her father, recognizing her unhappiness, gave her a farm and built a house for her. She lived there in familiar surroundings for a few more years, until her death during an epidemic.

It saddens me to think of this woman, my grandfather's first wife. She was brave and kind. She enabled my grandfather and other children to become educated, yet I don't even know her name. In her memoir, my mother referred to her only as "the good daughter of the Duke Oginskis."

Jokūbas married again at age forty-nine. This also was an unusual union. Julija was twenty-four years younger than he, and she could barely write her name, whereas he was a cultured man. Why did he choose her? That's a question that must remain unanswered. He met her at the home of a friend, where she was visiting one of that friend's servants. From what I have learned of their relationship, it was more like that of master and servant than of husband and wife. Julija called Jokūbas by his last name.

After Bronė's birth they had another child, a boy. Jokūbas sent him away to a farmer family so that he wouldn't have to hear him crying. The baby died.

My grandfather was an honorable man, but he was selfish and had a fierce temper. His wife and little daughter feared him. He berated Julija for the slightest misstep or infraction, even for things beyond her control.

"What do you mean there was no more bread at the bakery?" he might fume. "You must have come too late. Why didn't you go earlier, you stupid woman?"

Trying to explain only fanned his fury, so Julija would never tell him that she had come as early as usual, but someone had arrived even earlier and bought twenty loaves. Instead, she might say, "Tomorrow I'll go earlier," then run into the salon, where she buried her face in the sofa to stifle her sobs. She would remember the floral pattern of the fabric covering that red plush sofa her entire life.

Jokūbas was also quick to punish their daughter, should she speak out of turn, wipe her nose on her sleeve, or be slow to do as told.

"To the corner!" he would shout.

Sometimes Bronė stood facing the wall for so long that she thought he must have forgotten her. Her mother would ask timidly, "*Pani Aleksandrovicz?*" Perhaps it's already enough?

Not surprisingly, Bronė was a fearful child. She was scared of bugs, spiders, spider webs, and cotton wool, the kind you put on a wound to stanch the blood. But what she feared most was being summoned into her father's study for an arithmetic drill. No matter how much she practiced the multiplication tables, she would inevitably freeze somewhere in her recitation, standing in front of him as he watched her sternly through a cloud of tobacco smoke. His gaze knocked the numbers out of her mind, so she fixed her eyes on the gas lamp above his head.

"Look at the person you're addressing!" he would order.

These drills left Bronė exhausted and confused. Like her mother, she sought refuge in the sofa, curling up in a corner under the afghan to escape her father's voice and her own self-reproach. Yet she did well in school in every subject, including arithmetic.

After one of the drills, during which she didn't stumble even once, her father looked at her with unusual warmth.

"So, Bronytė, tell me," he asked, "do you dream of what you might want to study later?"

"I want to be a nurse," she answered without hesitation.

He bristled. "Out of the question! Nurses are ignorant. Many of them are loose women. Perhaps you can become a pharmacist or doctor—those are honorable occupations—but a nurse? Forget about being a nurse."

Bronė did not reply. A professional nurse was known as a "merciful sister." Bronė imagined herself in a white uniform, her head covered by a white scarf with a small red cross over the forehead, walking softly through hospital wards, sitting at bedsides, holding aching hands. Blood did not scare her, and she knew she could overcome her childish fear of cotton wool. Her father's disapproval would not kill her dream.

The family's daily routine didn't vary much. Jokūbas drank two cups of tea in the morning, then left for work. He returned in midafternoon, took his main meal with a glass of whiskey, then went to the bedroom for a long nap.

"That's when we had to be completely quiet," my mother wrote in her memoir.

After a couple of hours he rose and retired to his study, where he stayed until supper. Bronė remembered that the three of them usually ate the evening meal in silence, her father at the head of the table with a glass of beer. Afterward, he often went out again, usually to the Lithuanian club, where men gathered to talk, read the newspapers, play cards and chess. On some evenings his friends came to their house, and from behind the salon doors Julija and Bronė heard the men's voices rise over their drinking and smoking. Julija often fell asleep with Bronė.

She was a dutiful wife, Julija, but she intensely disliked two of her tasks. One was making the *papirosai*, the cardboard tubes with tobacco stuffed into one end that her husband smoked. She detested his smoking. Even more, she detested having to drink whiskey or beer with him, as he demanded she do when he wanted company. Drinking alcohol was a sin to her. She obeyed, though, and then she prayed. Her rosary, going to church on Sunday, and her love for her daughter sustained her.

Looking at what I have gleaned of this family's life, I see that both Julija and Bronė were mistreated by Jokūbas. But perhaps this was not unusual for people of my grandparents' station in life in the Russian Empire. Jokūbas was a bureaucrat in the vast civil service, moving slowly up its ranks, changing uniform with each rank, looking forward to a peaceful retirement in his native land. He was respected among his peers and he provided for his wife and child, at least materially.

Bronė remembered that the family did have some happy times together, during summer vacations on the farm Jokūbas had inherited from his first wife. He would take Julija and Bronė by train to the town of Raseiniai, where a hired hand would meet them with horse and wagon to deliver them the rest of the way. After Jokūbas's vacation ended, he returned to Riga, but Julija and Bronė stayed at the farm the entire summer. That was the best time for them. Bronė loved to visit with her father's sister and her family, who worked their land, and who in the evenings sang and told stories.

Her father's longing to return to Lithuania to live was eventually fulfilled. He did not even have to wait for retirement. He was granted permission to transfer to a post in his native country as part of his reward for discovering and exposing a financial scandal in the department of roads and bridges. He moved the family first to Vilnius, and four years later to Kaunas.

Each move brought them closer to the farm, where Jokūbas had long expected to spend his retirement. He had only two more years to work to qualify for his full pension when bad luck intervened. He suffered a cerebral hemorrhage, and his doctor advised him to stop working immediately, even though that meant losing much of his pension.

The family settled in at the farm. Jokūbas tried to introduce some agricultural reforms, but didn't succeed. At least partly because of his foul temper and domineering ways, his workers would not cooperate. Expenses rose, farm income slacked. Eventually, Jokūbas sold the farm and bought a home in Raseiniai.

He sent Bronė to primary school in the town, but when she reached age twelve, he added grievously to his wife's unhappiness by deciding to send their daughter to secondary school in Saint Petersburg. How difficult that must have been for Julija!

Surely he could have enrolled Bronė in a local school. Even though non-Russian children were not easily accepted, his excellent civil service record should have made it possible. Perhaps with his health in peril he simply wanted the girl out of the house. But the reason he gave his wife and child was that students in the local school were "too free," and, as Bronė recalled, "he wanted to bring me up as a 'decent girl.'" She was sent to a boarding school run clandestinely by Polish nuns in Russia's capital.

Catholic convents and schools were illegal in the Russian Empire, so the sisters at the Santa Katarina school took care to be discreet. They wore dark blue suits rather than habits—all except for the director, who dressed in black and covered her head with a scarf. The girls were not allowed to roam far from where they studied and lived. Only after her schooling ended would Bronė have an opportunity to explore the beautiful parks, grand museums, and palace gardens for

Bronė, top right, and classmates at Santa Katerina school in Saint Petersburg

which Saint Petersburg, Peter the Great's "Window on the West," was famous.

Young Bronė arrived at the school speaking three languages: Polish, which the family spoke at home; Russian, the official language in schools and other public institutions; and Lithuanian. Cloistered at the convent school, she studied Latin, French, and German, which would have lifesaving value for her and her children more than three decades later, during World War II.

She loved literature and history, particularly the history of Napoleon, who introduced just laws in the lands he conquered, and the story of Joan of Arc, the French country girl who heard voices instructing her to rouse her countrymen and lead them to overthrow alien rulers and restore their legitimate regent. Riding a white horse, sheathed in armor, the Maid of Orleans led the French troops, sword held high.

Bronė learned that the soldiers and common people loved the Maid, but the priests feared her, seeing her as a threat to their power. They imprisoned her and ordered her to renounce her voices. She refused. Rejecting the Church's authority, she stayed true to her own heart and soul. Consequently, Joan was burned at the stake. Bronė wondered whether she would have Joan's courage if someone tried to force her to deny her own truth.

She hoped that one day, in some way, she would have a chance to test herself.

ON JUNE 28, 1914, in Sarajevo, a nineteen-year-old Serbian nationalist shot and killed Archduke Franz Ferdinand of Austria and his wife, Sophie, shattering a complex alliance among several European powers and releasing unimaginable forces of destruction that would rage across Europe for the next four years, taking some twenty million lives.

Bronė was home for summer vacation when the Great War broke out. Her father nevertheless decided to send her back to Saint Petersburg for her final year of school. Whether his wife and daughter agreed with his decision was irrelevant; their opinions did not count. Julija prayed to the Virgin Mary for her daughter's protection.

No doubt Bronė's father did not see the war as a great threat to her safety. The czar's armies were advancing against Austria and Serbia to the south, while the Germans had not succeeded in making headway into Russia from the west. The general opinion at the time was that this war would soon be over.

By June 1915, however, when Bronė's final school year ended, German troops had occupied Lithuania, and her way home was blocked. Stranded in Saint Petersburg with no place to live, little money, and no friends outside of the school, which was now closed, she had to fend for herself.

Her best option, she figured, was to find a position with a family as tutor, the traditional way to earn one's keep while studying far from home. That was how her father and his brother had gotten by as students in Riga. Many tutor positions also provided room and board with the family.

One day she spotted an ad in a newspaper for just such a position. The address given was in a remote part of the city, an area she did not know, so she hired an old man with a horse-drawn cart to take her there. The place was even more remote than she had guessed. As the horse clopped on, Bronė began to worry. They reached the outskirts of the city. The little houses they were passing looked shabby; the streets were not paved. Would a family living in this neighborhood be able to afford a tutor? When they arrived at the address listed in the newspaper, they saw no house, only buildings that looked like warehouses, among weedy lots.

"Girl, this does not look good," the old driver said. "Better go back." They turned around.

Bronė was frightened by that experience, but soon she felt relief. Living with some family she did not know, in a place she did not know, was not something she wanted to do. She had been acting out of desperation. But why not try to find work she did want?

For years she had wanted to become a nurse. Her father might sneer, but he was far away and she couldn't consult him even if she wanted to. She knew that nurses were desperately needed to care for wounded soldiers, and she was free to choose her own path in life now. She had seen a notice about an accelerated training course for nurses, with room and board. She applied and was accepted, even though she was still below the required minimum age of eighteen and had no money. Because of her situation and her father's name, she figured, but perhaps also because of her own qualities and her excellent academic record.

Two months later, she was working as an intern at a small private infirmary in Saint Petersburg, tending to soldiers injured in battle, as well as to civilians with a variety of ailments. She felt useful and strong.

One day, as she was leaving the infirmary, she saw a girl she knew from boarding school. They soon became close friends, working and studying together.

Helke Muraska was a Byelorussian, like Bronė's mother. She was easygoing, liked to laugh, and was not at all shy, as Bronė was, especially with young men. Perhaps she had grown up in a large family, not alone under the frown of a stern father. With Helke, Bronė met other young people. One day her friend introduced her to a medical student, whom Bronė liked right away. They started going on walks together, always in a foursome with Helke and the young man she was seeing. Bronė fell in love.

She knew she had to be careful. Her mother and father and the nuns had warned her of the dangers lurking for a girl out in the world without protection. Even if they hadn't, she knew what could befall a young woman who let her emotions rule her. She had decided already, before she even met this medical student: no kisses!

Alas, "after a while it seemed that he didn't care for me all that much," she later wrote, "and that, of course, was very sad." Not until after the war ended would Bronė give her heart to someone again.

In the summer of 1916, she and Helke decided they wanted to work closer to the battlefront, where nurses were needed more urgently than in Saint Petersburg. They also wanted to see more of the world, and this was their first opportunity to venture, independently, beyond the confines of home, school, and the city. They were assigned for duty on a train that transported wounded soldiers from field infirmaries to hospitals in Minsk, Moscow, and a few other cities.

Most of the wagons on the train were cattle and freight cars. The wounded lay on pallets. Only the most severely injured traveled in special hospital wagons. When the two friends started working on the train it was summer and the weather was hot. Inside the wagons, the air was heavy with sweat, the smell of dirty clothing, and the foul odor of wounds that had not been tended for days. They moved through each car in a team that included a physician and a few medics, changing bandages, distributing medicines, soothing feverish brows with cool, wet cloths. The train journey lasted two or three days, during which the medical team could not offer much beyond simple emergency care. Yet Bronė would recall, "We felt good when these men sighed and breathed a little easier, and thanked us for easing their pains."

When the medical team had to get from one wagon to the next, they would wait until the train slowed down, then jump off and catch the next car, holding on to their boxes of medications and supplies. A few times they missed and had to wait alongside the tracks until another train came along. This made the medical care on the trains erratic, but it also gave the team a precious spell of rest and companionship in the fresh open air. They stretched out in the grass and closed their eyes, taking turns, keeping watch.

Blowing black soot and steam, whistling occasionally, the train filled with wounded soldiers traveled across the fertile, black earth of Ukraine and Byelorussia, through deep forests, stopping sometimes at small stations in little towns where gaunt villagers came to the windows offering warm water to the travelers. Month after month Bronė and Helke watched the changing seasons, traveling through fields of grain—first light green, then golden, then denuded. Autumn came, painting maple trees red and yellow, and then winter, shrouding the land in white.

"We saw all kinds of places and all kinds of things," Bronė remembered. "Once we stopped at a forest at night, somewhere near Vitebsk. The forest was burning. Huge trees were falling, aflame, like giant torches."

When the train arrived at its destination, local medical teams took charge of the wounded men. The train stayed at the station a day or two, was restocked and repaired as needed, and the medical crew had a rest. Helke and most of the others usually went off together to dance and carouse, but Bronė stayed behind. On the one occasion she did join the others, she disliked the drunken company. Instead, she explored the city by daylight and went to sleep early.

Then Bronė lost Helke, who had been having an affair with a married doctor. Their supervisor found out and her friend was sent away. Helke's departure left Bronė forlorn, so she asked to be transferred too. In her new post, a field hospital, everyone lived and worked in large tents. The wounded were brought straight from the battlefield in two-wheeled handcarts. Surgeries went on day and night, even during air raids. Sometimes the exhausted staff thought they were about to get a break, but when they looked up they saw yet more handcarts lined up outside the surgery tent.

"At night, almost every night, the alarm," Bronė wrote.

Air raids. Whoever was not at a surgery ran to the shelter. You go in there and it's full of pale, frightened people. I went a couple of times, then told the others that if I'm sleeping when the alarm sounds not to wake me. Sometimes I'd go into the barracks where the wounded lay, that they should feel better. Somehow, I was simply not afraid.

Bronė was the youngest of the medical crew; the physicians looked out for her. When she was working especially late at night, they would sometimes tell her, "Go to bed, little girl."

THE WINTER OF 1916–17 was especially severe and the war was going badly for Russia. At the same time, revolution had broken out. At the field hospital, the staff heard that people were starving and that troops were abandoning their regiments and going home. In March 1917, the czar was forced to abdicate. A provisional government was formed, committed to continuing the war, but it was overthrown in October by the Bolsheviks, whose leader, Vladimir Lenin, wanted an immediate peace with Germany. Germans had smuggled Lenin into Saint Petersburg in April to help the Bolsheviks. He had declared that soldiers need no longer obey officers and urged them to form committees of comrades to replace them. Chaos ensued.

At military infirmaries, Bolshevik medics drove out physicians and other medical professionals who were not members of their party. In the field hospital where Bronė was working, supervisors told staff they could stay or leave, as they wished. Bronė joined the family of one of the departing doctors on a train to Moscow. She was unprepared for what she found.

Food was on ration cards. That is to say, there was no food. All you could get with the card was a quarter kilo of heavy bread that some-

times stank. Sometimes instead of bread we were given potatoes.
Public soup kitchens had been set up in neighborhoods, where we
sometimes could get soup.

Farmers were forbidden to bring food to city markets; they were
required to relinquish almost everything they produced to Bolshevik authorities. The punishment for hiding and smuggling food was
death. "At night we heard the sound of gunfire at the police station,"
Bronė wrote. "People who had smuggled in food were being shot."

Bronė found lodgings with a family and a job as typist for a judge,
an older man who had not yet been removed from his post by the rev-
olutionaries but, not being a Bolshevik, enjoyed no special privileges,
such as better food rations. After work she stood in one of the long
lines in front of a soup kitchen, but often, by the time she reached the
table with the kettles, the soup was gone.

She was hungry all the time. "I got used to that, as others did—
our stomachs shrank," she wrote. Occasionally an acquaintance
would treat her to horsemeat soup, and sometimes she found a few
potatoes to buy. Meanwhile, policemen and others with special privileges had plenty to eat.

Sipping her small portion of soup one afternoon, she could not
help staring at a man sitting across the table, slicing a piece of bread
off a huge loaf. As he was handing it to a companion, his eyes met
Bronė's.

"Would you like some?" he asked, and gave her a thick slice. She
nodded her thanks. This was real bread, true bread, dark and heavy.

"Where do you live, girl?" the man asked.

"With a family," she answered.

The man stood up, walked out of the hall, and soon returned carrying another loaf, which he handed to Bronė.

"We work on the railroad," he said. "We can get you more. All we
will ask in return is that you store a box or two of conserves for us."

"And show us the town," said the other man.

Recalling the gunshots at the police station, Bronė thanked the men but declined their offer. But oh, how she wished she could have accepted. That bread! What fragrance! She resolved to make the loaf she was given last for a week by eating it slowly, one small piece at a time. But she shared it with the family she was staying with, and it was all gone by the next day.

"How a person changes with long starvation," my mother reflected, telling this story many years later. "Sometimes I asked myself, 'Will I be like this from now on, thinking only about food?'"

She had been slim, but strong and healthy. After a few months in Moscow she was skinny and often felt weak and dizzy.

"The revolution was boiling," she wrote. Once she found herself in a crowd listening to Lenin, but he was too far away for her to make out his words, and she did not like the tone of his voice.

ON MARCH 3, 1918, the Bolsheviks signed a peace treaty with the Central Powers (Germany and its allies) at Brest-Litovsk, ending Russia's participation in the Great War. They renounced claims to a major swath of the former Russian Empire's territory, including the Ukraine, Finland, the Baltic States, and Poland. The terms of the treaty were highly unfavorable to Russia, but it gave the Bolsheviks some temporary relief, enabling them to focus on the civil war they were fighting.

After the treaty was signed, people in Russia whose homeland was in an area ceded to Germany were allowed to go home. While she lived in Moscow, Bronė almost always went to Mass on Sundays. The congregation was mostly Lithuanian and Polish; the pastor was Lithuanian. That autumn, she missed a couple of Sundays because she felt too weak to walk to the church. That was why she heard the announcement for the first time when it was almost too late.

"Tomorrow the last echelon leaves for Lithuania," the priest told the congregation. "Be at the station on time."

Dear God, did this mean that she could go home? To her parents! Four years had passed since she had last seen or heard from them.

Early the next morning, Bronė was at the station, with her belongings bundled in a bedsheet: a pair of shoes, two dresses, a piece of cloth, a few more small items.

At the gate to the train platform the Lithuanian priest stood, holding a piece of paper.

"You are registered?"

"No. I did not know you had to be." She almost broke into tears. "I'm alone. I gave up my job. I will sit right here because I have nowhere else to go."

"Write your name at the end of the list," said the priest. "Who will know when you wrote it?"

She ran to the train, a freight train like the military trains she knew so well. The wagons were already crowded. She climbed into one that seemed to have a bit of extra space. What a joy to settle down in a deep pile of straw, sweet-smelling straw, among her own people going home.

During the long ride from Moscow to Vilnius the train slowed and stopped many times, not only at the stations but in between. Nobody explained why and nobody asked. What mattered was that they were going home. At some stations hot water was available, and people stepped out to fill bowls and other containers.

Bronė lost track of the days and nights. Her head ached. She felt feverish and began to sweat. But no, she was not sick, she could not be sick. Word had reached the travelers that the Germans were keeping sick people out of areas they occupied to prevent the deadly influenza known as the Spanish flu from spreading.

A doctor traveling in the same wagon as Bronė noticed that she was hot and shivering and moved her into a dark corner. He gave her water and medicine, and by the time the train reached Vilnius she felt much better. She passed inspection, thanks to this doctor's kindness.

As the tired and hungry passengers poured out of the train at the Vilnius station, they found that a reception had been prepared for them by fellow countrymen: soup, dark rye bread, white farmer cheese—enough for everyone. Someone who was traveling on to Raseiniai invited Bronė to join him. Almost home.

She opened the garden gate.

The plants in my mother's garden have grown tall. I enter the house. My father is sitting at the table, as usual, reading. And here is Mama. She does not believe her eyes—she does not believe it is I, alive. They have not received the letters I sent, and, not hearing for so long, they thought I was dead.

Lithuania had been under German occupation since the beginning of the Great War. The country had also suffered from lack of food, although not as severely as Russia. The Germans had demanded part of everything farmers grew, much of which they sent to their starving home country. But people managed to keep enough to maintain themselves.

Bronė's parents had been compelled to give up half of their house to German officers. But the men billeted there had behaved respectfully with their hosts, both of whom spoke German. "For some reason, the officers thought that my father was a pastor, perhaps because he was old and had a beard."

Within a few weeks, walking in the orchard, sleeping in the sunlight, she regained her strength and soon began to look for work so that she could help her parents. Without the pension her father had counted on, he was borrowing from a lender to cover living expenses.

A three-month job on a large estate preparing three children for school restored Bronė fully to health. The food was abundant and rich. In the evening the children brought her milk still warm from the cow. "I began to get fat, for the first and last time in my life," she wrote. "When I came home, Mama said, 'Nah, you are now completely a country girl, fat, with red cheeks.'"

When the influenza arrived in Raseiniai the toll was heavy. Up to sixteen funerals a day were held in the Catholic parish, according to a memoir, *Glimpse into the Past*, written by Konstantinas Žukas, a Lithuanian veteran of the imperial army who had come home after the Bolsheviks made peace with the Central Powers. Not a single Jew was among the fatalities, he wrote. Before the epidemic had hit the town, the Jewish physician had called a meeting of the Jewish community and announced that he was old and would not go to any sick person's house. He ordered that everyone stock up in advance on medicine: aspirin, quinine, and linden blossoms. Anyone who felt ill was to go to bed right away and stay there for two weeks, even if he felt better. Although most Jews in Raseiniai caught the flu, according to Žukas, they all survived.

Bronė found a job in a pharmacy, but she soon grew restless. She began to suffer from migraine headaches. From people who stopped by she heard news that made her want to head for Kaunas. The Germans were withdrawing; young men who had been conscripted had found their way home and joined the new Lithuanian armed forces. Scholars, poets, and teachers were returning from abroad. Young people were coming back from faraway Russian cities where they had moved to complete their education after the secondary schools they had been attending in Lithuania closed in 1915. Kaunas was where the excitement was.

Bronė packed a suitcase and, once more defying her father, walked to the railroad station. She had managed to take care of herself, all alone, in Saint Petersburg and Moscow. She would manage in Kaunas.

In one of the photographs in our family album, my mother is standing with another young woman between two young men in military uniform on the shore of a lake, smiling in a bemused, relaxed way. She's wearing a loose skirt and blouse and long beads—I would guess amber. A light-colored scarf is wrapped stylishly around her head. During my childhood I loved to gaze at that photo because she looks so happy and so at ease. Under the photo she had written: "One marquisette dress and a pair of rope-soled shoes, but how we danced!"

In Kaunas, Bronė at last began to enjoy life as a free young woman.

A PASSION FOR FLIGHT

In early 1919, when Bronė arrived in Kaunas, Lithuania was fighting for her existence as an independent state.

Even as German troops still occupied much of the country, the Red Army was moving in from the east to reclaim a land that had been under imperial Russian rule for 124 years. Meanwhile, from the northeast, a military force self-designated as Russia's Western Volunteer Army, but generally known as the Bermontians, was making incursions with the intent of establishing a separate state in the Baltics. This stateless army, led by Lieutenant Pavel Bermont, a former officer in Russia's imperial army, was composed mostly of former Russian prisoners of war and Germans. It was supported by Baltic German landowners and well armed by German industrialists who hoped to secure within the Baltics an industrial region similar to Germany's Ruhr Valley.

Lithuania's predicament was perilous, to say the least. Unless the fledgling state succeeded in repelling the attacks and securing its borders, its Declaration of Independence, proclaimed on February 16, 1918, would be merely a footnote in history, its vision of "an independent Lithuanian state on a democratic foundation" no more than wishful thinking.

AS THE BOLSHEVIKS came close to Lithuania's capital, Vilnius, the Lithuanians moved their military headquarters from that city to Kaunas. Funds for essential expenses were raised by appeals to friendly countries, including France, Germany, and Sweden.

A call went out for volunteers, and many young men responded. The nascent government had little to offer its recruits except a chance to fight if they believed Lithuania's freedom was worth fighting for. They had almost no arms or equipment beyond what could be scavenged out of the disarray of the departing occupation troops.

Among those who rallied to their nation's defense was Leonardas Peseckas, a tall, upright youth with deep-set eyes and a craggy forehead who later became one of my father's good friends and trusted colleagues. In early 1919, he was nineteen years old, had finished six grades of school, and was a teacher in a village elementary school.

One winter day, he wrote in his memoir, *Tales of a War Pilot,* his sister Adele came to visit him from Vilnius, hauling a huge, oddly shaped package wrapped in cloth and tied with rope. She dropped it on the floor in the middle of his room.

"For you, Levuk," she said.

Leonardas removed the cloth and was amazed to find a saddle, a beautiful military saddle with brass fittings. Adele pulled a folded piece of paper from one of the saddle bags and handed it to her brother.

"Read," she ordered.

Leonardas unfolded the paper and read.

Lithuania is in danger. A foreign Russian army has already intruded into our country's eastern precincts. The Muscovites are

coming to suck up Lithuania's last men and, with flashes of fire,
bring us starvation, torture, and ruin.

Let us all rise up to defend Lithuania.

"We have the saddle and I will also buy you a horse," Adele said. She was five years older than Leonardas and, as usual, spoke to him with authority in her voice. "Lithuania is rising. Boys who are healthy and brave are riding to war."

They sat down together and Leonardas's sister brought him up to date on the news. Lithuanian military bases had been established in Kaunas and two smaller towns. People who lived near the bases were bringing food to the troops. Women were knitting socks and sewing shirts for the soldiers. Adele and a few other young women had sewn a Lithuanian flag, which had flown above Gediminas Hill in Vilnius, flanked by a guard of honor.

In his mind's eye Leonardas saw the tricolor banner: yellow for the sun, green for the land, red for the blood shed for the country.

"I will join the hussars," he told his sister.

A few days later, the promised horse arrived. Leonardas stepped up into the saddle and set off across the snow-covered countryside toward Kaunas.

The sun was rising as he crossed the wooden bridge spanning the frozen Nemunas River and rode along the riverbank into the old part of the town. His horse's hooves clopped along on cobbled streets. German soldiers were milling about and he heard several languages being spoken—Russian, Polish, German—but no Lithuanian.

When he found the hussars in an abandoned stone building that had once housed a brewery, he was dismayed. They bore no resemblance to the hussars he had envisioned, the fearsome light cavalry that led the forces of the Grand Duchy of Lithuania and Kingdom of Poland to victory over the Muscovites in the Battle of Orsha in 1514.

Instead of smart uniforms, the men in the brewery wore ill-matched military clothing, some of it Russian, some German. Lithuania's armed forces had no money to spare for uniforms; they made do with what they could scrounge. Leonardas was issued a military cap, a belt with a German clasp, a horse brush.

Not every hussar had a horse. Those who didn't as yet were called "wooden hussars." Two of them, Vytautas Rauba and Juozas Kumpis, told Leonardas they had been visiting an officer who was organizing an aviation school, and urged him to come with them. Their eyes glowed, Leonardas remembered, as they talked of their new acquaintance and of flying. He was tempted, but loyalty to his sister and his horse led him to decline.

Aviation was by now vital to defense. Aircraft provided views behind enemy lines and were highly useful in communicating with the largely rural population. Because few people had radios, leaflets floating down from the sky reached more people than radio transmissions. The Bolsheviks were dropping flyers over towns and villages calling on the inhabitants to join the world revolution, the Bermontians urged them to fight the Bolsheviks, and Poles scattered propaganda alleging that the Lithuanian state had betrayed the people by collaborating with Germans.

Yet in early 1919, the Lithuanians had not a single usable plane or qualified pilot.

To remedy that situation, the defense ministry announced that an air corps was being established within the army's engineering battalion. It purchased eight German-built two-seater aircraft (LVG C.VI) and hired eleven Germans from the aviation detail that had been stationed at the Kaunas garrison since 1916: five pilots, five aviation mechanics, and one scout. These mercenaries were to fly reconnaissance and bombing missions, and also provide flight training to Lithuanian aviation students, who would replace them as soon as possible.

The ministry also announced that a military aviation school would be established, headed by Konstantinas Fugalevičius, a twenty-five-year-old officer, native of Kaunas, who had been in charge of reconnaissance at the Kaunas garrison before the Germans seized the city in 1915, and had flown missions to the front for the czarist forces during the Great War.

Fugalevičius had searched in vain for men with aviation experience among those who had flocked to Kaunas to volunteer for military service. Various characters who loitered near the airfield had wings stitched on their sleeves and across their chests, and claimed to have fought heroically in air battles of Russian imperial forces with the Germans, but they turned out to be mere braggarts who knew how to trade a good story for a beer. No Lithuanians knew how to fly.

IN HIS MEMOIR, Peseckas recalled a February day when word came from the eastern front that Bolshevik contingents were moving toward Kaunas and that the route they were taking was undefended. The hussars (those who had horses) slung their rifles across their shoulders and set forth. What happened that day shaped Peseckas's life path.

> *The cold seeps through our flimsy clothing, pierces to the bone. We gallop, trying to warm up. At one point we meet enemy riders. We shoot at them. The enemy slumps and hides in the winter mist, while we place our numbed palms on the warm pipes of the rifles. . . . The infantry, being ahead of us, occasionally fires. We veer into a forest clearing to make sure the enemy's cavalry is not about to attack from the wings. Empty ice fields. The crazed cold burns. Endless snow and roads vanished in the drifts.*

In the clearing, Leonardas saw a cluster of dark figures. They turned out to be Lithuanian soldiers gathered around an airplane.

Few if any of them had ever seen an airplane except in newspaper photographs.

The hussars approached.

"Our eyes pop," wrote Peseckas. "In its nose a yellow propeller glows. A red sign—five-pointed star. A Bolshevik airplane!"

The Russians had run out of fuel. They had commandeered a horse and cart from a farmer and sped off to the east. The Lithuanians agreed that the plane had to be taken to the Kaunas airfield right away, before the Bolsheviks returned to reclaim it. They pushed it to the nearby road, but then had to stop because roadside telephone poles blocked passage. What to do?

Agreeing that their trophy was worth much more than the wooden poles, the troops proceeded to cut them down with axes and saws.

Thus we had knocked out about two kilometers of the telephone line when a German soldier on a military bicycle appeared out of nowhere, jumped off, inspected the aircraft, walked around it, and informed us we "don't know from the devil." What we had here was an English-made Sopwith [Sopwith 1½ Strutter], he told us, and everyone knows that you don't transport an airplane on a road without removing the wings. He said he knew how to do that and would show us.

We watched him closely. The Germans had lost the war and were demoralized. They were selling military goods or trading them for food. But it seemed that this German was simply a diligent craftsman who wanted to show us his skills. The wings sagged like a donkey's ears and soon separated from the body.

As soldiers accompanied the trophy to its new home, Peseckas continued with the other hussars in pursuit of the Bolsheviks. But new thoughts arose in his mind: How does the earth look, when you rise high above her? What emotions govern a man when he tries to force his way into the pathways of birds, to break through to the shining road beside the sun?

The Russians were repelled that day; Kaunas was at least temporarily saved. A few days later, an enemy's bullet hit Peseckas's horse. He just managed to jump off and roll away in time to avoid being crushed as his steed fell. Now a wooden hussar, he felt free to sign up for aviation school, joining Rauba and Kumpis, whom Fugalevičius had already begun to instruct in aviation basics at his home. The school was officially opened there, then moved, in April, to wooden barracks next to a giant zeppelin hangar the Germans had built during the Great War.

ANTANAS GUSTAITIS VOLUNTEERED for military service on March 15, and was admitted to the aviation school. That school was the beginning of what was to become this small country's outstanding air force, which my father would eventually head, and for which he designed and built nine models of aircraft within walking distance of where we lived until I was six, when World War II began, all his work was destroyed, and he was wrenched from our lives.

My father left no journal or memoir, so in trying to tell the story of his life I searched accounts by his contemporaries for shards of information that might enable me to piece together a portrait. The memoirs of Peseckas and of another fellow airman, Simas Stanaitis, titled *Twists of Fate*, conveyed a particularly vivid impression of the early days, when daring young men rose toward the sky in rickety aircraft they barely knew how to fly.

Stanaitis recalled his first impression of my father as a "stocky broad-shouldered man of medium height," who arrived at the school wearing the kind of long coat the czar's cavalry and artillery had worn. Word quickly got around that he was a whiz at mathematics, and before long he was teaching trigonometry to his classmates. In his free time he liked to play the mandolin, but "his greatest passion was chess. Nobody could match him."

"Flying in a squadron was not easy for him at first," Stanaitis wrote. "We joked, 'Hey, this isn't algebra or trigonometry. Here you have to feel how to hold the stick.' Later he discovered the pleasure of flying and became an excellent pilot."

When the list of thirty-four students who graduated with the rank of lieutenant was posted in December 1919, the name Antanas Gustaitis was at the top. Like most of the others, however, he had yet to complete flight training. The only available instructors were the hired Germans whose main job was to fly missions to the front. All the students were hungry for air time, Peseckas remembered.

> *Afternoons, when the planes returned from the front and the pilots and scouts went to eat and sleep, we, the student aviators, climbed into the LVG planes, which were still exhaling heat. We moved the steering column, imagined we were flying. . . . Everything smelled of enchanting secrets.*

Albatros II at airfield in Kaunas

When the German pilots did find time for the students, they didn't take them up in the LVG fighter planes but in one of the double-winged Albatros aircraft acquired from the Germans or reconstructed from wrecks gathered as war booty.

"What a pitiful sight these were," wrote Peseckas, with "canvas on the wings torn, ribs protruding, still marked with black German crosses for lack of paint for the Lithuanian colors."

The only fuel available was heavy, low-grade benzole, which gave off greasy black smoke. "You get out of the Albatros after a flight black as the devil's brother," Peseckas recalled. "In your shiny face, spattered with oil and soot, only your eyes gleam, protected by goggles."

Even that fuel was scarce. Students bought it in small quantities on the black market for their training flights.

Accidents were frequent. Most happened close to the ground. Many propellers were broken. The airfield was bumpy, boggy in some places, and puddled after heavy rain. The student flyers—as well as instructors—stalled in mud, slammed into embankments and haystacks. Peseckas's instructor crashed into an oak. His student, riding behind him, found himself upside down, tangled in the branches, and broke a leg as he fell to the ground.

Not infrequently, equipment malfunctioned. Stanaitis's flight instructor had warned him, "Never forget to follow the speedometer. If you don't see 120 kilometers an hour you'll fall like a rock."

Proud and excited, Stanaitis had climbed into an Albatros for his first solo flight and started the motor. He felt the wheels lift off the ground and the plane begin to rise. But when he glanced at the speedometer, the arrow was on zero. In his memoir, he wrote,

Oh horror, my plane is driving upward. I push the steering column down, don't let it rise—I don't have any speed. Staying close to the ground, halfway across the airfield I look again—still zero. The

plane hits a clump of dirt and jumps; it wants to rise, but with all my strength I force it to stay low. I keep checking. Zero. The railroad tracks are now devilishly close, and beyond them the trees lining the road to Suvalkija. My hand automatically yanks at the steering column and I jump over the tracks. Still zero. The trees now are right in front of me. At the very last moment I pull upward and clear the treetops.

Realizing that the instrument was simply not working, Stanaitis stopped looking at it. The old Albatros coughed, seemed to stop in midair, jumped forward—and at last he experienced the pleasure of flight.

From that harrowing test of mind and mettle, Stanaitis wrote, he learned more than he had in all the many hours with his instructor, who had trained him to rely only on instruments, not on his own perceptions. It turned out that the speedometer—of which the air corps had only one—was moved from one aircraft to another as needed, and had been screwed on so tightly that the indicators were stuck.

Among the student aviators' major duties was keeping an eye on the foreign mercenaries, who could not be expected to be Lithuanian patriots. Even so, they were unprepared for the betrayal when it happened.

On October 16, 1919, a monoplane was caught in an ice storm and forced to land at the edge of a forest. The pilot was ready to take off again when a group of armed Lithuanians emerged from the trees, asked to see documents, and found that the pilot, a German, had no flight permit to cross Lithuanian airspace. He was carrying three passengers, two Turkish pashas and a soldier.

The Lithuanians ordered the captured pilot to fly the aircraft to Kaunas, accompanied by one of the Lithuanians. The German complied, not realizing that he could have flown in any direction, for the Lithuanian with him had never been in an airplane before. In Kaunas, the pilot and one of the three passengers, the soldier, were released to make their way home, while the two pashas were interned in Kaunas pending further decision, and the plane was confiscated.

It turned out that the Lithuanians had captured the former Turkish war minister, Enver Pasha, "who had dragged the Turks into the First World War on the side of the Kaiser," wrote Peseckas. "Now, with the Western Allies having won the war, he was unable to go home because the young nationalists, led by Kemal Atatürk, had sentenced him to death in absentia as a war criminal." The other Turkish passenger was his adjutant.

The captured aircraft was also a prize. It was a Junkers F 13 prototype, built of metal and clad with aluminum. The Germans had named it *Annelise*, and were keeping its existence secret. They wanted it back. The Allies also wanted it. The Lithuanians chose to keep it.

During the ensuing days, the Turks were quartered in a hotel in Kaunas and permitted to move about freely. That was a big mistake. They became acquainted with the hired German pilots.

"One midday, we were hurrying to our meal," recalled Peseckas. "At the door to the dining hall, one of the hired German aviators stopped us and asked, with a smile, 'Test flight?' That meant that he was going to do a test flight and if a student wanted to come along, he could."

The German took the first young man who spoke up and walked away with him. Before long, that student came running back and reported what happened.

Soon after takeoff, the engine had begun to knock. The pilot landed in a nearby field and told the student to get out and check the carburetor. As soon as he stepped out to do that, three men emerged from the bushes. The student recognized them as the two pashas and the soldier who had arrived with them. The pilot turned, a pistol in each hand pointed at the student. The Turks boarded, and the plane took off. Later the Lithuanians learned that the German had prearranged the knock in the engine.

Mourning Juozas Kumpis, the first aviation school graduate to be killed in battle.

That same day, a telegram arrived, stating that the plane was fine, but required fuel, and giving the location where it could be retrieved. The German also requested that someone bring the possessions he and the Turks had left behind, and the pay due to him up to that day.

"We were all very surprised," wrote Peseckas. "The evening before, we had enjoyed a friendly evening together. He told us of his adventures above France . . . and we sang folk songs accompanied by mandolins." The German had been my father's flight instructor.

After that betrayal of trust, all the German airmen were dismissed, and flight instruction ceased completely. Some British pilots were hired to replace them, but they spoke none of the languages the Lithuanians knew, and the Lithuanians did not speak English. Instruction resumed only in 1921, when Pranas Hiksa, a Lithuanian who had completed aviation school in England, joined the air force. My father was assigned to be his adjutant and completed his flight training with him.

By the end of 1919, about a hundred aircraft, in various conditions, were parked inside the dirigible hangar. Twenty-four had been delivered by train from Germany as part of the reparations to Lithuania demanded by the Allies. Several were purchased from the Germans as they withdrew from Kaunas in July. Others were seized as war booty. Many of these planes were seriously battered, but mechanics quickly set about making repairs.

When historians tried to make an inventory of these aircraft, they couldn't determine the origin of some of them. These had most likely been traded for bacon and other necessities. The postwar years were a time of hunger in Germany, as well as in the Soviet Union. Bacon was an untraceable universal currency—as it would be again during World War II.

BY THE BEGINNING of 1920, the Lithuanians had driven the Bermontians and the remnant German troops out of the country. Now, however, they were at war with Poland over Vilnius. Fledgling aviators were sent to the Polish front. In October 1920, with Vilnius in

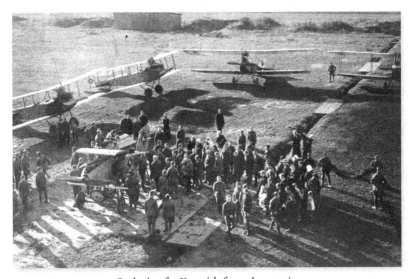

Gathering for Kumpis's funeral procession

Polish hands, a commission representing the Western Allies ordered that fighting stop. Failure to resolve the issue of Vilnius kept the two neighboring countries hostile to each other. Germany and Soviet Russia would crush them both.

On May 29, 1921, the air corps staged a celebration, Aviation Day, to mark the second anniversary of its existence and show off its achievements. Some of the guests would be treated to short flights.

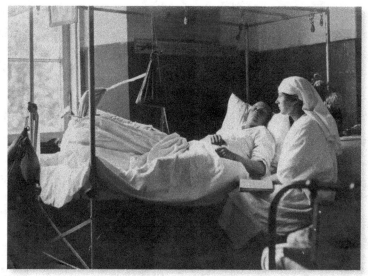

Bronė with Lt. Simas Stanaitis, injured in plane crash

Stanaitis had promised to give a ride to the attractive nurse Bronė Aleksandravičiūtė, whom he had met at a dance. Before flying with a passenger, however, he was required to practice flying with a squadron. He found it difficult to stay in formation because he was piloting an Albatros C III, which was faster than the Albatros B II that all the others in his squadron were flying. To keep his plane from jumping ahead of the others he had to stay at minimum speed. This was risky, because at minimum speed the aircraft was in danger of plunging to the ground at any moment. At the altitude of three hundred meters, one of the other pilots panicked and accelerated, creating an air current that propelled Stanaitis into a horizontal spin. He managed to right the plane but could not regain altitude, and crashed, losing consciousness, breaking a leg and a kneecap. He would spend the next two months in the hospital, where the nurse he had planned to impress with his flying skills tended to his injuries.

Aviation Day began at ten a.m., with Mass in the zeppelin hangar, and did not end until ten p.m., according to a report written by General Kraucevičius, chief of the air force. It featured a parade of aircraft and demonstration flights, much feasting and dancing, and fireworks. After the guests finally dispersed, twenty-one of the proud, irrepressible young airmen walked en masse through the streets of Kaunas.

"Watch out, men, women, and children," they shouted. "The air force is coming!"

They were arrested by city police and jailed for the rest of the night for disturbing the peace.

"The eagles behind bars" took the matter in stride, Peseckas wrote. "They sat at chess boards while Antanas Gustaitis, lying on a bunk, played against all twenty of them."

BRONĖ AND ANTANAS MEET

My father, Antanas Gustaitis, was born on March 26, 1898, at six in the morning, to Kazimieras Gustaitis and his wife Petronėlė, in the village of Obelinė. He was baptized in a nearby church, and his name was entered into the official book of the Marijampolė region's permanent residents as a member of the peasant class. That much was officially recorded. The few other facts I have gathered about my father's early years are only a springboard for the imagination.

It was still dark outside when his parents first held him, their sixth child, in their arms, in the light of a kerosene lamp. The windows were frosted. It is likely that snow still covered the fields and ice lay on the pond and on the puddles in the roads. But inside the house, the tiled woodstove spread plenty of warmth.

I picture the baby—Antanėlis (little Antanas, as everyone called him)—asleep in a cradle set in a patch of sunlight in the kitchen, or, in the evening, watching shadows cast on the whitewashed walls by flickering lamps. He heard the rain, the steady rhythm of the shuttle of his mother's loom, the voices of his parents, three brothers, and two sisters. Crows cawed in the bare trees outside. His mother sang to him.

Antanėlis

Soon, rivulets of snowmelt began to flow in wagon tracks, ushering in the mud season. Antanėlis's ears picked up the songs of birds courting noisily among the apple trees. Swallows built a nest under the eaves above the kitchen window that faced the orchard. Trees burst into bloom, and on warmer days, when his mother took the baby outside, pinkish white petals flew in the breeze and floated to the ground.

I imagine my father as a child, running barefoot in the grass, playing with his brothers and sisters, feeding chickens and pigs, living within his large family according to the cycles of the sun and the seasons.

The name of my father's village is derived from the word for apple tree, *obelis*. Kazimieras Gustaitis was a relatively prosperous farmer who was known among neighbors as an excellent source of advice on apple cultivation. Like most Lithuanian farmers of that time, the family produced almost all its basic necessities.

By the time I was born, my father's father had passed on, as had my maternal grandfather. Of my grandmother in Obelinė I have only

The parents of Antanas Gustaitis

a dim memory. I do have an eloquent photograph of both my father's parents, however, taken in their flower garden, with a picket fence in the background, and beyond the fence a glimpse of a field, then woods. Only a corner of the house is visible, at top right, with traditional decorative wooden carvings along the eaves.

I don't know the date of the picture, but my grandparents look to be past middle age. My grandmother is seated in a chair, in a long dark dress, her head covered by a scarf tied under her chin in the traditional manner for country women. Her hands lie lightly in her lap, fingers loosely intertwined, holding a prayer book. It's easy to imagine a small child on that ample lap. My grandmother's oval face, framed by the scarf, shows patience and something more. Mild curiosity maybe. It's a soft expression. She's in repose.

My grandfather stands to her left, arms hanging somewhat stiffly at his sides. He's intense, sharply focused. His hip-length jacket and dark shirt with high collar are, like my grandmother's dress, of home-grown flax and wool. His substantial mustache turns downward at the sides of his mouth. His deep-set eyes beneath a high forehead and a receding hairline are traits that would be passed down his lineage. My father was nearly bald by age twenty-four.

This photograph, in our family album, is next to the portrait of my mother as a young girl with her parents, taken in a studio in Riga, carefully posed in garments that are exquisitely tailored and fitted. They are a city family. Different as they are, though, both my grandfathers have a commanding presence.

On a farm, before mechanization, healthy children meant more hands to do the work, but Kazimieras Gustaitis wanted his boys to have an education, and he could afford to provide it for them. He enrolled Antanas in the elementary school his older brother Juozas was already attending. One teacher taught as many as a hundred children of all four grade levels in one room, with the older and more advanced pupils helping the others. Antanas was often one of these more advanced pupils, so here began what was to become a lifelong practice, learning and teaching at the same time. Instruction was in Russian, though sometimes the teacher would explain something in Lithuanian. One hour a week was officially allotted to study of the Lithuanian language.

The parents of Antanas appreciated their youngest son's love of reading, and—the story has been passed on by the his siblings—sometimes let him sit in a tree with a book while everyone else was busy in the orchard or fields. He followed his brother Juozas to the Marijampolė Gymnasium, a secondary school in a spacious two-story brick building surrounded by trees and a black iron fence in the town of Marijampolė, twelve kilometers from Obelinė. More than a century later, I would stand in front of the heavy wooden doors of this school and read my father's name on a wall plaque, listed among graduates who played a significant role in Lithuania's history.

The Marijampolė Gymnasium offered a classical education preparatory for university study. From my twenty-first-century American perspective, the depth and breadth of the curriculum is astonishing, especially for a provincial school in a country where the vast majority of the population was illiterate. It included mathematics, physics, Russian and Polish history and geography, religion, nature, Latin, Greek, German, French, and Lithuanian. Also gymnastics, drawing, and music.

Some particulars of my father's time in the Marijampolė Gymnasium were recalled by his classmates in interviews years later, and recorded in articles and a book. One of his fellow students said that Antanas "was the most talented in the class, especially in mathematics," and that he gladly helped students who struggled. "He could have been first in the class, but apparently he was not interested in that: only in mathematics and Russian did he have the highest grades."

My father did not always follow the teachers' rules, this classmate told the interviewer, recalling a day when the math teacher became enraged because Antanas had not brought his textbook to class. "Nothing comes of these talented students!" the teacher declared. "They have too much self-confidence. They lose the habit of working attentively, get lazy, and end up as failures."

Russian was the language of instruction, as it had been in elementary school. According to another alumnus, however, some of the Lithuanian teachers made sure that their students, 80 percent of them Lithuanians, also learned about their own nation's past. Speaking carefully, lest they fall afoul of Russian censors, these teachers sought to inspire students to seek their people's liberation.

Antanas learned—if he hadn't already, from his parents—about the 1410 Battle of Žalgiris (Grünwald) in which the Lithuanian Grand Duke Vytautas and King Jogaila (Jagiello) of Poland decisively defeated the Teutonic Knights, who had been raiding pagan Lithuania for about a century. The crusader knights never fully recovered from this defeat.

Antanas also learned that Vytautas was considered to have been a wise ruler, governing by strategy rather than force. He expanded the borders of the Grand Duchy of Lithuania to the Black Sea and nearly as far east as Moscow, but allowed conquered people to follow their customs and religions. He invited Jews, who were being persecuted in Russia, to come to Lithuania, seeing an important role they could play by bringing skills as merchants and craftsmen to a land of farmers and woodsmen. In the future, an astonishing number of Lithuanian children would be named Vytautas.

Because Obelinė was too far from Marijampolė for Antanas to go home every day, he boarded at a farm within walking distance from the town during the school year. A fellow boarder remembered that in his free time he played chess, strummed a mandolin, and read copiously, "books he borrowed from the school library or obtained elsewhere," and that he followed a rigorous physical fitness routine, starting every morning with a fifteen-minute set of exercises, then washing his whole body and massaging it with a towel dipped into cold water. Antanas also organized a soccer team at the school.

Such details gleaned about my father's early years led me to conclude that he must have been an all-around outstanding human being.

THE OUTBREAK OF the Great War in 1914 interrupted the peaceful course of Antanas's education.

In March 1915, as German troops advanced toward Marijampolė, the school was evacuated to Yaroslavl, a city northeast of Moscow on a trade route to Asia, known for its golden onion towers and monasteries. Each student was allotted ten rubles of travel money. Although many chose to move instead to Voronezh, where a Lithuanian community existed and some outstanding Lithuanian literati taught at a secondary school, Antanas opted for faraway Yaroslavl.

When he graduated in spring 1916, he was prepared for university study in the humanities, but applied to take the examination for entry into the prestigious Emperor Alexander I Engineering Institute in Saint Petersburg, which turned out engineers for transportation infrastructure projects, including railroads, water systems, and bridges. Admission was highly competitive.

Antanas easily passed the entrance exam, was admitted, and in September 1916 received a student certificate, along with official permission to live freely in Saint Petersburg and vicinity. But after his first year at the institute, the war interrupted again. In December, foreseeing that he was almost certain to be drafted into the military, he asked for a deferment so that he could enter artillery school.

Like many other young Lithuanians scattered throughout Russia, he returned to his native land after the Bolsheviks made peace with Germany, signing the Treaty of Brest-Litovsk, and Lithuania began the struggle for independence.

THROUGHOUT MY CHILDHOOD and youth, when my mother talked about her years with my father as the happy time in her life, it never occurred to me to consider how long they were together. My mother's life seemed to be divided into a before and after: before 1941, when the Soviets invaded Lithuania, and after, when she lived for her three daughters, cherishing her memories of the time before. My mother lived 101 years. She had only 13 of those with Antanas, yet as I heard my mother talk, they seemed like forever.

Soon after her arrival in Kaunas in the winter of 1919–20, Bronė returned to her professional work as a nurse.

"There were announcements everywhere, calling attention to a great shortage of nurses," she wrote. She volunteered at the military hospital and was immediately sent as a member of a five-person medical team to a border reception point for Lithuanian prisoners of war returning from Poland.

Medical team ready to receive prisoners of war released by the Poles.

"They were in terrible shape," my mother wrote. "Many were sick with typhus, and six had cholera." The medic and the other nurse on Bronė's team fell ill with diphtheria. "I stayed healthy, I was very careful never to eat anywhere but in our mess hall." Five of the cholera patients died. After three weeks, back in Kaunas, Bronė was assigned to work in a ward at the military hospital.

There were fifteen soldiers in my ward, young men, most of whom could barely sign their names. I offered to teach reading, writing, and arithmetic during my free time to anyone who wanted me to. All of them wanted that. Some whose wounds required a lengthy stay at the hospital did learn a little. Years later, a man stopped me in the street. "Madam, do you remember me? You taught me how to count, and I now have a good job in a cooperative. Thank you." That was a pleasure to hear.

After work, Bronė now also had time for fun. Sundays she often went with friends by steamboat on the Nemunas River to a lake in the woods. Some evenings, the aviators put on dances in the zeppelin hangar.

At one of these events, someone pointed out a lieutenant named Antanas Gustaitis, saying he was "our star." But by that time she was already in love, with the handsome Lieutenant Vytautas Jablonskis, whom she had met while he was hospitalized after an airplane crash.

"It was a beautiful love," she remembered, "which led to marriage. But I was too naïve and did not understand that he was already drawn into cards and drinking."

Before long, she was miserable. Her husband almost always went out after dinner to enjoy himself in company that shared his tastes, while she stayed home, waiting up for him. Her health began to fail, and she began to suffer from migraines again.

"At about this time my father died," she wrote, "and we brought my mother to live with us. She took care of the cooking and housekeeping while I worked."

To supplement the family's income, they invited two of Vytautas's fellow officers to eat dinner with them as paying guests. One of them was Antanas Gustaitis.

Antanas in his first ANBO, in front of his parents' home

Bronė's husband continued to leave right after dinner. The guests often stayed to keep her company. Antanas asked her if she would give him some German lessons, and she gladly agreed. They found they had a lot to talk about.

"I came to love Antanas," my mother wrote. "A strong, beautiful friendship developed."

Antanas was just then planning to build his first airplane. Although he would use his own funds, money he had saved, he was worried that the chief of the air force, General Kraucevičius, might not allow him to build it at the air force's plant.

To improve his chances of support from his chief, Antanas thought he might invite a nephew of the chief to be a partner in the project—in name only, because this nephew was not qualified to contribute to the design or construction. Bronė advised against such a move, arguing that it might well lead to Antanas's losing ownership of his creation.

"Better just ask for yourself—take the risk," she urged. "He followed my suggestion, and the general staff approved. Antanas was grateful to me and called his plane ANBO," which combined letters of their names.

He launched his single-seat monoplane successfully on July 14, 1925. Perhaps not coincidentally, July 14 is Bastille Day, France's independence day. He might have already set his sights on study in Paris.

When asked what ANBO meant, he would not tell. This makes sense, given that Bronė was married to Vytautas Jablonskis at this time. The airmen devised their own interpretation: *Antanas Nori Būti Ore* (Antanas wants to be in the air), and that explanation stuck.

Over the next fourteen years, before the curtain fell on Lithuania's independence, my father would design a total of nine different ANBOs and supervise the building of sixty-six aircraft he had designed for the growing Lithuanian air force.

After the success of his first plane, which he built with only such

ANBO II above Kaunas

aeronautical engineering knowledge as he could find in books, the Lithuanian government funded his study at the École Supérieure d'Aéronautique et de Construction Mécanique in Paris. He was not the first Lithuanian aviator to enroll there. A fellow graduate of the aviation school, Jurgis Dobkevičius, had preceded him, using his own means.

Dobkevičius had designed three airplanes, which had been built at the air force's facilities in Kaunas. All three shared one serious flaw: poor visibility for the pilot on descent. An improved version of Dobi III was ready for its flight test on June 8, 1926, the day before its creator was scheduled to return to Paris. He promised his mother he would not fly it, but couldn't resist. Early that morning he eluded her by climbing out a window, made his way to the airfield, and took the plane up.

Stanaitis, a good friend of Dobkevičius, was walking toward the field just then. He saw the pilot try twice to land, then, on his third attempt, crash into a lone oak tree on a slope. The first to reach the mortally injured flyer was his mother. A cross made of two propellers was erected above the new grave.

BEFORE LEAVING FOR France, my mother recalled, "Antanas told me that he would be waiting for me to be free, so we could marry."

Recently, I learned that my father had written a courtly letter to my mother's then-husband, telling him he had observed that their marriage was no longer happy, and if Vytautas had no objection, he, Antanas, would like to ask Bronė to be his wife. Whether or not Vytautas replied is not known, but he kept the letter. It was found among his effects after his death many years later.

The divorce was amicable. On September 28, 1927, while Antanas was home from Paris on vacation, a small wedding took place. Soon after, with Bronė's encouragement, Vytautas married Vera, a Russian woman who had fallen in love with him and enjoyed the same forms of recreation as he did. The first time the two couples appeared together, at a dance, they caused a stir, for divorce was uncommon at

Wedding of Antanas and Bronė, 1927

Newlyweds in Paris

that time in Catholic Lithuania, and friendly relations between former spouses even more so.

After the wedding, Bronė Gustaitienė came to Paris with her new husband. "We found a room with kitchen privileges on Montmartre, near Sacre Coeur church. We lived simply as students and were happy," my mother wrote.

How romantic that must have been, to be in Paris, in love, in the late 1920s, that legendary time of artistic rebellion and creation. Bronė studied French at the Alliance Française and took piano lessons. Antanas, in his free time, had already designed his second airplane, the ANBO II, a two-seater monoplane. He was permitted to build it in the air force plant while home on vacation, and took it on its test flight on November 10, 1927.

After completing the three-year course of study at the École Supérieure d'Aéronautique, ranking third in his class, Antanas came home with a diploma in aviation and mechanical engineering. General Kraucevičius assigned him to be his aide on technical matters. In April 1928 he was put in charge of the air force's technical division, which was responsible for supplies, fuel, repairs, and aircraft construction. His predecessor in this post had been building copies of German aircraft that had come into Lithuania's possession. Five of these, all built in 1927, had poor flight records. Antanas ended the practice of copying and began serial production of planes he designed.

He was especially proud of the ANBO IV, a two-seat parasol-type monoplane, designed for reconnaissance purposes and also as a light bomber. He tested the prototype on July 14, 1932, flew it to Latvia, Estonia, and Finland, and then began to prepare for a longer journey, around Europe, to twelve European capitals to display his small country's aeronautical capacity.

That longer European tour, two years later, also commemorated two Lithuanian American aviators, Steponas Darius and Stasys Girėnas, who had crashed and died in a German forest the year before, having nearly completed the first nonstop flight from New York to Kaunas.

Darius was one of several Lithuanian Americans who had come to Kaunas during the early days of independence and joined the air force. After Charles Lindbergh landed the *Spirit of St. Louis* in Paris after his solo flight from New York in 1927, Darius decided to undertake a record-breaking transatlantic flight as well, flying nonstop— farther than Lindbergh—New York to Kaunas. In 1931 he took a leave of absence to visit his mother in the United States and secure veteran benefits due him for serving in the U.S. Armed Forces during the Great War.

To raise money to buy a suitable aircraft, he performed aerial acrobatics at air shows organized by Lithuanian American communities. He chose as co-pilot another American Lithuanian flyer, Stasys Girėnas. With their own funds and contributions from relatives and others, they bought a six-seat Bellanca CH-300 Pacemaker high-wing monoplane, named it *Lituanica,* and dedicated their flight to Lithuania. They took off from Floyd Bennett Field in Brooklyn on July 15, 1933, and flew 6,411 kilometers in 37 hours 11 minutes without landing. They crashed just 636 kilometers from their destination. Tens of thousands of people who had gathered to greet Darius and Girėnas at the Kaunas airfield walked in a funeral procession instead. The two aviators became national heroes.

My father headed a commission of inquiry into the cause of the crash. It found no evidence of foul play. The pilots were fully prepared to accomplish their mission, the inquiry found; they had suitable technical equipment and had completed the most difficult part of the journey accurately and on time. The tragedy was blamed on "difficult atmospheric conditions, to which engine trouble contributed." It happened on a rainy night, and the pilots were tired. To this day, however, some people continue to suspect that the *Lituanica* was downed by Germans, mistaken for a spy plane.

ON JUNE 25, 1934, five weeks after I was born, three ANBO IVs with a total crew of five took off from the airfield in Kaunas on a nine-thousand-kilometer tour, visiting Sweden, Denmark, Holland, Belgium, Great Britain, France, Italy, Czechoslovakia, Hungary, Rumania, and the USSR.

Antanas Gustaitis had been appointed commander-in-chief of military aviation a few weeks before that flight. He was promoted to the rank of brigadier general in 1937. Although his administrative duties increased with his rising rank, he continued to design and build new military aircraft, and piloted each one on its test flight. He also encouraged the development of sports aviation. In 1932, he had become Lithuania's chess champion, but now he no longer had much time for chess.

With visiting British aviator Jean Batten

LITHUANIA BECAME A modern European country during its years of independence between the two world wars. The government introduced its own currency, the litas, and stabilized it, linking its value to the U.S. dollar. It instituted land reform, reducing the size of the largest estates and allotting land to country people for small farms. Agricultural cooperatives were formed, enabling farmers to collaborate in processing and marketing their products. Education was a priority. As of 1927, four years of elementary school was compulsory.

In Kaunas, which in 1919 was a provincial garrison town with streets impassably muddy after heavy rain, about ten thousand modern buildings were constructed during this interwar period of independence. The government sent talented young people to Italy, Germany, and other Western European countries to study architecture. The city is now known for its excellent collection of international modernist styles.

My mother recalled that the government found creative solutions to some of the inevitable economic setbacks. One year, she said, a huge order for geese was cancelled by a foreign buyer after the farmers had already begun to raise goslings. To avert economic catastrophe for the farmers, the government ordered all public employees to buy geese or goose meat, setting the quota according to salary size.

"If you were invited somewhere for dinner," my mother said, "you did not wonder what would be served. 'Guess what we're having?' the hostess would joke. There was no need to guess."

Creative though they were, the Lithuanians did not succeed in maintaining a democratic government, however. In June 1926, the Party of National Progress, which had been in power since 1920, originally led by Antanas Smetona as president, lost the election to a coalition of national minorities and the left. The new government severely cut the military budget. In December 1926, a group of military officers, mostly from the air force, overthrew this elected government and returned the Party of National Progress to office. Smetona was president again—the country's first and last president during this interwar time of independence.

Bronė Gustaitienė with her firstborn daughter

Bronė with Jūratė and baby Rasa

In the Baltic surf

My father did not take part in the military coup. He was in Paris when it took place. He also believed that the military must obey civilian authorities and play no role in politics.

ACCORDING TO MY mother, our family life was simple and peaceful. She and my father liked to go to movies and to walk. They attended various official dinners and balls but didn't entertain much at home. I remember moments: Tėtė picking up Mama, one of his arms under her knees, the other around the waist, as he twirled with her and they laughed. Mama scolding me for getting into her makeup and the roughness of the cloth with which she wiped the lipstick and rouge from my face. The fragrance of dried apples from the bag kept behind Mama's dressing table. Sitting on Tėtė's lap at the table before breakfast. All the while, darkness was descending on the world.

In January 1940, and again in May, my father was sent on secret missions to Moscow. He returned from the last one of these just three days before the Soviet invasion. En route, he told my mother, he had seen a buildup of Soviet troops east of our country's border. He tried to meet with President Smetona, to plead for joint defense with Latvia and Estonia. The air force was ready.

"In his opinion," my mother said, "even if a Soviet occupation could not be avoided, there had to be at least some resistance, so the world would know that we were taken over by force."

But Lithuania's president would not make an appointment with him.

When the Red Army marched into the country, Smetona fled to Germany. He would die in 1944 in Cleveland, Ohio. Several other military and political leaders fled, and my mother pleaded with her husband that we do likewise, but he refused.

"Everyone can't escape, even if they wanted to," he responded. "Life will be difficult. But why should the intelligentsia save itself, abandoning the people? The more educated people remain, the harder it will be to take over the country completely."

On June 17, two days after the invasion, General Gustaitis issued an order urging that the Soviet military be treated with politeness. The invaders did not respond in kind. They demanded that the air force turn over airplanes, supplies, and buildings—including officers' housing—to them. Most of our apartment was subsequently occupied by Russian officers. Aircraft were pushed out of the hangars. My father complained that they would soon be ruined unless they were covered, to no avail.

The new masters of Lithuania's air force grounded it, barred the airmen from airfields, and began dismissing officers, several at a time, or sending them into the reserves. They set up a commission charged with dismantling the air force and appointed my father, who had built it, as its chairman. Only after he had completed that task was he permitted to resign from active duty.

That was the end of The Time Before, the time my mother's memory would return to in the difficult years that lay ahead.

5
....

ESCAPE

My sister Jūratė remembered what happened during the night after my parents parted, the beginning of the Time After.

"Mama woke me, holding a finger to her lips. She said, 'Get up, don't get dressed, do as you are told.'

"She wrapped a blanket around me and led me outside.

"The car was there, with Baba, holding the baby, and you and the chauffeur inside. You were sleeping. It had snowed and the road was muddy. We got stuck, and then we saw a Russian soldier approaching, with a rifle. Mama said, 'Jesus Maria!' She spoke to him in Russian, told him that I was very sick and she was taking me to the hospital. He helped us dig the wheels out."

We spent the rest of that night with people Jūratė didn't know. She and Mama were in one house, Baba and I in another. Tėtė's friends were taking precautions. Later Mama learned that men in a truck had come for us the following morning, but found us gone.

I remember only that the train we took to escape was crowded, and that it moved slowly through the flat, sparsely populated, frozen landscape, stopping at small stations and sometimes at places where no buildings were in sight, only fields and forests. The wheels clattered and smoke flecked with coal ash blew past the windows. Each time the train started or stopped, metal clanged against metal. We saw Russian soldiers guarding each station, and the red flag with a hammer and sickle flying from poles.

Then—I have no idea how much time had passed—we came to a station with a different flag: two crossed black hooks in the center of a white circle on a red background. A woman sitting across the aisle from me sighed deeply and signed herself with the cross.

Very soon after, a railway official pressed through the crowd and approached Mama. I did not hear what he said to her, since she was sitting on the other side of the aisle, but as she heard his message, she stood up, the baby in her arms.

"*Ich muss zurück! Ich muss zurück zu meinem Mann.*" I must go back. I must go back to my husband.

"*Das ist night möglich, gnädige Frau,*" said the official. That is not possible, madam.

STIFF FROM LONG hours in cramped positions, hungry, thirsty, and sleepy, we struggled out of the train in Lodz, the Polish city the Nazi occupants had renamed Litzmannstadt in honor of Karl Litzmann, the general who led German forces into this region in 1914. All the passengers on this train were officially *Umsiedler* (resettlers), coming home to their *Vaterland*, although for many who had German roots, Lithuania had been home for generations. Others, including us, had claimed German ancestry only to escape from the Russians.

As we were getting off the train, Jūratė was stopped by a uniformed man. After inspecting her closely, he measured the circumference of her head and photographed her before allowing her to rejoin the rest of us. Jūratė's skin tone is darker than our father's and mine, although it's about the same as that of our mother, who was not scrutinized. Nobody explained why the Nazi official singled out Jūratė.

It was nighttime and cold in the dimly lit station. Food and a place to sleep awaited us in a nearby school that had been converted to a transit camp, but first we had to pass through the delousing station to rid ourselves of any bugs we might have brought with us. Men and women with Red Cross armbands on their brown uniforms directed us to a huge shower room, where we stripped, handed all our clothing to attendants for disinfection, and picked up towels from a stack. As we stepped under the showers, we stretched out our palms to receive gobs of a green disinfectant paste.

I was shivering by the time the warm water flowed over me. My mother massaged the slimy soap all over my head and body. When I whimpered, she told me to stop complaining. We retrieved our clothing, now stinking of chemicals, from a bench in the dressing room.

Our next stop was the school gym, already crowded with fellow passengers and their baggage. Babies were sniffling and wailing; old people were coughing. Mama led us to an unoccupied spot against a wall, and we built an enclosure for ourselves with our luggage. Then she went off to register. Women in uniform came around with milk for babies, and someone handed out blankets from a cart. Little Elena slept in Baba's arms, while Jūratė and I, keeping on our coats and caps, curled up miserably on the rough gray blankets. After a long while, Mama returned.

"We have beds on the second floor. And there's a nursery for infants," she said. Baba looked alarmed.

"You will take her there? And stay with her? Or should I?"

"They won't let us. But don't worry, she'll be under a nurse's supervision." Mama was a nurse, and she trusted nurses.

She lifted my five-month-old sister from our grandmother's arms and went off with her. She returned empty-handed.

"The nursery is quiet and clean," she said. "It will be better for her than being with us. I'll be going there to feed her."

We made our way upstairs to a classroom. School desks were stacked against a wall, replaced by bunk beds standing head to head. Jūratė took an upper bunk; I took the lower. Baba was in the adjacent lower bunk, Mama above her. Strangers filled the rest of the room. The overhead lights went out, voices hushed, sounds died down.

I wanted my father to say good night to me. Where was he now? Mama had learned on the train that the Russians had stopped him. What did they do to him? An image of a dark room without windows surfaced under my eyelids, but I immediately banished it and called up another.

I'm standing beside the birch tree outside Jūratė's bedroom window. Mama and Jūratė are beside me. I hear Tėtė's plane, purring softly in the distance, then louder. I look up and there he is. I see the wings of the ANBO, silver against the light blue sky. The sound of his engine grows into a roar. We wave, he waves to us, and I watch him disappear in the direction of the airfield. The sound of his airplane fades, then again grows louder, and there he is once more, flying right over our heads. The sky is my favorite shade of blue. Soon he'll be home for the midday meal. The hum in the sky lulls me to sleep.

Jūratė told me years later that the next morning she sat up, looked out the window, and saw a street with a barbed-wire fence and elevated railroad tracks farther on. On our side of the fence she saw several men walking in the gutter, single file. A German soldier with a rifle slung over his shoulder walked on the sidewalk, parallel to them. The men in the gutter kept their heads down, and on their dark coats, front and back, Jūratė saw yellow patches in the shape of a six-pointed star. She was frightened, although she didn't know the meaning of what she was seeing.

After a few days we were transferred to Kirschendorf, a former children's camp in the woods. Spring had barely begun. It was cold and damp outside and also inside the cabins, which were usually inhabited only during summer. Later Mama wrote,

It wasn't bad: we were given food; the children got milk and vita-mins. An epidemic of chicken pox broke out. Immediately all the children were sent to the camp hospital. Because I was still nursing Elytė, they put a bed for me next to her. Jūratė also went through mumps during this time.

Every afternoon the smaller children were rounded up to learn German songs and play vigorous games. Older children, including Jūratė, went on hikes in the woods, singing as they walked. Through loudspeakers attached to camp buildings and trees, we heard that the German armies were winning the war.

What I remember most distinctly from this camp is a set of colorful postcards the woman who taught us songs distributed to all the children, with instructions to honor *Der Führer,* who was a father to us all. I stared at my three cards with portraits of Adolf Hitler, an unpleasant-looking man standing on a podium in a brown uniform, against the background of the Nazi flag. He certainly was not *my* father.

Spring arrived. Mud puddles left by winter snowmelt shrank and dried. Firs sprouted light green tips. Little blue-and-white flowers appeared in sunny spots.

Mama dreamed of Tėtė often.

"When I see him in a dream, I know something is about to happen and I should prepare," she told us. "He is warning me. He is protect-ing us."

When I heard her say that, I felt that my father was somehow almost with us, yet that feeling only sharpened my longing for him and for home.

"He was so real in my dream," Mama said sometimes.

Did that mean that he was dead, I wondered, and his spirit was now our guardian angel? I didn't ask. But my father's absence was a dark empty place in my heart.

ON JUNE 22, Germany attacked the Soviet Union, breaking Hitler's nonaggression agreement with Stalin. The attack stunned Stalin. Soviet armies were completely unprepared. The Germans marched quickly through the Baltics, the Ukraine, and Byelorussia, and by midsummer were deep in Russia.

As the leaves of maples were turning to gold, we were moved to Duderstadt, a thousand-year-old walled town near Göttingen in Lower Saxony. There we were quartered in an apartment shared with another family, parents and a young boy. There was a common kitchen down the hall, but food rations were skimpy.

I remember the cobbled streets, red geraniums in window boxes of half-timbered houses, and a spiral tower, like something out of a fairy tale, above one of the old town gates. The people of Duderstadt were proud of their town and kept it very clean. Women aired out comforters on balcony railings on sunny mornings and scrubbed their front steps on their hands and knees.

It was here in Duderstadt that I began to attend school. Although I didn't speak much German, I had been hearing it spoken around me and understood quite a bit. We sat at little desks lined up in rows facing the front of the room. The teacher was a Catholic nun. She wore a long black skirt and a black veil, and her face was framed in white cloth.

As she entered the classroom, we had to jump to our feet, stretch out our right arm, and say *Heil Hitler.*

After we sat down, the teacher told us to hold up our handkerchiefs. A child who failed to bring one, or raised a dirty one, had to walk to the front of the classroom and extend the right arm, palm up, so the teacher could smack it with a ruler. That only happened to me once. It stung. But I never incurred the next level of punishment, which was to have your face dunked in the bowl that held the chalky water used for squeezing out the sponge that wiped the blackboard.

The teacher walked up and down the room, inspecting the letters in the angular Gothic script we were writing in our lined notebooks. We wrote the same letter over and over until she was satisfied. Then she would mark a check at the end of the last line, and write another letter on the next line for us to copy.

Gothic letters do not flow easily, unlike the Latin alphabet. Your hand cannot run with them. Writing them is more like walking stiffly or marching. But I enjoyed shaping some of the letters and pretending I was a nun in olden times, writing on parchment.

After school, walking back to our temporary home, I passed a shop under a stone arch with interesting things in its display window: notebooks and pens, carved wooden dolls, and little stickers with flowers, animals, and fairy-tale figures; also stickers that children collected and pasted into special notebooks. Mama bought me a notebook and told me I could choose one or two stickers. The sticker I wanted was bigger and more expensive than others, so I only took that one, a pink rose.

What stayed most vividly in my sister's mind from our time in Duderstadt was being hungry. Watching others eat while she was ravenous was especially hard. She had to do that on days she had piano lessons.

"Mother knew how important the piano was to me, so she somehow managed to arrange lessons for me," Jūratė said. "The teacher taught me during her lunch hour, while she sat next to me on the bench, eating enormous sandwiches. I tried to play, with my mouth watering."

ON JUNE 22, 1941, when Hitler attacked the Soviet Union, German troops replaced the Red Army as the occupying power in the Baltic countries, and Mama started trying to go home, hoping she would find out what happened to Tėtė. She never considered continuing without him to Argentina, or any other country. But to return she needed a permit from a commission that had sorted all the *Umsiedler* into two groups. Those found to be authentic *Volksdeutsche* were classified as group A, the rest as B. This sorting was in keeping with Hitler's *Lebensraum* plan. He intended to replace the populations of Eastern Europe with Germans. People in the A group were permitted to go back to the countries they had fled, and could expect to be given land and property seized from Jews and other people whom the Nazis despised. Our family was labeled B and denied permission.

But *nicht möglich* (not possible) was not in Mama's vocabulary. She had the address of Petras Karvelis, the father of my best friend, Ugnė, who was now living in Berlin with his family. Before the war he had been, at various times, Lithuania's foreign minister, a banker, and a businessman. What he was doing in Berlin Mama was not sure, but she had heard he was working with the Lithuanian resistance, and had connections, so she wrote to him. He suggested she come to Berlin and appeal to officials in person. Berlin was 150 kilometers from Duderstadt. She took a train.

In her notebook, Mama wrote,

I followed his directions and went to various offices, but everywhere the answer was the same: "We will help you settle here, your children will go to school, but we cannot allow you to return home."

Finally Karvelis said, "You have made the rounds, only the top man remains, Rosenberg. Try, perhaps you can reach him."

Alfred Rosenberg was Reichsminister for the occupied eastern territories, which included the Baltic States. His name would go down in history as one of the most fanatical Nazis. Born in Estonia to wealthy Baltic German parents, he moved to Munich during the Russian Revolution and there wrote for a racist newspaper, fulminating against "Judeo-Bolshevism," and blaming Jews for the Bolshevik victory, which had disrupted his life.

It was Rosenberg who devised the Nazi racial theory, putting "Aryans" at the top of the human ladder, Poles and other Slavs beneath them, and Jews, Roma, and Africans at the bottom. Later, with Heinrich Himmler and Reinhard Heydrich, Rosenberg planned for the "final solution of the Jewish question" in two stages: concentrating them in designated areas, and then, in Rosenberg's words, the "biological elimination of Jewry in Europe."

It was the beginning of that first stage—roundup and removal—that Jūratė had unwittingly witnessed that morning in Lodz.

The Nazis first intended the Lodz ghetto to be a holding cage for undesirables, to keep them from contaminating the Aryan super-race while the rest of the city was modernized. Later the ghetto was turned into a labor camp where thousands of people, including children as young as eight, worked twelve hours a day producing goods for the Nazi war industry.

But much of this was still in the future. Right then, my mother needed permission to go home, so she set out to see Reichsminister Rosenberg. She talked her way past several guards and came as far as his secretary. Perhaps because she spoke German, or for some other reason, she evoked the man's sympathy. She told him that her husband had been captured by the Russians and she was alone, a woman with three children and an elderly mother. She showed him a petition she had written to Rosenberg and pleaded to be allowed to present it personally to the Reichsminister.

He was very pleasant, she wrote in her account, but said, "I cannot let you in to the minister—you surely understand that he is very busy. I will take your petition to him."

The secretary's refusal to let Mama deliver her plea personally may have been a piece of luck. She might not have succeeded face to face with Rosenberg himself, since she didn't look at all like the stereotypical blonde "Aryan" beauty. Mama wrote,

He went into Rosenberg's office, and returned moments later with Rosenberg's signature. Permission was granted with one condition: that I work for some kind of German office in Lithuania. Because I could type and knew German, I was immediately assigned to Zentral Generalgesellschaft Ost (Central General Company East), and we soon left for Kaunas.

RETURN TO KAUNAS

When we arrived back in Lithuania, Mama found an apartment in Kaunas, near the office where she worked as typist and translator in the German military command office. The job came with a major benefit: superior rations. I remember her bringing home a loaf of bread one day and saying, as she showed it to Baba, "Look. The regular ration for this week was half this loaf. Who can live on that?"

People managed because Lithuania was an agricultural country. Almost everyone who was not a farmer had relatives who were, and knew from experience—most recently during World War I—how to hide food from invaders.

LATE ON THE night after we had finished our Christmas Eve dinner in 1942, I woke from a nightmare that has stayed with me for my entire life. Throughout my childhood, it filled me with dread every time I thought of it. Even now, as I recall it, my chest constricts.

It's night. The lights are out in the hall and on the stairs. I'm in the candlelit dining room, standing near the door to the dark hall in the apartment. All the rest of my family except my father are across the room, gathered beside the Christmas tree that reaches almost to the ceiling.

I hear a rasping buzz. It's the doorbell at the bottom of the dark stairs to the front door. Something horrible is waiting to enter. I look across the room at my family and see that they are all frozen with fear.

Nobody moves. Nobody speaks. Nobody goes to answer. Again I hear the doorbell buzz, louder.

Someone is trying to come in from the street. I hear thumps on the stairs. Someone is climbing, slowly, with the help of a cane. I hold completely still, barely breathing. The thumps are coming closer. Whoever entered is in the corridor that leads to the dining room. Everyone's eyes are turned to the open door. The thumps stop. In the doorway a skeleton woman has appeared, leaning on a walking stick. Her skull is covered by a scarf, tied under her chin the way old women wear them, but hers is not the customary black, it's bright red.

In Lithuania, the word for Death is female. She is now in the room. I see that everyone in the room has turned into a skeleton, long-boned and tall, much taller than I, and all of them are moving, slowly, across the shiny parquet floor, past the upright piano, along the window wall toward the door leading to Jūratė's room. They are leaving me. I too am now a skeleton, but when I try to follow the others, my legs won't move. I try to call out, but can make no sound.

The struggle to walk and scream wrenched me awake. My heart was pounding. From the other side of the room, past the door open to the dark hall, came the comforting sound of my grandmother snoring. I summoned my courage, leapt through the dark into Baba's bed, slipped under her down comforter, and snuggled against her warm softness. She turned toward me and stopped snoring. My ears stayed alert, yet all I heard was Baba's peaceful breathing. Eventually I fell asleep.

In the morning I asked my grandmother if she had heard the doorbell during the night and she said she had not. The dream was too frightening for me to evoke it by telling her about it, so I checked the dining room. The Christmas tree stood in the pale winter sunlight pouring in through the windows, its straw stars, angels, colored paper chains, and candles undisturbed. But the nightmare burrowed deeply into my mind. It kept ambushing me, pouncing out of my memory, bringing the same dread. Each time it surfaced during the days that followed, I tried to banish it. It was not so much the figure of Death as the sound of that rasping doorbell that held the terror.

Did I have this nightmare before or after the boy carrying a grenade blew up in front of the Vytautas the Great War Museum? I can't remember. That happened one afternoon as Baba and I were walking home from the museum park, with Elena in a stroller. We had just passed the path leading to the main entrance to the building when I heard the explosion, turned to look in its direction, saw something drop to the ground and then, because a low wall blocked my view, saw only the boy's knees, pulled up the way I would pull up my knees while lying in a meadow and looking up at the sky.

Baba hurried us away, so I didn't see the boy's stomach blown open. I only heard of that later—perhaps Baba herself told me. I just remember hearing the explosion and seeing his knees. But when I try to trace the vague anxiety that sometimes overcomes me, especially at dusk, I get to this moment, and to the Christmas Eve nightmare.

Perhaps the anxiety had a less specific cause. It's impossible to know. Unfathomable evil was ravaging Eastern Europe, and surely an awareness of its presence crept into every child, no matter how our families tried to protect us. The doorbell—or more typically, the pounding of a rifle butt on the door—announced Death's emissaries, at night or just before dawn. Hundreds of thousands, if not millions, woke in terror, first under the Soviet occupation, then under the Nazis, and later under the Soviets again.

The Lithuania we had returned to was haunted by the missing. In the course of three days, June 14–17, 1941, the Soviet occupiers had loaded an estimated 325,000 Lithuanians into cattle cars and shipped them to Siberia, the Ural Mountains, and other locations in what people referred to as "the cold lands." Among those deported were educated people, civic leaders, some of the more prosperous farmers, university students, and others suspected of being "enemies of the people."

The same was happening in the other two Baltic States, Latvia and Estonia. Stalin was attempting to root out resistance. The czars had practiced a similar policy, though not on such a massive scale.

These deportations would almost certainly have continued—lists of thousands of targeted individuals were later found—had the Nazis not launched Operation Barbarossa on June 22. Hitler meant it to be a lightning strike, one that would quickly vanquish the Russians. Napoleon had had the same expectation.

After the Germans had replaced the Soviets in Lithuania, Death continued to roam at large, hunting down people the Nazis considered to be *Untermenschen* (subhumans), especially Jews. Carrying a gun rather than the traditional scythe, the skeletal manifestation of Death sometimes leaned on a walking stick as she invaded children's dreams.

MAMA'S HOPE OF finding my father when we returned to Lithuania was soon dashed. About his fate, she learned only this: He had been captured, imprisoned in Kaunas for three days, then transported by special convoy to Moscow. She reasoned that the Russians would not be so foolish as to kill him, a man with so much talent and knowledge.

He was probably taken to a secret location, perhaps in the Urals, she thought.

Mama held on to that hope. It guided her life till long after the war ended.

During the three and a half years we lived in our country under Nazi occupation, I was mostly oblivious to the violence beyond our immediate surroundings.

Because we had returned to Lithuania when the school year was well under way, Jūratė and I were at first tutored at home. A university student came to our house five mornings a week to prepare me for entering the appropriate grade of primary school in the fall. She was a few years older than Jūratė, and she taught me to read and write in Lithuanian, using the Latin alphabet. Often she arrived with illustrated books from the city library, and wondrous characters began to enter my life through reading.

Through the story of a bee named Maya, I learned about the life of a bee colony. With a book about a magic beanstalk, I climbed into the sky, higher than my father had ever flown. In a story by Wilhelm Hauff, I found Mouk, who wore a turban, as was customary in his country. His family was poor and he was very short, and other children mocked him. But he was brave and had a good heart, and after long journeys and many adventures, came home rich and wise.

Books revealed that the world was full of wonders, and they lifted me beyond daily life in the city, which was often constrained and boring, except on the Sundays when my friend Ugnė came to visit. She and her family had also returned from Germany. I envied her for having her father with her. He invited me to call him *Tėtinukas* (little father), but I could not do it. Ugnė and I shared our most intimate secrets and played games we made up. Sometimes we assumed romantic identities, becoming spies, or partisans who emerged from the forest to lay grenades on railroad tracks. I have a photograph of us in oversized adult clothes, looking very serious.

I didn't see Mama much. She worked long hours, and I was not allowed to wander on my own the way my older sister did. So I was with Baba and Elytė much of the time. On warm afternoons we would go for walks in the oak woodland uphill from where we lived, or to the park beside the museum.

Baba liked to sit on a bench in a small plaza near the museum entrance that was flanked on three sides by inspiring bronze sculptures. On a pedestal behind the bench she preferred stood the *Sower*, a man in midstride, right arm outstretched, flinging seeds in a wide arc. To his left, on the side of the plaza facing the street, a woman in traditional garb sat at a spinning wheel with a boy kneeling beside her, poring over a book that lay open on her lap.

On the side facing the *Sower* stood the *Book Carrier*, a young country man, his right hand raised to shield his eyes as he gazes into the distance. A bag full of books is slung over his shoulder.

I loved the *Book Carrier*. Looking up at him, I studied his boots, laced up to midcalf; his wide peasant trousers, tucked into the boots; the tunic tied at the waist with a woven sash. I studied his face. What did he see in the distance?

BOOK CARRIERS ARE heroic figures in Lithuania's history. During the 120 years when the country was a province in the Russian Empire (1795–1915), most Lithuanians were illiterate. Russian was the official language, Cyrillic the legal alphabet. Schools were primarily for Russians, although Lithuanian children could be admitted if their parents agreed to convert to the Russian Orthodox religion. To most Lithuanians such conversion was unthinkable. Lithuania was the only predominantly Roman Catholic province in the empire, and its religion was inseparable from the long struggle for independence from Russia.

After one of a series of insurrections during the reign of the czars, the regime had outlawed the Latin alphabet and publications in the Lithuanian language. The ban lasted from 1864 to 1904, and may have had an effect directly opposite to what was intended. Lithuanian intellectuals and priests abroad published books, newspapers, and pamphlets, which were delivered to towns and villages by book carriers traveling on foot or in horse-drawn carts that could appear to be loaded with potatoes or apples. How brave the book carriers were! Could I be so brave, I wondered as I looked at the bronze figure of the *Book Carrier*. Among my secret fears was that I was a coward.

The boy who exploded was not carrying books; he held a grenade. Was he brave? I had no answer. On that particular afternoon, as Baba and my little sister and I left the museum park and began to walk home, leaves shimmered in the sun. The explosion drained all light and color from the world. Dread tasted like dust in my throat.

I saw other troubling things that went unexplained. I remember a poster plastered on a wall depicting a small girl in a cage. Her eyes were big and dark, her dark hair tied back with a ribbon. She was holding both hands, clenched into fists, in front of her lips. Blood was trickling down her forehead. Who was she? The poster suggested that she was a victim of the brutal Soviets. On the same wall, and on many other walls, bigger posters featured the silhouette of a man with a hat—a spy. Across the image, in bold letters, was written "Shhh!"

One day, through the window of a bus, I saw a man in a gray coat running alongside the road, running very fast. He jumped the roadside ditch and ran into the field that extended to the edge of a forest. Behind him, in pursuit, came two German military men on a three-wheeled motorcycle with a sidecar, bouncing over the rough ground. I saw the running man fall. As he fell forward I saw a yellow patch in the shape of a six-pointed star on his back. I was frightened, just as Jūratė had been frightened at seeing men with yellow stars out the window in Lodz.

Someone on the bus said, "A Jew."

Nobody talked about the people with the yellow stars. I saw small groups of them in Kaunas, walking in the street, escorted by soldiers carrying rifles. Then I didn't see any more.

Children witness things adults don't want them to see, so they don't tell the adults, they only tell other children. One day we were visiting a family outside the city, people I did not know. Maybe we were there to buy eggs. The house was dark and I did not like being in it. A boy somewhat older than I said he had something to show me. He led me to the edge of a woodland and pointed to a grassy mound.

"This is where they shot Jews last year," he said. "They covered up the bodies, but I saw blood coming out of the ground, and I saw a hand. Later they came back and put more soil on, and sowed some grass."

I told my mother what the boy had told me.

"What a story!" She bristled. "Boys shouldn't invent such stories to scare other children. I hope you don't believe it."

I told myself that, of course, that story could not be true. I spoke no more about the mound the boy had shown me.

Things that could not be spoken but could not be forgotten became secrets. Now all of us were carrying secrets that we did not share. Jūratė, who was not only older but also more adventuresome than I, witnessed more. Only years later did she tell me the following story.

She liked to wander, alone. One day she was heading for the oak woodland uphill from where we lived, taking a shortcut by climbing over a low wall. As she was about to jump down on the other side, she heard voices and stopped. Through the trees, some distance away, she saw people standing in front of a ditch. They were naked. It was winter; there was snow on the ground. She saw German soldiers, and then she saw the soldiers begin to shoot the naked people, who then fell, one by one, into the ditch.

She ran home and told nobody what she had seen.

This woodland was only one of several places in Kaunas where the Gestapo and its accomplices shot men, women, and children, most of them Jews. Thousands were shot in the Ninth Fort, one of the fortifications built around the town in czarist times. Maps now exist showing mass murder sites throughout the country.

Jūratė was passionate about the piano and played for several hours a day. Chopin études, she remembers, but what I remember hearing most often was a funeral march. I remember Mama scolding her once, in an impatient voice, "It's enough. Enough!"

But Jūratė would tell me, years later, "It was the piano that saved me."

This too she told me only recently: Walking to her lesson at the Conservatory of Music one day, she saw a bonfire in the middle of a square. Soldiers were throwing sheet music into the flames. They were burning Mendelssohn's work because Mendelssohn was a Jew. She told her teacher, the director of the conservatory, what she had seen.

"From that day on he had me come to his house for my lessons," she said.

After a time, the teacher's sister took over the lessons. She was widowed, lived with her mother, and had dreamed of becoming an opera singer, but her voice, though pretty, was not strong enough.

"I loved to go to her house," said Jūratė. "It was so light and lovely. On the walls there were flower prints and colorful paintings of the Himalayas. She was a gentle soul and a follower of the Russian philosopher and artist Nicholas Roerich, who became a Buddhist scholar in Tibet."

My sister paused, thinking back. "She loved flowers. I remember her holding up a blossom and exclaiming, 'Look! How beautiful.'"

But Jūratė also recalled the woman speaking of the German soldier she had been compelled to take into her house. "One day she burst out, 'I can't stand this anymore. He screams at night. He has horrible nightmares and screams, "They are coming to kill me!"'

"He was one of those assigned to shoot Jews," Jūratė said.

Only decades later, when she was a great-grandmother, did Jūratė tell me these things.

WHILE MY OLDER sister found solace in her piano during these years, I found religion. I developed a fervent desire to become a Catholic. Nearly everyone in Lithuania was Catholic. On the first day of school, the teacher asked anyone who was not Catholic to stand up. I was the only one. In Jūratė's class, she too was the only one. She told me that before the war there had also been a Jewish girl in her class; the two of them had sat together in the hall during religious instruction. Now she sat alone.

"What is your religion?" my teacher asked.

"Evangelical Lutheran," I replied, as Mama had told me to do, although the only church we ever attended was Catholic.

The teacher asked me to repeat what I had said. I stood mortified. Everyone was staring at me.

As a non-Catholic, I was an outcast, excluded not only from religious instruction in class, given by a priest, but also from all the heavenly beauty that my best friend Ugnė and all the other children were enjoying. Like them, I wanted to make First Holy Communion, when girls wear veils and white dresses, and carry white candles decorated with white flowers. But that was not the only reason. What I really wanted was to unburden myself of my sins by confessing them.

Baba went to church every Sunday, and I liked to go with her. Mama sometimes came too, but she never walked to the altar rail for Communion. In the cool vast space of the space of the Church of Archangel Michael, known as Soboras, incense smoke drifted in rays of sunlight slanting down from the great round stained-glass window behind the altar and through the side windows depicting scenes from the lives of saints.

Dead Jesus hung on the cross to the left of the altar. I contemplated the pain he had felt when the crown of thorns was pushed onto his head, sending streams of blood down his forehead, like the blood on the forehead of the caged girl I had seen on a poster. I looked at the bleeding gash on Christ's chest, at his dead hands pierced by nails, and imagined nails being hammered into my palms, all the way through the hand, to attach them to the cross.

From what my grandmother had told me, and from the catechism Ugnė studied for her First Holy Communion and let me borrow, I knew that Jesus suffered and died for our sins. For my sins. His mother suffered because he suffered. And all of this was our fault. Catholics could go to confession, tell the priest they were sorry, and be absolved. But I carried it all with me, my sins and the sins I had witnessed.

In Kaunas, one day after a heavy rain, I had seen a man whipping his horse because the wagon it was pulling was stuck in the mud. The horse was trying with all its might to pull the wagon forward, its mouth foaming under the bit that cut into its lips. The man kept lashing the horse, which stumbled and fell onto its knees. Still the man kept lashing it. I burst into tears. My grandmother, standing behind me, put her hands on my shoulders. We did not save the horse. *Mea culpa, mea culpa, mea maxima culpa.* In church, I knocked my right fist against my chest, bowed my head. *Mea culpa.*

No evil existed inside the church. It was the safest place I knew, except for my grandmother's bed. The aroma of incense and flowers intoxicated me. Banks of little candles flickered beside the altar rail, in prayer for people dead, lost, or suffering. Mama and Grandmother lit candles in front of the Mother of Jesus, praying for the well-being and safe return of my father.

The priest, in his gold-embossed robes, chanted in Latin, and the choir responded. Then everyone, together, sang in Lithuanian, "Marija, Marija, purest lily. . . ." The music lifted my prayers toward the sky.

"Lighten our existence," came from the choir, and I added, silently, "Please, Mother of God, bring back Tėtė and persuade my mother to allow me to be Catholic."

For she would not. "You are too young," she said. "When you're older you can choose for yourself."

So I resorted to more extreme measures. In a tiny chapel atop an old stone tower in Kaunas there is an icon of Mother Mary that is believed to be miraculous. People, mostly old ladies with black kerchiefs, climb the steep stone steps and circle the icon on their knees. Some bring a piece of tin imprinted with a heart, leg, torso, whatever is relevant to their petition, and tack it onto a wall in this chapel. I made that pilgrimage, but had no money, so I couldn't leave a heart.

The miraculous Mary did not intervene with my mother, so I appealed to Little Saint Teresa of the Flowers, fondly known as The Little Flower. She was one of my favorite saints and beloved by Jesus, who sent a shower of roses down to her deathbed. I had seen a plaster statuette of the saint in a shop and wanted to buy it and make an altar for her. Though I had no money, I had a notebook filled with stickers, mostly flowers. After Mama bought me the first one in Duderstadt, I had acquired many more. Ugnė had money and agreed to trade my album for the cost of the statuette.

In a closet-sized hall between the dining room and Jūratė's room, Ugnė and I made an altar. We covered a wooden box with a white cloth and placed Little Saint Teresa on it, surrounded by candles and flowers. We lit the candles and prayed, watching the smoke. If the saint heard us, the smoke would rise; if she didn't, we would have to pray more. Jūratė peered through the door from her room and snickered. I angrily drove her away.

My mother remained unyielding, and eventually I learned why.

A woman who came to clean house told me, but made me pledge not to tell Mama that she had. As I've written above, my mother had been married to someone else before she married my father. She had been the wife of Vytautas Jablonskis, who was a neighbor and still a good friend of my parents, and whose two daughters were friends of Jūratė's and mine. The Catholic Church does not permit divorce, so Mama was excommunicated, and when Jūratė and I were born, she had us baptized in a Protestant church we never attended.

The family album contained proof of what the house cleaner told me: a small picture of my mother in a nurse's uniform, signed *Bronė Jablonskiene*. Excommunicated Catholics go to hell, so I realized that my mother was in great peril. What to do? If only I could talk with her about it. But I had promised not to tell.

I came upon a Catholic pamphlet with a story titled "The Protestant Woman and Marija," in the house of a family we were visiting.

This woman's case was not as difficult as my mother's. She was simply Protestant, not a divorced ex-Catholic. Still, Mary had saved her, and Mary was merciful. I copied the story on lined paper I found on a desk in that house and placed it by Mama's bed, in case, in some way, it might help her.

She never mentioned it.

"SHHH!" WARNED THE posters near bus and tram stops.

Some of my secrets would have been of no interest to spies, yet I wished I could share them with someone because they disturbed me.

One afternoon, in the early winter dark, I was startled by a man, a German soldier, as I stepped into the unlit hall of our apartment building. I couldn't see his face.

"Don't be frightened," he said. "I'm here to check if there is a shade on the window above this door, but I can't reach it. I'll hold you up so you can check and tell me."

I didn't like the way he smelled, and I didn't like the way he stepped behind me. He reached up my skirt, pushed down my tights, pushed his hand into my panties and felt around in my most private places. Then, with his left hand across my belly, he put his right palm between my legs and lifted me. I reached up.

"The shade is there," I said, pointing to it with my free hand, and he put me down.

I ran upstairs and straight into the bathroom to wash. What had happened was strange and dirty, yet somehow exciting.

I told no one.

WE DIDN'T VISIT the seashore in the years of Nazi occupation. The Baltic coast was a military zone, off limits. In summer, we moved from the city apartment to the tiny cottage in our orchard across the river Nemunas, not far from where we used to live before the war. Mama had planted this orchard on a plot of land the Lithuanian government had given to my father for his service as military pilot during the 1918–19 war with Poland. My father's good friend, the architect Vytautas Landsbergis-Žemkalnis, had designed the cottage for the gardener to live in. Mama had planted plums, cherries, and apple trees; also currants, red and yellow, and gooseberries. After we moved in we put in a vegetable garden, and I had my own little plot, where I planted radishes and peas.

It was during our time in the orchard that I began to appreciate that my mother was resourceful and brave. When the apples were ripening, she got ready for thieves. She hired a woman who was to take turns with her standing guard at night. They both wore trousers and a man's hat and tied their hair in back. The plan was to patrol the orchard carrying a long stick that someone might mistake, in the dark, for a rifle.

One night Mama was startled awake by noise outside. The thieves had come. She jumped up and started shouting in German. The intruders quickly departed, leaving behind a big bag of our apples. The woman who was supposed to be on patrol that night had gone to sleep.

While we lived in the orchard I walked barefoot all day and didn't range much beyond its gate, except to play with children of another former aviator, who lived across the road. But we were not sheltered completely. One day a haggard, bearded man came to the gate with some clothes to sell. He opened the bag he was carrying and pulled out a girl's dress made of marquisette. As we were looking at it, Mama came up. She told the man to wait a minute, went inside the cottage, came out with some bread and cheese and gave it to him, declining the dress.

Later she told Jūratė, "The little girl whose dress this was is probably dead."

ONLY YEARS LATER did I learn what was happening in the larger world while we lived in Nazi-occupied Lithuania. On September 15, 1941, the Wehrmacht encircled Leningrad but could not break its defense. The people of the city held out heroically for almost nine hundred days. More than a million died, mostly of starvation, during the Siege of Leningrad. Among the dead were guardians of the seed bank, who might have extended their lives a little if they had eaten the seeds, but they did not betray their trust. Like Napoleon in 1812, Hitler had underestimated the willingness of the Russian people to sacrifice their lives for their motherland.

Hitler had been so confident of a quick victory in the Soviet Union that his troops had not been equipped for winter. The season of rain and cold began; dusty dirt roads turned boggy, then icy. The heavy German Panzers and other vehicles kept getting stuck in the mud. The Russians' smaller tanks were more maneuverable, and of course the Russians knew the terrain. The Germans were unable to get food and supplies through to their troops at the front.

THE BATTLE OF Moscow began with the invaders hungry and suffering from frostbite, yet still pressing on. In early October 1941, they were closing in on the Soviet capital. Evacuation had begun. Would Hitler's troops burn Moscow as Napoleon's had?

But the Soviet troops regrouped and, with reinforcements from the east, counterattacked. By December 13, the attempt to seize Moscow had been repulsed.

The battle most fateful for the Germans, however, was still to come. In mid-August 1942, they had reached the Volga River north of Stalingrad. Their bombers set the city aflame and reduced it to rubble. The Soviets built a defense system in the ruins and held out. The Volga froze. Field Marshal Friedrich Paulus, commander of the Sixth Army, asked Hitler for permission to pull back to winter positions, but der Führer refused. On November 18, 1942, the Sixth Army attacked one last time in morning fog. Four days later it was encircled. Some three hundred thousand soldiers were left to die of starvation, lack of medical care, and the cold. On January 31, 1943, the remnant of the Sixth Army surrendered.

Later some letters were found, written by German soldiers who knew they were about to die in Stalingrad. The *Washington Post* published some of them while I was a reporter for the paper.

Well, now you know that I shall never return. Break it to our parents gently. I am deeply shaken and doubt everything. . . .

Even for me this letter is difficult. How much more difficult it will be for you. Unfortunately, there will not be any good news in this letter. . . .

In Stalingrad, to put the question of God's existence means to deny it. I must tell you this, Father, and I am doubly sorry. . . .

In spring 1944, "the news spread that the Russians are pushing back the Germans," my mother wrote in her notebook, "and that Kaunas might be bombed. I took the children to the farm."

I was ten years old now, had completed primary school and was ready for secondary school in autumn. Jūratė was preparing to enter the Conservatory of Music. That was the plan. But as it turned out, the weeks we spent that June at Aunt Antanina and Uncle Jonas's farm in Raišupis would be our last weeks in Lithuania.

Hitler's Third Reich was collapsing. The Russians paraded thousands of German prisoners through the streets of Moscow. Millions of soldiers and civilians were dead or dying. But I was oblivious of all that. My world was contained in Auntie and Uncle's wonderful farm.

I helped with daily chores, though not much. It was easy to feed the chickens, but my hands were not strong enough to milk a cow; I couldn't squeeze hard enough, and the cow stomped in annoyance and swatted me in the face with her tail. I tried churning cream into butter, but became bored before yellow flecks began to appear in the cream.

The baking of bread was a major event in the cycle of farm life. Twice a month the kitchen floor was scrubbed, and a huge wooden tub was placed beside the kitchen stove. The dough was mixed in the tub, covered with a cloth, and left to rise overnight.

It was fun to punch it down in the morning. When it was ready, Auntie spread flour on the kitchen table, broke off hunks of the dough, and shaped them into oval loaves. Before sliding them into the oven on a spatula with a handle as long as a broom, she glazed the top of each loaf with egg white and placed it on reeds gathered the day before at the edges of the pond. The fragrance of the baking bread suffused the house. Shiny dark loaves emerged. For me, this rye farm bread was and continues to be the only true bread. Never mind that uncounted other kinds exist and are delicious.

My uncle sat on a bench by the kitchen door on many evenings, smoking his pipe and talking with the Russian prisoner of war who was living and working at the farm. He was a farmer and beekeeper too, like my uncle. I liked to hear the men's quiet deep voices.

Nobody kept me from roaming freely, so I explored. Following gullies through a field of grain that rose above my head, I came upon a little pond inhabited by frogs. It became one of my secret spots, a place to go where nobody would find me. Another was up in the big haystack, next to the haybarn, where I dug a cozy nest for writing stories in my notebook. One, as I recall, was about a girl who understood the language of animals. One night she learned from a horse that the house was about to catch fire. With his help, she woke everyone up and saved the whole family.

When Mama's two-week vacation started, she came to join us, bringing worry with her. I remember her sitting with Uncle in the dining room, listening to a little radio he had set on a shelf. I heard Hitler's harsh and penetrating voice ranting about a new weapon that was soon to be deployed and would win the war. I gathered that neither Mama nor Uncle believed the weapon he was boasting about existed. But they looked worried.

On June 22, 1944, the third anniversary of Hitler's attack on the Soviet Union, Stalin mounted a major counteroffensive and began rapidly recovering invaded territory. Mama wrote, "I took the bus [to Kaunas] to find out what was going on. The Germans were fleeing, and many Lithuanians too . . . by car if they could, in wagons, on foot."

My mother could not decide what to do. She retrieved her mother and daughters from Raišupis and took us back to the city. We too would flee, she decided. "I tried to attach us to someone, but nobody had space. Finally I had this thought: I will stay. Maybe I'll find Antanas. I told my family. The children were silent, frightened."

My mother decided to return to the farm. She packed a suitcase with warm clothes and sent it by train to Marijampolė. Uncle could pick it up there for us with a horse-drawn wagon. We would soon follow, on another train. She needed a few more days in Kaunas.

The bombing was now more frequent. The siren woke us nights, and we kept having to get up to go to the cellar. Jūratė refused. She stayed in bed.

A good friend of Tėtė's came by to talk to Mama.

"What are you doing? You can't stay, they will kill you all," he warned.

"Antanas might come back," she answered.

"You must go. Think of the children," the friend said, just as my mother had said to my father when he argued that he had to stay with the people. She began to question her decision. What finally persuaded her to flee, however, was a dream. In her notebook she wrote,

Antanas is standing beside my bed, gazing at me, and he says, "Consider what you are doing!" He disappears. It was like a vision. I was shaken. I had to flee, as fast as possible, to save the children.

The streets are empty; there are no more trains. Then I see that an ambulance is standing in front of the next building, taking the last Germans. The driver agreed to take us too, with very little baggage because there was little space. We sat down on our bundles. En route we saw burning farms, fleeing people, German trucks.

The driver agreed to make a detour to pick up the suitcase Mama had sent to the railway station in Marijampolė. Jūratė was assigned to look for the turnoff toward that town. She peered through the little window in the panel separating the front seat from the back, where we all huddled. It was nighttime and rain was coming down hard, but my sister recognized the turnoff and pounded on the panel to alert the driver. He stopped but immediately saw that the road to Marijampolė was impassable, jammed with German vehicles and equipment stuck in the mud. I looked back in the direction we had come from and saw flames. We had to forget about that suitcase. Whatever we had with us would have to suffice.

SUDIEV LIETUVA
(GOODBYE LITHUANIA)

The wheels of the train kept repeating *Sudiev Lietuva, sudiev Lietuva* (goodbye Lithuania). Occasionally the rhythm varied, gaining a beat: *Sudiev brangioji Lietuva* (goodbye my dearest *Lietuva*).

From a window seat facing backward, I watched my country re—ceding, forests and lakes and meadows slipping into the past. A few dry bread crumbs were lodged under the short summer dress between my sweating thighs, but we were so tightly squeezed together on the seat that I couldn't move, so these crumbs just stayed where they were, irritating but also somehow right because the physical discom-fort helped to relieve my sadness.

On my lap I held a small brown leather purse that contained the personal treasures I was taking with me: One tiny green celluloid box in the shape of a book, which opened on hinges and held a miniature light blue rosary inside. Another such box, white, with a picture of the *Book Carrier* pasted inside the front cover and a series of tiny photo-graphs of Kaunas on an accordion-style foldout. Three glass animals wrapped in embroidered handkerchiefs—a delicate white elephant, a polar bear in milky pale blue, and a miniature green elephant on a blue stick that was made for lifting lemon slices from a saucer to drop into a cup of tea.

Tucked against the back of the purse was a holy picture of Saint Teresa, the Little Flower, and a portrait of my best friend, Ugnė, sitting on a windowsill dressed in the Lithuanian national costume, hands folded, looking away with downcast eyes.

Just about everything else had been left behind. I mourned for the fluffy little duckling my dear uncle had given me. It was the smallest and sweetest of several he had selected at a neighbor's in exchange for two egg-laying hens. When he handed it to me its heart was pounding, and I assured it silently that I would take good care of it. But now we were on this train, and I had no idea where we were going or when we would return.

"I'll keep it for you," he had said as we were leaving the farm, my favorite place in the world. "I'll have it here when you get back." Uncle always kept his word. But a fluffy duckling soon grows feathers. He would not be able to prevent it from becoming a duck. I knew that.

We had been on this train for many hours already. *Sudiev Lietuva* repeated the wheels.

Of course, I thought, the war would soon end. Then the Russians would leave our country; Lithuania would again be free. And then my father would return. Wherever the Russians had taken him, when the war was over he would find his way back, and so would we.

The thought of a different future never entered my mind.

The train slowed and stopped, then jerked forward and speeded up again. When it resumed its steady rhythm, my mind drifted back into the world that was slipping ever farther behind us. I felt myself atop a swaying wagon, sinking into fragrant fresh hay gathered under a darkening sky, just before the first raindrops fell. An apple came within reach, so I picked it, held it against my cheek, inhaled its aroma, and drifted off to sleep.

➤ ➤ ➤

SOME KIND OF disturbance on the train jerked me awake. The door at the end of the wagon slid open and in came a familiar-looking man. Could it be?

Yes, it was Ugnė's father, Mr. Karvelis, and she herself was right behind him. He greeted Mama, who was also surprised to see him, then told his daughter she could stay with me for a while as he made his way to the front of the train to talk with some people and get some news.

With my best friend aboard, life suddenly brightened.

"Do you know where we are going?" I asked.

"No," Ugnė said, "but I'm sure my father is taking us to a safe place."

The seat next to me had become vacant; she slid into it and we talked. Her departure from Lithuania and the trip thus far had been quite different from ours. They had traveled to the train station at Lithuania's border in a hired horse-drawn wagon, not stuffed into the back of a van. They had twenty-one pieces of baggage.

"My job has been to keep track of it," Ugnė said.

Many years later, in her fictionalized memoir *Tomorrow There Will Be No More Trains*, published in 1991 in France, Ugnė wrote that as she and other Lithuanians were about to board this train, a wave of grief swept through the crowd.

> *Men and women on their knees kiss the ground as though it were a relic. They take a handful of earth, knot it in their handkerchief. . . . An old man held some grains of rye in his open palm and was watering it with his tears.*
>
> *"Take some, little Lithuanian girl. Keep them: if I don't return, you will sow them in my stead," the old man said.*

She put five grains into her coin purse. They would accompany her through life, she wrote, but she never sowed them.

As the train was about to leave, a voice struck up a familiar song: "Beloved Lithuania."

Mr. Karvelis returned shortly, collected his daughter, and went back to the compartment where Mrs. Karvelis was waiting for them. Before leaving us he gave my mother the name of the hotel where they would be staying in Vienna, and expressed his regrets that he could not secure a room for us there as well. Even if he had been able to, Mama wouldn't have been able to afford it, since it was a luxury hotel.

MY MOTHER CARRIED a zippered black leather handbag, which she never let out of her sight during our flight through the German Reich. She called it by its German name, *Tasche,* despite the fact that she was a purist about language and would invariably chastise us if we used some Russian or German derivative rather than the academically proper Lithuanian.

This handbag contained our documents, the papers vital to safe passage. When we arrived at the Vienna train station, Mama slung that handbag over her right shoulder and told us to wait on the platform with the suitcases while she inquired about a place to stay. The wind was cold; we were tired and hungry. A voice over the loudspeaker kept repeating: "*Achtung! Achtung! Frauen und Kinder. . . .*" It seemed that shelter was being offered to women and children. Mama returned with the name of a hotel where we could stay for three nights.

Vienna was wide streets, gray stone buildings with geraniums on wrought-iron balconies, formal parks and castle gardens with many fountains—and dark nights pierced by the swooping wail of air raid sirens. In the hotel we went to bed dressed in our day clothes, shoes within easy reach, so we'd be ready to join the procession of guests down to the underground shelter as soon as we heard the siren. Feeling our way along the walls in the dark, we descended first on carpeted stairs, then on concrete steps into the cellar, where dim lamps glowed. One night I looked back for my grandmother, who was lagging, and saw her coming down in bare feet.

"Baba!"

"I couldn't find my shoes," she mumbled.

Jūratė and I burst out laughing. Baba's calloused pale feet were hilariously out of place on the cold concrete, and laughter was such a relief.

We sat on benches in the cellar until we heard the steady all-clear sound. On our second night in the shelter I met a Latvian girl about my age, who wore four dresses, one on top of the other, because her mother wanted be sure she had more than one if the family needed to escape again and she couldn't get to her suitcases.

Vienna was no longer far from the front when we arrived. The war was closing in on the Third Reich from several directions. As the Red Army pushed the Wehrmacht back across the Baltics, Poland, and Czechoslovakia, the Western Allies were attacking from the west and south. The aircraft bombing Vienna were British, and their bombs were more powerful than the Soviet bombs dropped on Kaunas. They were more likely to knock out a whole building than just a few floors, people said. But to us, these bombers were friends. We expected them to liberate us. So we wished them well, but hoped they wouldn't hit us.

Despite the unfavorable conditions, Mama made the best of our stay in Vienna. She herself had never been in this great city before and was interested in visiting some of its famous sites. So she took us to the vast formal parks and gardens of Schönbrunn, the summer palace of the Habsburg Dynasty, which had ruled from Vienna for six hundred years. We visited the Church of the Augustinian Friars, where Napoleon married Marie Louise, princess of Austria, in 1810. The giant Ferris wheel in the Prater amusement park was, unfortunately, not turning. But I would see it in action years later in the great 1949 British postwar film *The Third Man*.

As we walked along tree-shaded avenues, I imagined plush-appointed rooms inside the apartment houses we passed. I envied the children kicking around a ball in a neighborhood park. They would go home to dinner, while we had to find someplace to eat.

It was Jūratė who spotted something far more exciting than any castle or palace.

"Come look!" she called out. "*Knödel!*"

Through the window of a restaurant, she saw a waiter bearing a tray of dumplings, drenched in gravy, toward a table.

"We have no meat coupons," said Mama.

But, amazingly, no ration coupons were required. We took a table, ordered. At first bite we discovered that, alas, these dumplings were made of nothing more than flour and water.

On our fourth morning in Vienna, when we had to leave our hotel, Mama found a room in a small, shabby pension. We fell into our beds as soon as it grew dark.

At first light, Jūratė woke up screaming. Her arms and face were speckled with red bites. She leapt out of bed, shaking her limbs. But of course, bedbugs don't stay on a person, they drink and then hide.

"I'm not staying here another night," Jūratė shouted.

"We're leaving Vienna," Mama declared.

She sought advice from Mr. Karvelis, who suggested we travel south to Graz, a town two hundred kilometers southwest of the Austrian capital, which he thought was less likely to be bombed.

IT WAS LATE in the evening when we arrived by train. Mama didn't know where to go, so she sat down with us all on the stairway from the station to the street. After a while a military officer walked up.

"You can't stay here," he said, "it's dangerous."

"Can you tell us where we can find a room?" Mama asked.

He said no, but then Mama reached into the bag she carried that contained a slab of bacon, and cut off a fat slice for him. That seemed to jog his memory. He escorted us to a shelter for women and children where we could stay till morning.

Someone there directed Mama to a compound of one-story wooden barracks at the edge of town, next to an Army garrison, where several other families from Eastern Europe were housed. There we lived for the rest of the summer of 1944, through autumn and winter, and almost to the end of the war in Europe in May 1945.

Our quarters had two small rooms, with a toilet and a shower. There was a woodstove, but wood was scarce. Next door lived a Ukrainian family with a girl about my age and a younger boy. My bed stood against the thin wall between us. They often sang in the evening, and I would fall asleep listening to beautiful, sad Ukrainian folk melodies.

Graz didn't seem to have been much damaged by bombs, except around the railroad station. Before long, however, the air raids began here as well. The British and the Americans seemed to be taking turns. Our air raid shelter was a trench cut zigzag into the ground and covered with dirt. Inside, we were not afraid even as we heard the bombers approach, not until there was sudden silence, for we believed that was when they were directly overhead. Nights when the siren didn't interrupt our sleep were rare.

For me, life was not wholly unpleasant that summer of 1944. I roamed in a rubble-strewn field with the Ukrainian girl and other children who lived in the barracks. We were free to play amid broken concrete and piles of brick that easily became fortresses and castles. Nobody compelled us to march or sing or organize, as had been the case in Germany during our first flight from home, in 1941.

We played Statues, a game in which one person takes the hand of another, spins that person around and releases her, then does the same with all the others, Those released must stay in the position in which they landed. The first to move becomes the next spinner. We found interesting twisted hunks of metal, probably pieces of exploded bombs, which we took home and gave to adults to use as paperweights. And we gathered strips of metal foil that we saw scattered all around, for decorating Christmas trees. Years later I read that these strips of foil were dropped by British aircraft to confuse German radar signals. As they fluttered to the ground they provided myriad false alarms that obscured the real echoes represented by the aircraft.

In autumn, when the new school year began, Mama took Jūratė and me to an office to be enrolled. That process required a physical examination, and my sister was found to have tuberculosis. So instead of attending the gymnasium, she was sent to a sanatorium in the mountains.

"I begged to be allowed to borrow the books I would have studied," she told me later, "and I received permission. That was the end of school for me. From then on, I studied on my own."

As for me, I was assigned to the first year of the Bundesrealgymnasium für Mädchen, a girls' school near the Schlossberg, the big castle rock in the city's center. The sixteenth-century fortress that had stood on the rock had been destroyed by Napoleon's troops, except for the clock and bell towers. At the base of the rock, tunnels had been dug to shelter people during air raids.

To get to school and back, I took the streetcar, by myself. After school I walked to a children's center near the barracks, where we snacked on milk and biscuits, did our homework, sang, played games, and learned various crafts.

I was proud of the little wooden cradle with a heart-shaped headboard that I made and painted, and the tiny checkered blanket and pillows I stitched for it, edged with white ruffled lace. I gave it to my little sister. I don't recall if there was a doll in it, although I vividly remember the doll I had left in Lithuania. She was about eight inches tall, and had curly blond hair and eyes that opened and closed. She also had a perambulator, and a blanket and pillow and mattress that my grandmother had made. I used to take her outside for fresh air, but tried to keep her out of the sun so that the color in her cheeks and lips wouldn't fade. When I thought of her later, I always saw her in her perambulator, in the orchard, in the sun.

Mama worked in the cafeteria at the army garrison, and sometimes managed to bring back extra food. She left early in the morning and usually returned after my little sister had gone to sleep and Baba and I were ready for bed.

Every Sunday, Mama visited Jūratė at the Hörgas Sanatorium, and once she let me come with her. We took a train, then walked partway up a mountain. It was a hot day and I felt I was wearing too much clothing, as Heidi did while being taken into the Swiss Alps to live with her grandfather, in one of my favorite books. The road passed fields sprinkled with wildflowers; the breeze carried their scent. We stopped at a beer garden on the way, and my mother ordered a mug and let me have a taste. I liked the bitter brew, and it quenched my thirst.

We kept walking until we arrived at a big white house with a veranda, where we found my sister lying in a lounge chair, covered with a blanket. Perhaps because I hadn't seen her for a while and this was such an unfamiliar setting, she seemed somehow different, distant. Mama gave her the books she had asked for and some sweet biscuits brought from work. Jūratė gave her a pretty box she had made of flower postcards inserted between two sheets of used X-ray film, the image washed away, stitched together with colored thread. It was strange and sad, seeing my sister at the sanatorium.

Winter set in. Graz has a much warmer climate than Kaunas. We didn't get snow, but some mornings the water in our washbasin was covered by a delicate layer of ice and the window panes were patterned by frost. That did not stop Mama from taking a cold shower before she went to work.

"You have to build up your strength and be resilient," she explained. "Your father washed with cold water every morning."

I admired my parents, but was not at all tempted to follow their example. Baba would heat up some water for us.

During this winter, the last winter of the war, bombings worried me far less than my poor performance in arithmetic. The teacher wore a jacket of wide vertical stripes, blue and black. His posture was stiff as a ruler; his black hair stood straight up several centimeters above his scalp. He never smiled. I was terrified of him, as well as of the subject he taught.

My greatest fear was that I might be called up in front of the class to work out a problem, because I remembered how once, in Lithuania, I went completely blank in such a situation. So I tried to be invisible, sitting way back in class, looking down, glancing only fleetingly at the teacher and the blackboard. Not surprisingly, I did poorly; in fact, I failed—the only time in my life I ever failed a class. Too embarrassed to go home, I wandered around until it was almost dark.

I didn't tell my mother that I hadn't passed the arithmetic class, or why I was late coming home, just blubbered some excuse and crawled into bed. It wasn't that I was afraid she would scold me. I just couldn't bear my failure, my stupidity revealed in this way. My father was brilliant in math. I felt I had brought shame on him as his daughter.

I was also intensely afraid of matches. Someday, I knew, I would be called upon to strike a match, and I knew what would then happen. The head of the match would fly off, aflame, sparking a fire that would spread, unstoppable. What brought on this paranoia I had no idea. Perhaps if I had been allowed to strike a match, I would have gotten over it. But I was not given that opportunity until, horror of horrors, I was selected to light the first candle on the traditional Advent wreath at the after-school center I attended near the barracks. In Austria and Germany, four weeks before Christmas, a wreath made of pine branches is hung from the ceiling, like a chandelier, with four candles implanted in it. One is lit each week, and when all four have been lit, Saint Nicholas comes, bringing presents. He is a forerunner of the Christ Child, who arrives on Christmas Eve.

Finding no way to decline the honor, I stayed away from the after-school place on the first day of Advent, then lied that I'd been sick. What a timid, cowardly child I was, so unlike my beautiful and brave older sister, the talented Jūratė!

OUR RELATIVELY STABLE life in Graz ended in spring 1945. The British and American bombers were coming more frequently, by day as well as at night. If the warning siren sounded during school time, we dropped our pencils, closed our books, lined up two by two, and were led across the street and into a tunnel within the Schlossberg, where we sat close together. Not only schoolchildren but many other people sought shelter in the tunnels—they were considered to be the safest place in the city. Once inside, you couldn't even hear the planes or the bombs or the all-clear siren; you had no idea what was happening. Someone would announce when it was safe to go outside again, and then we would return to the classroom, where the teacher gave every child a spoonful of honey. If the school day was not yet over, we continued with lessons.

One afternoon, while I was still savoring the honey, a woman whom I recognized as a neighbor walked into my classroom, looking distraught. I heard what she said to the teacher: She had come for her daughter because bombs had hit the barracks and the shelter. Some people were dead.

Oh my God! I leapt up and ran down the stairs and to the street.

My family! They were dead! Oh dear Jesus, don't let them be dead. Dear Mother Mary most holy!

I ran, following the tram tracks, past houses ripped open, their guts exposed, their fronts torn off—buildings that had been part of the street this morning now skeletons with stairs leading nowhere. Bathtubs and beds stood as if on shelves. Strings of bricks dangled from cracked walls. I ran past people searching through the rubble, ignoring the pain in my side, shutting off the thought of what I might find, a sob choking me.

Smoke was rising from two chimneys that stood above charred remains of barracks I had passed in the morning on my way to school. But—*oh God, oh God, oh Mary*—our building was standing. Weirdly, crookedly, but still standing.

"Mama, Baba!" I flung myself forward. The door opened and there they were, my grandmother, my mother, my little sister. I fell into Baba's arms. Mama's enveloped us both. They held me tight as I sobbed, unbelievably happy.

Next door there was weeping. The little Ukrainian girl and her brother were dead. A bomb had made a direct hit on the air raid shelter. Just before it fell, the two children had been visiting another child some distance from their mother, around a zig in the trench. When their mother sensed that a bomber was overhead, she had called them to her and they had come. That other child, whom her two had been visiting, was alive, but hers were dead. Through the thin wall between our apartments I heard the Ukrainian mother wailing.

The next morning I went next door. My playmates' bodies were laid out on their beds, covered with blankets up to their chins. Their faces were waxen white. The girl's golden hair was spread smoothly on the white pillow; the mother had combed it carefully. Her mouth was open and full of dark red congealed blood. The white face, the red open mouth. I remember that family every time I hear a sad and beautiful Ukrainian song.

> ► ► ►

WITH THE BARRACKS wrecked, we needed another place to stay. The walls were still standing, the roof was still on, but everything had been thrown topsy-turvy by the bomb blast and was now rickety and unsafe. Fortunately, it was now late spring, no longer cold. We would stay until Mama found some other place.

She left early in the morning and returned in the late afternoon. By the grim look on her face I could see she had no good news.

"I went first to a Lithuanian family we know," she said to Baba. They have two rooms and a kitchen. I asked if they could let us stay for a little while and they said no. Their daughter is of an age where she needs a room of her own, they said. Can you imagine?"

Baba drew in a breath, clasped her hands, and brought them up to her lips.

"What are you saying, how can that be?"

"There are all kinds of people in the world," said Mama.

That night was windy. The loosened walls swayed and rattled. I kept waking up, afraid they would collapse on us. But then I would hear Baba's regular breathing, with an occasional snort. If she could sleep, I need not worry.

Mama went out again early the next morning. I knew she'd find something, she always did. And indeed, she returned excited.

"We are moving to a beautiful apartment, with parquet floors and a grand piano," she announced. "It was a German doctor's, but he has fled and left everything. Get ready. We don't need to take any of these pots or dishes, only our suitcases. Everything is there."

Later I would wonder how she managed to find it and who helped her. Probably she went to the office that dealt with refugees, the one that directed us to the barracks, I figured. I also wondered why the doctor had fled, but the answer to that soon became clear: the Nazis were losing the war.

There was much to explore in this house, especially in the doctor's study, where I found medical books that explained matters of anatomy I had not known much about. I checked out the accuracy of the illustrations with a small mirror, in secret. The space under the piano became my space, a place to sit with a book or a sock to darn while Mama and Baba went about their business. That was where I heard Mama say that the Germans were on the run and the war would soon be over.

One morning—it was May 1, 1945—my mother brought a newspaper into the kitchen while Baba was making pancakes. On the front page was a formal portrait of Hitler, with a thick black border around it. The headline read, "Der Führer killed in battle in Berlin."

"In battle? . . ." said Mama. "I wonder."

8

············

THE VALUE OF LANGUAGES

Someone was knocking on our door. Mama looked up but didn't rise from the couch in the living room. A man's voice shouted in Russian, "Open or we'll break the door!"

Mama opened. A thin young man stood before her, in khaki uniform, with red stars on his epaulets.

"*Dobriy den,*" she said. Good day in Russian.

He was surprised.

"*Gavarite pa-ruski?*" You speak Russian?

"*Gavaryu.*"

The Red Army had arrived in Graz. We had hoped for the British. For some days nobody seemed to know who would occupy this region, as Soviet troops moved in from Yugoslavia and the British approached from the west. My grandmother had been praying almost constantly to the Mother of God, begging her to persuade her Son to send the British. During the past night we had heard tanks and trucks rumble through the dark streets. Russians. We had fled from them, and they had caught up with us.

"We heard rumors that they were deporting refugees to Russia," Mama wrote in her notebook.

The slim officer who stepped into the living room did not seem hostile. He said he had come to tell us that we must move from the apartment because it had been assigned as officer quarters.

"How soon?" Mama asked. "And where can we go?"

She wrote,

I showed him the bed where my mother and the two girls lay. He looked under the bed.

"You're one of ours," he said. "Why are you here, so far from home?"

"The Nazis brought us here by force," I answered.

"Well, now we have liberated your country and we'll help you get home," he said.

"Thank you. But we will have to wait a while because my oldest daughter is very ill. She's in a hospital."

Mama wasn't sure he believed her, but before leaving he told her another place would be found for us. And he did return the next morning, to say that we could move next door, to a smaller apartment that had been vacated.

The move was quick, for we had little to carry. Our new place was dingy and dark, but it had a small kitchen that opened to a balcony, and a room with a big bed plus a cot.

That evening, when Baba, my little sister, and I were already under the covers, and Mama was getting ready to join us, we heard a knock on the kitchen door—the door that opened to the balcony. That was odd.

Mama looked scared. "Who is it?"

It was the young officer. The balcony to the apartment now occupied by the Russians was right next to ours and he had climbed over the railing separating the two.

"Get your heads under the blanket and don't talk," Mama whispered. "Lie still."

She glanced at the wall mirror by the bed, fluffed her hair, then stepped into the kitchen, closing the door behind her.

I stayed awake and alert. She greeted him in a friendly voice. Chairs scraped. They were sitting down at the kitchen table. They talked for what seemed like a long time. They laughed. I heard a clink of glasses. He had brought a bottle, and I heard his voice begin to slur.

Then my mother's voice changed, and she spoke sharply. She seemed to be telling him to leave. Not knowing Russian, I didn't get the words, but she spoke again, more severely, and I heard a scuffle, then the door to the balcony closing.

The next morning Mama told us that the officer was a good man, that he had come to visit her because he was lonely and she spoke his language and was from his part of the world. Soon after, he returned to apologize.

MOTHER'S LANGUAGE SKILLS again proved lifesaving. The Russians desperately needed translators. She was assigned to work at a military office responsible for agriculture. Farmers were coming in to complain that Russians were robbing them of food and equipment. Part of Mama's job was to put their protests and pleas on paper in Russian and take them to the *komandant*.

Some farmers, grateful for Mama's efforts on their behalf, brought her gifts of food. After she persuaded authorities not to confiscate one man's tractor, he invited her to come to his farm the following Sunday for fresh potatoes, which were difficult to come by.

Mama and I took a tram to the end of the line at the edge of the city, where this farmer met us with a big sack and filled Mama's backpack to capacity. But on the way back we almost lost this precious gift. Mama had just stepped into the streetcar, and I was behind her, still on the sidewalk, when one of the leather shoulder straps of her pack broke. Potatoes tumbled out, some falling inside the tram, some rolling down the steps and into the street. We had to choose. The tram wouldn't wait.

"Come back, there are more down here," I yelled from the sidewalk.

Mama picked up a few potatoes from the tram floor, tossed them out the door toward me, and stepped back out. A passenger tossed down a few more. This was true kindness, for food was scarce for everyone.

Mama was walking a fine line with the Russians. Every time she went to the komandant's office, she worried. The komandants changed frequently, and each was curious about her excellent Russian speech and writing. They wanted to know more about her. She kept saying that the Germans had deported her from Lithuania, but sensed that they didn't believe her.

One day she felt herself in imminent danger.

"The komandant and another officer began to cross-examine me," she wrote.

"Where is your husband?"

I said, "I don't know. He went to Moscow."

I had a strong feeling this could end badly. I had seen a large camp for Ukrainians in Graz, fenced in like animals. Fortunately my inquisitors were interrupted by some kind of important announcement and left.

As it turned out, the Soviets had to withdraw from Graz. The Allied Joint Military Command had divided the former Third Reich into four zones: British, American, French, and Russian, each administered by the military command of those nations. Graz had been assigned to the British.

One evening, Mama was summoned by the Russian general who

occupied the next-door apartment, the big one from which we had been evicted. She had helped him as interpreter in various dealings he had with Austrians, but this time he didn't have a task for her. Mama wrote,

> *"We are leaving; the British will come here," he told me. "If your*
> *political baggage is small, come with us, but if it's large, stay here."*
> *I thanked him. He could have taken us away, but it is clear that*
> *he was a good man. That night we saw horse-drawn wagons full*
> *of Ukrainian families. The men walked, with guards. They were*
> *being taken back.*
> *The next day the British arrived.*

Oh the wonder of those tanks, those flags! We hurried out into the street to greet them. Now it was Mama's command of English that was useful. Again she found work translating.

Jūratė was back with us. Mama had decided it was time for her to leave the sanatorium after learning that her sixteen-year-old daughter was having a romance with one of the doctors, a man twice her age. Jūratė's recent X-rays had looked good, the disease had been arrested, and in light of the precariousness of our situation, it was best to have the family together.

The danger of being forcibly returned to Lithuania was over, but we had to find someplace to live while waiting for the Soviets to withdraw from our country. Contrary to our expectations, the Western Allies were not compelling the Russians to relinquish the Baltic States immediately. Staying in Graz was not an option. The Austrians were short of food even for their own people.

It was Jūratė's job to go out early every morning to stand in line for an hour or more until the food stores opened, then buy whatever was available. She hated this task because Austrian women were hostile to us foreigners, blaming us for the food shortages. My sister usually returned with bread, peas, onions sometimes, and occasionally blood sausage. Once she brought back cherries. I jumped to taste them and found that they were wormy.

"I'll make dumplings," Baba offered.

Jūratė looked at me with contempt, reached for a cherry, and bit into it. We both saw the worm. I shivered with disgust and admiration.

Occasionally Jūratė came back from her food hunts with items that had not required ration cards, such as a tough-skinned yellow squash, which was growing in abundance around Graz in the summer of 1945. We ate so much, prepared as Baba best could without butter, that years would pass before I could appreciate squash again.

A FEW MONTHS after the war ended in Europe, the possibility arose that we might be able to go to America, there to await our country's liberation. One of my father's sisters, Kastė, had married a Lithuanian American and was living in New York.

Mama took a train to Vienna, hoping she could get Kastė's address at the offices of the Allied Command. With her usual combination of hard work, perseverance, and good luck, she met an American soldier who was about to go home to New York on leave. He agreed to take a letter and try to find the address in a New York telephone book.

A response from Aunt Kastė soon arrived. She invited us to come. In fact, she had already taken steps to obtain the affidavit we would need, in which she guaranteed that we would make a living on our own, without any public assistance.

After the affidavit arrived, the Allied authorities arranged for us to move to a refugee camp near Salzburg, in the American zone, where we would await our turn to travel to America.

➤ ➤ ➤

THE GLASENBACH DISPLACED persons, or DP, camp was within walking distance of Schloss Goldenstein, a medieval castle built on a rise, overlooking the Salzach River and a wide valley south of the Berchtesgaden Alps. Since 1897 the castle had been a convent, home to the Order of Regulated Choirwomen of Saint Augustinus of the Congregation of Our Loving Ladies.

In spring and summer 1946, I walked to Schloss Goldenstein almost every Saturday to meet one of the nuns, Mère Michaela, for catechism lessons. Mama had relented and agreed to allow me to convert, at age twelve, rather than wait till I was older, as she'd long insisted I needed to do. What broke her resistance was my older sister's announcement that she had also decided to take the Catholic faith.

Jūratė was now seventeen and living in the convent, rather than with us in the camp. Mother had persuaded the nuns to take her in as one of their student boarders, because she thought Jūratė would have better food there to restore her health—and perhaps also because she worried about exposing her younger girls to tuberculosis, although Jūratė's was no longer active. Also, in light of my sister's romance with a doctor at the sanatorium, she probably thought her rebellious daughter would be safer with the nuns.

One Sunday afternoon Jūratė came to visit and told Mama that she had been attending Mass with the sisters and other boarders, and was receiving religious instruction from one of them.

Mama did not try to dissuade her. She nodded, then looked into my pleading eyes.

"Mamute . . . please?"

"All right," she said. "You have wanted this for a long time."

I threw my arms around her.

And so it was decided that my greatest desire was to be fulfilled.

Mère Michaela agreed to prepare me as well as my older sister, separately. If I learned the catechism and passed the test, both of us would be baptized as Catholics and receive our First Holy Communion together at summer's end.

MY ROUTE FROM the camp to Goldenstein led past a stinking garbage dump in a gully, then followed footpaths through meadows that in early summer turned into a dense carpet of bluebells. Soldiers from the American Army base next to our camp pulled up in trucks to the edge of the gully and shoveled trash and garbage out the tailgate. Children from the camp found interesting stuff there—American comic books and copies of *Life* magazine.

One time when I was walking by, two soldiers were spreading the garbage, and one of them called to me. I stopped but didn't come near. He held up a pack of cigarettes, smiling.

"*Komm, komm*," he said, assuming that I was Austrian, I suppose, or at least spoke German. Cigarettes were better than money. Like nylon stockings, they could be traded for food and other things of value. Yet I didn't respond to the soldier's beckoning, recalling the drunk Nazi soldier behind our door in Kaunas. Later, I regretted my timidity, for when I told Mama, she said we were in the American Zone now, safe from danger, and these soldiers surely just wanted to be kind to a child. Mama could have sold those cigarettes, or traded them for something we needed.

Once past the dump, my path to the convent led across green meadows sprinkled with wildflowers to the austere castle built in about the year 1400. It was eight stories high, square-based and austerely vertical, topped by a steep roof with turrets at the corners. Walking toward it, I looked north toward the Untersberg, where the remnants of a glacier lingered in a south-facing hollow. Inside this mountain the Emperor Charlemagne sleeps, tended by gnomes.

He wakes up once every hundred years, and if he sees ravens flying around the mountain, he nods off for another century. Barbarossa sleeps there too, at a round table. His beard keeps growing, wrapping itself around the table legs. When it has wrapped them three times, the world will end. When I lived in Glasenbach, it had already circled them more than twice.

The Untersberg straddles the border with Germany. Behind it, in Bavaria, rise the three jagged peaks of the Watzmann Familie, dazzling white. Closer in, at the edge of the meadow I crossed on my way to the convent, a small forested hill rises off to the left.

Before we left for America, I intended to explore that hill, and to climb the Untersberg and search for the rare Edelweiss blossom. I also wanted to see my friend Ugnė again. But there was nothing I wanted more than to kneel at the railing in the convent chapel and receive Jesus into my heart.

I walked into the coolness of the castle through a high and heavy wooden door. Mère Michaela met me in the garden. We sat at a table, under an arbor. She questioned me, always gently, about the assignment for that day, and answered my questions. I needed no coaxing to study, for I was cultivating a garden in my heart for Jesus. Every day I considered how my actions, thoughts, and words either nurtured or harmed the flowers growing in this interior garden. Sometimes I came in troubled by some misdeed.

"I took an apple from an orchard," I confessed to Mère Michaela one day. "I climbed a fence and picked it off a tree on my way home from school."

"Was it on a branch that leaned outside the fence?"

"No. I reached inside the fence. I stole it. Stealing is one of the seven deadly sins."

"Well," she said, "it was stealing, but not very serious. Did you just take that one?"

"Just that one."

"Reaching into the orchard was not all right. If you had found the apple outside the fence, or even on a branch that leaned beyond the fence, that would have been fine to take, but climbing the fence and reaching in. . . . Well, don't do it again." She paused.

"Did the apple taste good?"

"Very good."

She smiled, and I felt forgiven.

The hardest work was avoiding impatience or disrespect toward Mama. When she scolded, her voice was harsh. I hated that voice, and I hated my own when I responded. Mère Michaela was always encouraging when I talked with her about this problem and said God forgives us if we only try.

I loved Mère Michaela, and she loved me too. Her blue eyes gazed at me kindly from a soft face squeezed into the white frame of her wimple, her full lips often parted in a smile. The rest of her was hidden in a voluminous black serge habit, right down to her black shoes, so her body didn't really exist, it was just a black softness within which she moved. Once, when she lifted her right arm to point at something in the distance, I was able to look into her wide sleeve as into a tunnel and was shocked to see the white skin and the cluster of hair in her armpit. Despite that, she was another kind of being, not like us. She was pure, as I wanted to be pure, as I would try to be. She came from Germany and her official name was Mater Michaela Rabener. But Mère suited her much better.

The terrain of the convent, and of Mère Michaela, was where I truly lived during this time. The camp, the school in Salzburg—they were part of the ordinary world. Mère Michaela transported me far beyond all that.

THE GLASENBACH CAMP was one of many in the former Third Reich set up by UNRRA, the United Nations Relief and Rehabilitation

Agency, to shelter refugees, mostly from Eastern Europe, who refused to go home because their countries remained under Soviet occupation or because they feared persecution if they returned.

More than a million of these displaced persons were scattered throughout Western Europe, mostly in Germany and Austria. President Franklin Delano Roosevelt had initiated planning for such a situation before the war ended to prevent the spread of epidemics and hunger, such as followed World War I.

Our camp was a compound of one-story wooden barracks; the residents were mostly Ukrainians and Baltic people. Our family had a tiny room, with a small iron stove, a small table, and two sets of bunk beds. Food was cooked in the camp kitchen, in a separate building. People brought pots to fill with soup, potatoes, whatever was served. Sometimes the soup was thick and nourishing, sometimes very thin. Later I learned that some of the food products allotted to the refugee camps disappeared before they reached the intended destination. Here, as in most institutions, there were some dishonest people and thieves. But at least meals of one kind or another were served daily to everyone. And soon we would be leaving, for America.

Aunt Kastė had begun to introduce us to life in the United States by sending a subscription to a Lithuanian newspaper published in Chicago, *Draugas* (*The Friend*), and an American magazine written in simple English, *The Reader's Digest*, which, having learned some English at school in Salzburg, I read and enjoyed.

She also sent a CARE Package: a large brown cardboard box filled with canned and dried foods, plus toothbrushes, combs, and a small pink rubber ball. We puzzled over the white paste in one can, which looked like whipped cream but was oily and much harder. This was Crisco, a solidified vegetable oil meant to be used instead of butter in frying. The most delicious item in the package was Spam, a pressed meat product we had never tasted before.

Lithuanians had organized a school at the camp, but my mother thought I would learn more by going to an established Austrian school, so mornings I walked to the road passing the camp and boarded a bus into Salzburg. Every day I had a stomachache, which vanished as soon as the school day was over. Aside from that, I remember little about the school and the DP camp. My real life was elsewhere.

ON SEPTEMBER 6, 1946, I spent the night with Jūratė at the convent. Before going to sleep we were both baptized, then went into the convent chapel to make our first confession. When I emerged from the confessional I felt that my soul had been completely purified.

The following morning, during Mass, we received First Communion and Jesus entered the garden I had prepared in my heart. It was my first ecstatic experience, something I realized only years later when I had a profound experience with LSD, which gave me a new sense of my place in the universe and relieved me of the last traces of my Catholic guilt.

Of course I wanted to go to Mass the next morning too, but Mama said no, Sunday's was sufficient—there was no need to become a religious fanatic.

Several weeks after our conversion ceremonies, Mama was notified that our visa applications had been approved and we would soon be transferred to a transit camp in Munich, and from there to Bremen, where we would board a ship for New York.

Again we took a train, this time going north.

MUNICH WAS A city in ruins. Along many streets, only rubble remained. The buildings that had stood there were either entirely gone or ripped open, their innards exposed. Where exterior walls had crumbled and floors were broken, stairways that had led to upper stories now ended in midair. Bathtubs and toilets stood anchored on bits of flooring two or three stories aboveground. Patches of rain-stained wallpaper hung in shreds. Here and there, men and women moved slowly around mounds of debris, collecting scraps of metal and piling old bricks into neat stacks.

That was what I saw of Munich through a window of the U.S. Armed Forces bus that transported us from the train station to the Funk Kaserne, a dark red brick military barracks now housing the DP transit camp, last stop for the refugees approved for travel to America for resettlement.

Soon we would be leaving all this behind and boarding a ship for New York, thanks to the affidavit sent by Aunt Kastė. We would stay in the transit camp only until all necessary documents were in order; then we would be taken to the port of Bremen, from which we would sail to America. The process would take no more than a few weeks, we thought. As it turned out, though, we would wait in Munich for several months, through winter, spring, and summer, until September 1947.

The Funk Kaserne stood next to a cemetery, where big trees spread over the pathways and flowers grew beside old tombstones. Baba and I enjoyed walking through this cemetery on our way to the church on its far side, Saturdays to make confession and Sundays to attend Mass.

This church, however, felt alien to me. It was not at all like the cheerful sunlit chapel in Schloss Goldenstein. The interior was cold and dark. The stained-glass windows, which had survived the bombing, failed to dispel the gloom. Whenever the altar boy rang his bell and we all sank to our knees, I closed my eyes, breathed in the incense smoke that wafted from swinging censers, and drifted back to Goldenstein. The sound of familiar Latin recitations helped, and after I took Holy Communion, with the host melting in my mouth, my soul again found its home.

EVERY FRIDAY AFTERNOON a list of those scheduled to sail from Bremen to New York on the next ship was posted on a bulletin board in the corridor outside the cafeteria. Week after week we joined the crowd that gathered in hopeful anticipation, searched for our names, and came away disappointed. Before leaving Glasenbach, we had given away everything we thought we would not need to take to America, including bedding and clothing, and now we were stuck here without things we could have used.

At the same time, there was still some uncertainty about whether we'd be allowed into the United States at all, since people with tuberculosis were categorically excluded. Jūratė was well now, but the scars on her lungs would be evident on an X-ray. If she didn't pass the medical examination given to every prospective immigrant before permission was granted to board a ship, we certainly wouldn't go without her. All we could do was hope that those scars would be too faint to see.

We had a great deal of free time as we waited. Adults and youth, including Jūratė, had work assignments, but not every day. So on days between the Friday list postings and the work days, we explored the beautiful Bavarian countryside and its legendary history. Jūratė sometimes preferred to go on her own; I went with Mama. We visited a deep blue mountain lake and took a little boat to a chapel accessible only by water. We marveled at frescoes on the high ceilings of a castle, in which the eyes of painted figures followed us as we moved around below.

One day we took a train to the town of Berchtesgaden, and walked up a road to the ruins of Hitler's inner sanctum, high above the lovely valley.

I had seen Nazi propaganda films showing Hitler standing in an enormous room in front of a huge plate glass window that offered views of snowy peaks. As we entered what was left of that room and walked across it, glass crunched under our shoes. Shards protruded from the empty window frame. If anything could symbolize the wreck of the Third Reich, it was this place. Later, the British would blow it up entirely, so no resurgent Nazism could claim it.

Hitler had harangued the world from here, but evil had been defeated. We walked around the ruins of the former secret Nazi compound, taking in the views in all directions. Looking south, I recognized the peaks of the Watzmann Familie, which we had seen to our north while in Glasenbach. Jūratė told me that from her room in Schloss Goldenstein she sometimes saw reflections of lights on a snow-covered mountainside, and that they came from this place. From here, the Untersberg, and Goldenstein, were behind the Watzmann Familie, and as I searched for them, I felt a spasm of longing for Mère Michaela.

She was as inaccessible now as Lithuania.

I did, however, get to spend some more time with the other person I longed to see—Ugnė. She and her parents were not in a refugee camp but had settled in Tübingen, an ancient university town some two hundred kilometers away, and my mother arranged for me to visit her for a few days. Ugnė's father was away much of the time, and her mother, a literary scholar, spent her days at the university or in a library, so Ugnė and I had the family's comfortable apartment to ourselves much of the time.

One afternoon we walked to a nearby park, climbed into a big tree, and sitting on one of its lower branches, pledged eternal friendship to each other. Ugnė had brought a needle and a scrap of white cloth. We each pricked a finger and let drops of blood fall on the cloth and comingle. Then Ugnė gave me three of six dried peas she had in a little cloth bag brought from Lithuania, and I shared with her the bit of soil I had been carrying in a tiny triangular purse I had made from ribbons in the three colors of Lithuania's flag—yellow, green and red. No matter where life took us, we promised, we would remain friends forever.

Back in Munich, the weeks dragged on. Cold seeped through the drafty barracks. I succumbed to a sinus infection, with excruciating pain in my cheeks and forehead. In the medical dispensary, a nurse dipped a brush-tipped metal stick into iodine and worked it into each nostril. I walked around in the corridor with these sticks in my nose for what seemed a very long time, dreading their removal, for the insertion had hurt. But after a few of these treatments, my sinuses cleared up.

ASH WEDNESDAY CAME, with the promise of the Resurrection in six more weeks. Baba, Jūratė, and I knelt at an altar rail to have the priest daub our foreheads with ashes. I prayed for my father, that he stay alive and return to us, and for my mother, that God keep her healthy and save her from hell; and I prayed that Jūratė be admitted to the United States despite having had TB, and for the well-being of Mère Michaela and of Ugnė. Soon, for the first time, I would celebrate Easter as a Catholic.

During Holy Week, I wanted to go to Mass every day, but Mama agreed only to Good Friday, known as Great Friday in Lithuania. That was the day Jesus died for our sins. As we entered the church, I saw that all life had left it. No candles glowed. The light in the tabernacle had been extinguished. All the statues were covered with purple cloth.

Before He died, Jesus had begged his Father, "Forgive them, for they know not what they do." At the altar, the priest recited a long prayer of forgiveness, dropping to his right knee each time he named offenders. We followed with a genuflection each time, our heads bowed. When the priest prayed for the Jews, however, he did not kneel—for the Jews had mocked Jesus by kneeling before him after they had pressed a crown of thorns onto his head. The Jews betrayed him. Jesus the Messiah had come to the Jews because they were God's chosen people, but they had failed to acknowledge him, they had rejected him, taunted and killed him.

"Let us pray also for the faithless Jews . . ." the priest began.

After World War II, the Good Friday Prayer for the Jews was revised several times, removing the accusation of collective guilt for the crucifixion. In 1970 the Second Vatican Council changed it completely, to begin, "Let us pray for the Jewish people, the first to hear the word of God, that they may continue to grow in the love of his name and in faithfulness to his covenant."

Before these revisions, however, the Good Friday prayer supported the popular idea that "the Jews killed Jesus."

I shivered as I joined the priest in praying for the Jews at the church in Munich. It did not occur to me that Jesus himself was Jewish. He didn't look Jewish in any of the holy pictures I had seen. In almost all of them he was depicted with blue eyes and light hair, and his nose was straight. It wasn't easy to forgive the Jews, but Jesus had forgiven them, so I tried. I also remembered the man in a long coat I had seen out the window of a bus in Kaunas, running, pursued by a German military officer on a motor tricycle.

There were many Jews in the transit camp, and I heard people grumble that they were getting priority, that rich Jewish organizations in America were pulling strings to get them visas ahead of non-Jews. "There, again," I heard a woman say one Friday as she ran a finger down the list posted outside the cafeteria. "Goldberg, Silverstein—they're going as Lithuanians. They don't even speak the language. They're Jews, but they're taking places from us."

In fact, as I would learn later, U.S. immigration law allotted quota numbers not according to nationality or ethnic group but according to place of birth. Mama would be traveling under the Latvian quota because she had been born in Riga when her father was working there, while we, her three daughters, born in Kaunas, were included in the Lithuanian quota. We were all Lithuanians, but that was the American law.

Early in September 1947, our names appeared at last on the list posted outside the cafeteria. Our visas were ready; there remained only the physical checkup. Almost miraculously, Jūratė was approved. Mama speculated that perhaps there had been a mix-up in the X-rays. I wondered whether Mama could somehow have arranged such a mix-up. But years later Jūratė told me what occurred.

"There was no mistake," she said. "I remember exactly what happened. The doctor looked at my X-ray, and he saw. Then he looked me straight in the eyes, and at you and our little sister, and said, 'Everything's fine, good to go.'

"I'm so grateful to that doctor, I still pray for him."

THE TRUCK STOPPED. A soldier dropped the tailgate and helped us down. An enormous gray ship loomed at the dock in front of us, tied to steel posts by gigantic ropes. To me it looked taller than a four-story building, and longer surely, I thought, than several whales. I had never been on the water in anything but the kayak we had in Palanga and a small boat on an excursion in Bavaria.

The ship's name, *SS Ernie Pyle*, meant nothing to me. Much later, when I was studying to become a journalist, I would learn it was named after an American war correspondent who reported from the Army's front lines in Europe and North Africa, telling in straightforward language what soldiers experienced. He was the first authentic soldier's voice, helping people back home to understand what the veterans would never be able to explain, that those who returned weren't who they had been when they left home.

The *SS Ernie Pyle* was a U.S. Merchant Marine vessel, built to carry cargo and troops. On each ocean crossing she had carried up to nine hundred men. After the war in Europe ended, President Harry Truman put this and four other ships into service to speed up the transport of refugees who had been waiting for months in camps for lack of transportation.

As soon as we had completed various sign-in procedures, I made my way to the deck and, leaning on the rail, watched the onshore preparations for departure. More trucks arrived and unloaded DPs. People were embracing, saying goodbye. Nobody was waving to us. We had already left behind everyone we knew.

As we pulled away from the dock, a wave of sadness swept over me, but soon it gave way to excitement. We were leaving the war behind us, sailing to a country that had not been trampled by foreign armies, a peaceful country where everyone had a home and plenty to eat, and the Statue of Liberty would welcome us as we arrived. I already knew the end of the poem inscribed on Liberty's pedestal.

> Give me your tired, your poor,
> Your huddled masses yearning to breathe free,
> The wretched refuse of your teeming shores;
> Send these, the tempest-tossed, to me,
> I lift my lamp above the golden door.

Wretched refuse we were not, but tempest-tossed surely.

I glanced at Mama, who was standing close to me to my right, and saw sadness in her face. I knew she was thinking of our Tėtė. Wherever he might be now, he would be much farther from us very soon. I wrapped an arm around her waist and pressed close to her, then stepped away. Now I could open the letter.

I found a wind-sheltered spot and pulled out the blue envelope Ugnė had given me when we last saw each other, with instructions that I must open it only on the ship. I lifted the small piece of blue paper from the envelope and unfolded it. Both sides were covered with her familiar handwriting, in green ink.

Dear Rasutė, my best friend always!

From my whole heart I wish you much happiness far from our country and people precious to you. Do what you wish in America, only remember that you are a Lithuanian, that Lithuania waits and expects much from us. Remember the bound hands of Lithuania, extended toward us. Write me at least one letter a month during the first year, and at least one letter a year after that.

You will be happy in a convent, behind walls. You will give up the world once, and that will be it. About myself I can say nothing because a liquid mass is boiling inside me, to be shaped by the artist. A great sea—the sea of life—is before my eyes, with its temptations, happiness, sorrow, pain, and joys. My ideal is to give up everything for our country, to cut the bonds from her wrists. Nobody will ever replace you, I will always be for you what I now am. Don't forget your poor Uga. Pray for her.

The letter irritated me. It seemed condescending. The life of turmoil Ugnė foresaw for herself was far more interesting than the life she envisioned for me. And how could she, my best friend and soulmate, even think that I might forget who I was and dishonor my father and my country?

We had both heard of Lithuanians who had emigrated to America after the First World War and lost themselves, whose children did not speak Lithuanian. Some had become Communists. But these emigrants were mostly poor peasants who left their native land in search of a better life. They weren't like us, fleeing for our very lives, going into exile unwillingly. Ugnė's patriotic exhortations annoyed me. But I reminded myself that her name meant *flame*, and mine meant *morn-*

ing dew. She was bold and dramatic, very different from me. I put the letter back into its envelope and slipped it into my skirt pocket.

THE SEA WAS calm on our first day aboard. We delighted in the substantial portions of good food served in the cafeteria, not at all like the meager meals often dished out in the camps. Jūratė was glad to find many young people aboard, and on that first day spent much of her time on deck with them. Then we entered the open ocean, and the ship began to sway.

On the second day at sea I felt queasy. I hurried down a steel stairway to my bunk belowdecks, but the nausea worsened in the dank windowless space. Afraid to throw up in bed, I hurried back upstairs and leaned over the railing. Someone was retching upwind. From then on, seasickness was all that existed, so awful I would gladly have died.

"All the flirting ended," Jūratė would remember. "We were all sick for the next five days. All except Baba and Elytė."

Elena remembered only one thing from that voyage: eating. Mama and Jūratė gave her their meal tickets, and she consumed all three portions.

A snapshot taken on board shows us all looking rather gaunt. Food had been scarce for so long that to refuse it when it was offered was unthinkable to me. I made it to the cafeteria most mornings, no matter how I felt, except once, when I lay curled into a ball, my head splitting, stomach churning. But Jūratė dragged herself up to breakfast that morning and returned with a prize: an orange.

"You can probably still get one," she said, "if you hurry."

My feet moved of their own volition. Soon I held my own beautiful orange, cool against my aching belly. And then, amazingly, a cafeteria worker came around, distributing oranges to those sick in bed. Hiding the one I had, I took a second one and—even knowing I shouldn't—was so pleased with myself that life seemed worth living again.

The nausea subsided.

WE ARRIVED IN New York Harbor toward evening on September 21, 1947, Elena's seventh birthday, only to learn that we had to stay at anchor until morning.

The Statue of Liberty was within our view, but disappointing. I had envisioned her as tall as a Gothic cathedral, dominating everything around her the way a cathedral dominates an old European town. The torch in her right hand would be piercing the sky like a spire, I'd imagined. But when I first saw her amid boats swarmed by noisy flocks of seagulls, Lady Liberty looked too small. Beyond her, as darkness fell, the lights of the city glittered like a thousand Christmas candles above the water. But when daylight returned, and we passed close to Liberty, she grew in stature.

All the passengers were on deck as we docked. On the wharf, a crowd was waiting to greet the ship, and men were wheeling carts laden with boxes and bags. The noise of people, machinery, and vehicles overwhelmed me after the long quiet days at sea.

Some people were holding up pieces of cardboard with names of arriving passengers or DP sponsor organizations: Catholic Charities, Jewish Family Services, National Council of Churches. We were sponsored only by Aunt Kastė, so Mama was looking for her.

Most passengers had disembarked; the crowd below had thinned out. Where was Aunt Kastė? We had no telephone number for her, nor directions to her house. What were we to do if she didn't come?

Someone told us to pick up our bags and get off the ship. It was warm. We took off our coats. Once again we were stranded in a strange place with no idea what to do.

At last we heard a man's voice, shouting in Lithuanian, *"Ponia* Bronė, *ponia* Bronė! Is that you?"

"Yes, we are here," Mama called out to the short roundish man in work clothes who was hurrying toward us. Uncle Felix had come; Aunt Kastė was waiting for us at home. He shook hands with Mama and Baba, and looked the rest of us over and nodded but did not extend a hand or a smile. Then he glanced at our bags, with what seemed to me disapproval.

"Is this all yours?" he said. "I will help. We have to take the subway."

He grabbed the larger suitcase and a satchel and started walking away. Mama picked up Father's small leather suitcase and the bigger brown one; Jūratė and I took what remained. Baba carried our coats over her left arm and held Elena's hand with her right. Uncle was walking fast, not looking back, threading his way through the crowds, past trucks and forklifts. We hurried to keep up.

Down a stairway we went, to the underground railway, the subway. When a train pulled into the station and stopped, Uncle Felix leaned into one of the open doors to prevent it from closing while we filed in. How dangerous the subway seemed to be—how easily people could be separated and left behind!

"Keep your baggage between your knees, hold on to the child," Uncle ordered.

The crowded train, with clattering wheels, moved at high speed through a dark tunnel, stopping at stations with white tile walls.

"Off at the next stop," Uncle said, nodding toward a door. Out and up to the sidewalk again we went, and then up another stairway, this one leading to tracks above the street. The bag I was carrying was growing heavier, but when we reached the elevated platform we stopped, at last, to wait for the next train. To my left, two young Black women stood chatting. I had seen a few Black soldiers in the camps, but never a Black woman. These two were both tall and slim, with sleek hair that bent below their ears to frame their faces. They wore bright red lipstick, high heels, and tight skirts. When they laughed, it seemed to me that their teeth were extraordinarily white. One of them noticed me staring, and I looked away.

We got off the elevated train on Pitkin Avenue, in Brooklyn, descended to a sidewalk, and started walking along the street below the tracks, passing people who all seemed to be in a hurry. After a short while we turned right.

Baba asked to stop for a minute.

"It's not far," Uncle said. He slowed down but kept going.

The biggest surprise on this first morning in America was the mess in the streets. Bits of newspaper, paper bags, and various other bits of trash were blowing around, and empty cans lay in the gutters. That wasn't something I had seen in Europe, even on streets in heavily bombed parts of town. But I also noticed that in all the houses we passed, without exception, the glass in every window was intact. No bombs had fallen here.

Auntie Kastė and Uncle Felix lived at 266 Montauk Avenue, in a two-story red brick house with white trim, and a stone lion on either side of the concrete front steps. A black wrought-iron fence surrounded a small front yard. As Uncle opened the gate, Auntie appeared at the door, beaming, and rushed down the steps to greet us with hugs, kisses, and laughter.

"Put your things in the living room; that's where you will be staying," Uncle said, and disappeared. It was clear he wasn't happy to have us all here.

"Come now, let's eat something," said our aunt. On the small Formica kitchen table she had put out soft white bread, white and yellow cheese, salami, oranges, and bananas. That was the latest wonder—bananas. And also a box of fat round pastries with holes in the middle, which she called chocolate donuts. Coffee. Milk. We filled our plates and carried them to the adjacent dining room occupied almost completely by a maple wood table, chairs, and a glass-front cupboard. Here we sat down.

Aunt Kastė's eyes were pale blue; her smile was gentle. Her pale skin suggested she did not spend much time outdoors. Her brown hair was pinned back carelessly, with random strands left loose. She wore no lipstick or other makeup. Her dress was a cotton print, with buttons all the way down the front, of a type I would learn was called a housedress. She folded her hands in her lap the way Baba did and, also like our grandmother, had a roundish belly. She spoke with the soft accents of Suvalkija, like my Aunt Antanina in Raišupis—which was only natural, as both were Tėtė's sisters—but with a twist. Her speech was sprinkled with odd words that I would soon decipher to be English words with Lithuanian endings tacked on. For example, by *karas*, which is the word for war in Lithuanian, she meant car. And *aisboksas* referred to the wooden cold storage box with brass fittings next to the kitchen sink, for which a delivery man brought a fresh block of ice once a week.

While the adults talked, I walked out through the kitchen door into the backyard, which was about the same size as the footprint of the house, as were the yards of neighboring houses, each separated from the others by a low wooden fence. The two adjacent yards had a few trees, and beds of flowers and vegetables. Aunt and Uncle's yard was bare dirt, with only a few straggly weeds here and there. It did have a lawn chair and table with an umbrella. Maybe I could help Auntie plant a garden, I thought. It was strange for a Lithuanian not to have one.

On our first night in America, and several days after, all five of us slept in the living room on the hideaway couch, to which a folding cot was added. It was stuffy and hot, so Mama got up and opened the three windows looking out onto the street. But Uncle Felix came around the front of the house with a long pole and closed them again. She loved fresh air. He worried about losing heat.

When I closed my eyes that first night, I again felt the rocking of the ship and, inside my eyelids, saw the glimmering ocean.

BROOKLYN USA

A few days after our arrival in Brooklyn, Mama took Elena and me to the neighborhood school, P.S. 64. I was thirteen years old and wore my best dress, a colorful flowered cotton print with long sleeves, and my braids were smartly fastened with shiny blue clips my cousin Bertha had given me for this occasion. My cousin's parents had given her the popular Lithuanian name Birutė, but she had renamed herself.

As we walked down Montauk Avenue, Elena was gripping Mama's right hand, while I walked a little ahead of them, on the left. Though I held my head high and my spine was straight, my mouth felt like it was full of cotton and a rubber band seemed to be squeezing my throat from the inside.

We soon arrived in front of a high chain-link fence surrounding a huge expanse of concrete. On its other side loomed a gray stone building, maybe three stories high, with tall windows. It was midmorning; school was under way and everyone was inside. We reached a stairway leading up to a tall, heavy door and entered.

"Can I help you?"

A woman with tightly curled yellow hair came toward us. I looked up at eyes outlined in black, with extremely long black lashes. Bright red lips smiled at us.

"Good morning," said Mama. "I am bringing my daughters. Where must I go?"

The woman's eyes passed over me, then my little sister, and then she led us down a long corridor with a shiny floor to an office, spoke to someone inside, and left us there.

Elena and I sat down on a bench by the door while Mama walked up to a high wooden counter, pulled some documents out of her hand-bag, and presented them to an older woman, who in exchange, gave her a couple of forms to fill out and a pen. We sat, waiting, listening to the clacking of typewriters and other unfamiliar sounds. Everywhere we had traveled Mama had presented documents and filled out forms. We were used to waiting.

Before long we heard the sound of voices and running feet coming down the corridor as children streamed down stairs and along halls, past the office door and into the concrete yard. So many, and moving in such disorder. Not walking in orderly two-by-twos but just crowd-ing out, laughing, talking, jostling. I swallowed a few times, trying to relax and appear calm.

"You must be Rosa," said a woman walking in the door and smil-ing at me. Rosa? It didn't even occur to me to correct her. She looked about my mother's age. Her face was not painted, her dark hair was pulled back, uncurled, and her eyes looked kind.

"You'll be in the eighth grade, with me," she said.

"And you're Ell-eena?"

A second teacher had entered.

"Elena," Mother corrected.

"In English that's probably Helen," the woman said. "Hello, Helen."

Elena hid her face against Mama's body.

"She'll be in my class, second grade. Does she speak any English?"

"Not yet. She speaks Lithuanian and a little German," said Mama.

"That's perfect! I speak a little German too. You'll see how fast she'll learn English. At her age, it will be quick."

She reached for my little sister's hand and, with Mama's urging, Elena yielded.

"Come, Helen."

I could see Mother wanted to correct the teacher on the name, but she didn't. "Your mother can come along to see your classroom."

Up a flight of stairs and down another hall I followed my teacher, toward the sound of loud chatter. At the classroom door I froze.

The chatter in the room ebbed. Heads turned and I stared back at the girls and boys sitting at school desks. They were my age, but the girls were dressed like stylish young women and looked much older, some with tight skirts, nylon stockings, and even heels. Who were they? Teachers? My eyes fixed on a pretty girl with light brown hair, shiny and smooth, that swooped down and under in a roll just above her shoulders in what I would learn was called pageboy style. She was wearing a white blouse and a tight brown skirt that reached down to midcalf.

"Class, this is Rosa. She's a new student."

I felt the nakedness of my legs, the exposed knees, the childishness of my braids. My flowery dress was faded and badly worn, I suddenly realized.

The teacher pointed to an empty desk near the back of the room, next to one of the tall windows, then walked to her desk in front of the room, on a platform.

"All right class. We will continue where we stopped yesterday. Now open your books. . . ."

She spoke with an accent that sounded terribly incorrect; it was different from the proper English I had been learning in Salzburg. I understood what she was saying, but her words just passed through my mind without leaving a mark as I was overtaken by fear of what lay ahead. What would happen after the class ended? Would I have to join a crowd of students?

A harsh, loud buzzing shocked me back to the moment. The teacher was still speaking—she hadn't yet dismissed the class—but everyone had already jumped up and was rushing toward the door.

"Arlene, Joan, Eileen! Come up here, please!" the teacher called.

Three girls walked to the front of the room. I stayed in my seat. The girls turned to look at me, then walked up to me. I needed no English to see that they were not pleased.

"Hi, I'm Arlene," said the tallest and prettiest of the three, the one with the smooth curled-down hair. "Come with us. We'll look out for you. Now it's recess, so let's go outside."

The concrete yard was teeming with noisy students running around, playing hopscotch and jumping rope, bouncing a ball, shooting baskets, or just standing in little groups. The girls to whom I had been assigned just stood together. A couple of other girls joined them.

Arlene introduced me. "This is Rosa. She's from Albania."

"Lithuania," I said.

"Lithuania. Where is that?"

"On the Baltic Sea," I said. "North of Poland."

That was the end of our conversation. They turned toward each other and chatted for the rest of recess. I stood with them because I couldn't think what else to do. My mouth felt dry, my tongue thick.

Fortunately, my aunt and uncle's house was only a few blocks away, so at lunchtime I ran home. Baba cut bread and cheese for me and poured a glass of milk. Aunt Kastė added a chocolate donut. I ate as fast as I could, then ran back to the school, arriving just before the next class began.

THAT FIRST YEAR in America was probably the hardest year in my life. Never before had I felt so strange and alien among my contemporaries. I was a creature from another world. In the DP camps we were among people of many nations, speaking many languages, but we had something important in common: we were all war refugees. Here at school in Brooklyn, I was the only one who'd come from somewhere else.

One day Arlene, Joan, and Eileen invited me to have lunch with them in an ice cream parlor, and I went, even though I was sure they only asked me because the teacher had told them to include me.

It was humiliating. I sat with them in the booth, trying not to stare at Arlene as she played with the delicate chain she wore around her neck, twirling it and passing it across her lips. I wanted to be like these girls, or else like Patsy in the Patsy Walker comic books my cousin Bertha had let me look at. Patsy had red hair, a blond boyfriend named Buzz, and a sidekick, Lois, with mousy hair. The three of them went to the soda fountain where Buzz worked after school. They lived in a neighborhood of small houses on tree-lined streets, where every family had a car. Even Buzz had one, a convertible.

Classwork was easy for me, on the whole. Arithmetic had always been my most difficult subject, but I had already learned in Salzburg what was being taught in eighth grade at P.S. 64.

But my English was apparently coming along too slowly, because one day, a few weeks in, I was told to report to the third floor to another classroom, where I would have a chance to catch up. This turned out to be a class for those having trouble learning to read and write. Most were boys. All were Americans. There weren't very many of them, so we sat around a long table instead of at desks. But they didn't pay attention to the teacher; they kept making jokes and fooling around. I knew I didn't belong in this group. I wanted to get back to my classroom, where we had been reading Henry Wadsworth Longfellow's long poem *Evangeline*. So every evening I memorized long lists of new words and then gave them to the teacher of the slow learners. Soon I was sent back to the regular English class, and Long-fellow.

> Behold the Forest Primeval
> The murmuring pines and the hemlocks . . .

The words were so beautiful I was happy to look them up in the dictionary.

We read Charles Dickens's *A Tale of Two Cities*, and Nathaniel Hawthorne's *The Scarlet Letter*. Books, dreams, and religion had been my escape from the daily world for as far back as I could remember, and these new books, in English, were taking me to new places in a new country.

Aside from the books we read in school, there were those in the library. Every Saturday I would bring back four, the maximum allowed. Mama would scold, "Get your nose out of the book and go outside, get some fresh air!" But outside, on the street, I was lonely, I had no friends and nowhere to go. In books my diffuse and inchoate longing found a home.

At the end of that year, various prizes were awarded. I was amazed when the teacher announced that I had been chosen as one of the two best students in English, together with Eddie Sutcliffe, a figure in my most private dreams, whom I adored at a distance. It seemed to me so romantic, sharing the prize, even though Eddie surely had no idea of what it meant to me. He never even noticed me.

I had learned a lot by the end of eighth grade. I knew that the paste that girls plastered on their faces was pancake makeup, though I never wore it. I only put powder on my nose so it wouldn't look so big and shiny. I wore white ribbed socks (bobby sox) and black-and-white shoes with laces (saddle shoes), like many other girls. I knew how to dance the two-step and the Lindy Hop. After a long struggle with Mama, I had succeeded in losing my braids and learned to do my hair in a pageboy. It wasn't easy to sleep comfortably in rollers, but was definitely worth the effort.

In home economics class I had learned to make things I had never tasted before: tuna casserole with cornflakes and mushroom soup, Welsh rarebit with melted cheese and that soft white bread, each slice cut into four triangles. I learned to sew with a machine and made my own graduation dress of white organdy, with lace on the sleeves and neck. I was as close to Patsy Walker as I would ever come.

Meanwhile, my little sister Elena, after being silent in school for a while, suddenly knew how to speak English.

THE SUMMER AFTER my graduation from eighth grade, we moved to an apartment of our own, in a basement in Queens. It was dark, with small windows just barely above ground level, too high to look through, and we entered it through the furnace room. There was no heat except what drifted in from the coal-fueled furnace if we left the kitchen door open. But it was ours.

Mother had found work in a cafeteria within a week of our arrival, so she needed no further help from Aunt Kastė. Before long she moved on to a job in a hospital as a practical nurse. Jūratė quickly found work in another town—Hartford, Connecticut—as an attendant in a mental hospital.

Kind strangers donated dishes, cooking pots, a kitchen table and chairs, beds and bedding. I especially appreciated the radio, a big thing that stood on the floor in the room where we slept. Saturday mornings I'd hurry through my chores so I could snuggle up next to it to listen to that day's drama on *Grand Central Station*. I had to keep the sound very soft or Baba would complain.

The least appreciated gift was the couch. It arrived in the bed of a pickup truck that pulled up in the driveway right outside our windows. We all came out to look. But what a shock! The driver tossed a cushion to the ground and a huge crowd of cockroaches swarmed toward the house.

"*Bozhe moi!*"

Baba tossed the pillow back into the truck. Mama explained that we did not need a couch after all. We tried to stamp out the roaches, but they were faster than our feet. From then on, we lived with them. I dreaded turning on the light in the kitchen and seeing them racing from the table to their hiding places. Squashing them didn't seem to diminish their numbers, and no effort to clean up crumbs and secure food in tight containers seemed to help.

The landlord had told Mama that he would fix up another room, one that would have more light, and after a while he did. That completely changed the feeling of the place. The new room faced the street, the windows were bigger, and sometimes sunlight shone in. We loved it and lived in it. Mama got another couch, and somehow obtained an upright piano, probably with Jūratė in mind. But Jūratė never returned to live with us, so I was the only one to play it. My repertoire consisted of two songs: "Heart's Sorrow" and "Anniversary Waltz."

Mama was working long hours at the hospital, bringing home $30 a week, and also studying for the registered nurse exam. Then she fell ill, very ill. Mama who never got sick—or never yielded to sickness—lay in bed with a cold towel on her forehead, covered with three blankets, day after day. Without her income, there was no way to buy food.

IT WAS MAMA'S collapse that brought a guardian angel, Mr. William H. Sudduth, into our lives. He was preceded by an emissary.

A knock on the door. Baba opened. A stately older woman stood there, a Russian woman with gray braids wrapped around her head.

"*Zdravstvuyte.*"

The visitor put the shopping bag she was carrying on the kitchen table and asked to see Mama. As Baba led her to Mama's bed, I peered into the bag: eggs, cheese, bread, honey, some cans. Apples.

Our visitor, whose name was Mrs. Bary, told us she was a volunteer with a committee that was helping DP students and their families. She wanted to know about each of us, asked Mama a lot of questions, and wrote things down in her notebook. As she was leaving, she said she'd be back in two days—and she was, with more food. By this time Mama was better and the two of them and Baba sat at the table, drank tea, and talked in Russian.

Mrs. Bary was aristocratic and beautiful; her blue eyes were bright above high cheekbones. The skin on her round face was smooth, her forehead high. She talked emphatically, with authority. She said that Jūratė needed to go to university and that she had a friend who was helping DPs and might be able to make that possible.

At this time Jūratė was working the night shift at the Institute for Living in Hartford, overseeing a dormitory for patients who had recently undergone electric shock treatments. Some of the patients were violent. One night, as Jūratė sat at a desk overlooking the ward, she felt someone behind her and turned just in time to see a woman with rage on her face holding a chair in the air, ready to smash it down on her head.

"She thought she was a Jew in a concentration camp and I was a Nazi guard," my sister later explained. "In fact, she wasn't Jewish, had been born in Connecticut, and had never even been to Europe."

The war was over, but its traumas lived on. Jūratė didn't tell Mama about that incident. But it made her want to leave her job as soon as possible.

Mrs. Bary set up a meeting for my sister with her friend Mr. Sudduth. He arranged for her to receive a scholarship to study at the University of Michigan, beginning in September 1949. It was sponsored by a group of students at the university and would cover tuition. She would have a part-time job on the campus to pay for room and board. A little photo story about my sister appeared in the magazine *Mademoiselle*, stating that she would be studying medicine and planned to research tuberculosis.

When Mrs. Bary told Mr. Sudduth about the rest of our family, he decided to help me get a scholarship too—at an excellent private boarding school.

We heard nothing more for some weeks. The school year began, so I reported to Franklin K. Lane High School, the public school to which I had been assigned. After taking a seat at the back of the freshman classroom, I listened to roll call with some unease. The students here included several tall boys who wandered around the room, ignoring the teacher's request that we all sit down. They talked among themselves, making it difficult for the teacher to get through the list of names assigned to his class. He did manage to finish it, though—but without calling my name. I approached him to ask whether he might have inadvertently skipped it, and he told me that my enrollment had been cancelled. Distressed and near tears, I left the classroom and, from the school office, phoned Mr. Sudduth.

"Oh yes," he said. I was to come to the apartment on East 87th Street the next morning and he would take me to an interview at the school he had in mind for me. "Bring a change of clothes in case they want you to stay overnight."

Who was this Mr. Sudduth? At this time, we only knew that he was helping DPs. Later I would come to think of him as an angel, one of several who appeared along my life's path to guide me—someone unique and marvelous to whom I would forever be grateful.

Mama packed a change of clothes for me into a satchel. She was working the afternoon shift, so she took the subway with me and delivered me to Mr. Sudduth before eight a.m. We set off, in a shabby Volkswagen with torn seats. Before leaving, Mr. Sudduth placed a gallon can of gasoline in the trunk: the gas gauge was not working, he explained. I sat in back. A friend of Mr. Sudduth's, a middle-aged college professor, took the passenger seat in front. He was coming along for the ride.

About four hours later, Mr. Sudduth and I were sitting in the office of Miss Stanley, the admissions director at Dana Hall. She was an older lady with small, pale blue eyes almost hidden in folds of skin, and an exceptionally full bosom that seemed to rest on the desk in front of her.

"When can she come?" Miss Stanley asked.

"She is ready to stay today. Her mother will send more clothing," Mr. Sudduth replied.

That's all I remember of the interview.

And so it was that I came to be a student at one of best private secondary schools in the country, not realizing how unusual my admission process had been. Dana Hall was founded in 1881 and was originally the preparatory school for Wellesley College. It was now an independent school, well-known for its high academic standards. We students lived in comfortable wooden houses shaded by big trees, and walked to the rambling main building to eat and attend classes. New York, with its rattling subways and dusty parks, was a world away.

Most of the students came from well-to-do East Coast families, but some were from other parts of the country and the world. For the most part, I was blissfully unaware of class distinctions. We wore uniforms on weekdays: dark blue skirts and white blouses in the cold months, pastel golf dresses with buttons down the front in warm weather. On Sundays we were free to wear other clothes, and I often put on the plaid skirt my mother had bought for me at S. Klein's basement. A classmate from India, a maharani, sometimes appeared at Sunday dinner in a colorful silk sari.

I loved my classes. In an attic classroom with creaking floors,

Miss Grimes discussed *Anne of Green Gables*, the 1908 Canadian novel by Lucy Maud Montgomery about an orphan girl sent to a farm on Prince Edward Island by mistake. All turns out well in the end because the girl is adventurous and competent.

Like most of my teachers, Miss Grimes was a lady in her middle years, unassuming, with kind eyes that gazed at her students with interest. She clearly loved both teaching and literature, and inspired me to put a lot of effort into my essays. I sat at the back of the class, partly out of shyness, partly because that location allowed my mind to escape now and then by gazing out the window at the trees. I missed my family and my language.

In my junior year I chose a seat near the front of the class of Miss Post, a tiny woman with graying dark hair pinned back and tucked into a hairnet. She walked back and forth in thick-soled black shoes that raised her height perhaps an inch—back and forth soundlessly and on tiptoe, between her desk and a bookshelf to my left, talking about *Silas Marner* and *Ethan Frome*. She would straighten a pile of papers on the bookshelf, but never quite enough, it seemed, because she did it again and again, absent-mindedly.

I dreamed of Heathcliff buffeted by the wind on the moors as Miss Post revealed literary marvels in bleak stories from a bleak country. She wore plain dresses in muted colors, and she never smiled, but she loved language. In Miss Gottfried's American history and government class, I began to learn what I would need to know when I became an American citizen. I appreciated all my teachers, even Miss Anderson, the Latin instructor, who terrified me.

First-year Latin was easy enough, but Latin II turned out to be a struggle, especially when we were called upon to translate out loud. I usually avoided Miss Anderson's homework, leaving it to the last when I was already too tired. Moreover, I found her class boring. So I sat in the back row with a couple of friends, and we entertained ourselves by passing notes. A day of reckoning was inevitable.

"Rasa, please see me after class."

I felt the blood drain from my head. Some of the notes were about her. The minute hand on the wall clock behind Miss Anderson ticked forward at a glacial pace. When the bell rang and all the girls stood up and left, I rose to face her.

She was very tall and, in her high heels, towered above me. I looked up at her dark cold eyes, then dropped my gaze to her black shoes, well-polished but rather worn.

"What was that you were doing today?"

Her voice always seemed to have a trace of anger behind it, and now the anger jumped out in front. She didn't expect an answer, and I had none.

"You cannot afford to play around in class. You have not been studying. And you have not been paying attention. Are you prepared to fail?"

I couldn't let her see the tears welling up in my eyes, so I fixed my attention on the lace border along the collar of her white blouse. Its tip veered outward a bit; it had been imperfectly ironed. I memorized that collar tip, the lace, the little pink roses at the edge of the lace, to keep myself from crying. On the left lapel of her navy blue suit, the iron had left a shiny mark. Miss Anderson kept talking, but her words no longer touched me. Not one tear brimmed over. This was, I felt, a victory. And being admonished had a healthy effect. I survived Latin II. I even improved my grade considerably.

During Christmas vacation of my first year at Dana Hall, Mama and I paid a call on Mr. Sudduth. Nobody answered the doorbell, but the door was not locked, so we entered. In the hall, suitcases and boxes stood stacked against walls, and donated clothing hung on a rack. In the living room, beside the piano, a couple of young men were wrapping and addressing packages to be shipped to DP camps in Germany. Ruth Praeger, Mr. Sudduth's assistant, rose from behind a typewriter on the kitchen table to greet us.

"Bill is away; he's with his family," she said. "He'll be sorry he missed you."

It was already after dark. We had left home after Mama returned from work at four.

"Let's go see the Christmas decorations on Fifth Avenue," she said. "I heard they are spectacular."

So we strolled along the avenue, marveling at displays in the showcase windows of Tiffany's, Lord & Taylor, and other famous shops. Some of the Dana Hall girls shopped there, I knew. In front of the brightly lit Plaza Hotel a huge Christmas tree stood, and a horse-drawn coach was waiting for passengers. Amid all the glitter, I felt forlorn. I was a stranger here, unsure where my home was or would be.

AN AMERICAN EDUCATION

During my first year at Dana Hall I began to question my Catholic faith. Two juniors rooming together down the hall from me, Sandy and Kathy, became my special friends and confidantes. After dinner, before or after homework, we would sprawl on their beds in pajamas and talk about things both silly and serious.

Kathy was Jewish, Sandy a Protestant, maybe Congregational. I didn't know much about their beliefs, and wanted to learn, especially about Judaism. I don't think I had ever met a Jewish person before. My two friends, in turn, asked me questions about Catholicism that seeded my mind with doubt.

"Why would God keep a special heaven just for Catholics," Kathy asked, "sending all other good people to some less desirable place?"

That question had already been troubling me. Even if my mother was forgiven for her divorce, she would not be permitted to return to the Church unless she confessed that her subsequent marriage to my father was invalid and her children were illegitimate. Without doing that, she could never earn her way to the best heaven. Could God be so cruel?

"It doesn't make sense to believe that Mary was a virgin. Mary was Joseph's wife. What about Joseph? Why would God ask him to stay celibate in his marriage?"

Quoting Mère Michaela, I answered, "It was a great gift and privilege to be selected to be the mother of the Son of God."

But my doubts persisted.

"I read somewhere that the whole idea of Mary being a virgin came from a mistranslation," said Kathy. "The word *woman* was changed to *virgin*. Plus, you know that the texts called Gospels were not written down until many years after the apostles had died?"

The Gospels were sacred texts, and the Church represented God on earth, so I simply had to believe what was in the Gospels. But I wanted better answers for my friends—and for myself. I resolved to talk with my older sister when I saw her next. Surely Jūratė would be able to clarify matters.

A different set of questions arose about the Church and the Pope. My friends told me more than I had heard thus far about the Nazi concentration camps. They put what little I knew into a perspective more horrifying than I had ever imagined.

"The Pope collaborated with Hitler," Kathy said.

I couldn't believe that, but began to wonder: Did the Holy Father use his power as representative of Christ on earth to stop the slaughter? Did he command Catholics to stand by the Jews? Mère Michaela had never mentioned anything about that. As our spiritual leader, the Pope had a duty, surely, to defend the evildoer's victims.

Jūratė would explain. I was eager to talk with her, but would have to wait for summer vacation for the opportunity.

DANA HALL WAS rich with possibilities. I started learning to play tennis; took part in a performance of *Our Town*, playing George in the headmistress's husband's clothes; and sang in Gershwin's *Of Thee I Sing*.

That was a lot of fun, even though I was only a voice in the chorus. Miss Glazer, who directed the glee club and theatrical performances, made us want to be the best. She was younger than most of my teachers, and quite unlike them, in that she was not at all stiff and proper. She wore her longish dark hair loose and sometimes unkempt, and once, when she lifted her arms to direct the chorus, I saw a hole in her maroon dress, under her arm, with a safety pin dangling to one side of it. For some reason, I found that reassuring.

The glee club was my only opportunity to meet boys. We collaborated with some boys' schools, especially Andover and Exeter, and after our concerts we'd have a dance. My schoolmates met boys during vacations, at various social events, but I had no social life at all. So when they came back to school with a lot of giggly stories, I didn't have much to share. Just to get mail from some boy, I cultivated a kind of friendship with a gawky Exeter kid after one of the dances. He wrote to me often, but even reading the letters was boring.

Mail, however, was a big thing. Mère Michaela wrote, but I could no longer reply. Knowing how unhappy my growing doubt would make her, I simply stopped responding. I read her letters over and over, though, with an ache in my heart.

Ugné's letters made me envious.

"I love walking in Paris at night with a pipe in my pocket," she wrote. She had left her parents, was living on her own and studying at the Sorbonne, even as I was in a girls' boarding school. It was not the convent she had predicted for me, but was nevertheless not glamorous, as her life seemed to be. Our correspondence slowed, then broke off.

Mama wrote frequently. She also sent special treats now and then, enclosed in the laundry box that traveled back and forth. All the girls packed their dirty clothes into a brown waxed-cardboard box, tightened it with two straps, mailed it, and got it back with everything fresh and well ironed. My dresses always returned folded and buttoned with care. I may have been the only student whose mother and grandmother did the washing and ironing themselves. Mama usually sent some baked goodies, too. The bacon rolls shaped like croissants were particular favorites among my friends.

Mama's letters told of big changes. Jūratė had left the University of Michigan after eloping with a fellow student, Jack, who was from Flint and played jazz piano. They soon had a baby boy and bought a house. Eventually my sister would give birth to five children. Jack worked for the Buick Corporation. He had been raised Episcopalian, but converted to Catholicism to marry my sister.

Just about everyone in Flint worked in the automotive industry. Jūratė told Mama she could readily get a job in a factory, where a nurse's duties were lighter than at a hospital and the pay was better. Mama had wanted to get out of New York all along, so, during my second year at Dana, she worked two shifts for a while, until she had enough money for the move. Jūratė found a place for her to rent not far from her home.

"We have a little house with a big veranda and a sunny backyard where we can plant vegetables and flowers," Mama wrote. "It reminds me somewhat of the little house where we used to stay in Palanga. You will see it when you come for your next vacation. I am working on the afternoon shift, but eventually they will give me morning."

The most precious letters I received in boarding school were from Mr. Sudduth, brief letters in a strong hand, usually including a $10 bill—enough to treat friends to ice cream sodas in town. Once he sent an invitation to come to New York, bringing a friend for a weekend in the city and a dance at the U.S. Army's military academy at West Point. I invited my roommate Sandy, and her mother gave permission.

Mr. Sudduth had instructed us how to get from Grand Central Station to the Biltmore Hotel, where we would meet by the big clock. I had just read J. D. Salinger's *Catcher in the Rye* and knew that the meeting place he chose was popular with prep school students coming in from out of town. He took us to the Russian Tea Room and then to the Stork Club, where he introduced us to the coat checker, a beautiful Ukrainian woman who wore a golden braid like a crown atop her head. She had gotten the job on his recommendation.

"One of my daughters," he said to her, nodding toward me, "and her school roommate, Sandy Habsburg." He referred to some of the girls he helped as his daughters.

Sandy was a refugee from Eastern Europe also, but she came from noble lineage. She was an archduchess of Austria, a granddaughter of Queen Marie of Rumania, a daughter of Princess Ileana of Rumania. Alexandra was her given name, but Sandy suited the girl who was my friend better.

A photographer came by and Mr. Sudduth asked him to take a picture of us. He ordered Shirley Temples for Sandy and me. The drink came with a cherry and a straw. Someone was playing jazz on a piano, but I was obsessed by the black ashtray on our table. The Stork Club was famous. An ashtray from the Stork Club would be a prize to show around.

"You can take it," Mr. Sudduth said, and I slid it into my purse.

We had dinner at Mr. and Mrs. Bary's, in their tiny East Side apartment, where Sandy and I also stayed the night. The next morning Mrs. Bary took us to the train to West Point, where two cadets gave us a tour of the campus and then escorted us to a formal dance. All this had been arranged by Mr. Sudduth.

The Barys were Russian aristocrats who had fled Communism in Russia before the war. They had been prosperous, but their property had been expropriated by the Bolsheviks. What was left of their wealth had vanished because Mr. Bary, who was an inventor, could not resist lending money to other inventors, none of whom were ever able to pay him back.

On an easel by the living room window lay plans for his own latest project, a circular runway that would allow airplanes to take off in much less space than a conventional runway requires.

"This would be very useful because airports will continue to grow and expand," he said. "People in government are interested, but they said I would have to produce a prototype to prove it works. That would cost a million dollars, and I don't have a million dollars."

In fact, so short of a million dollars were the Barys that they bought their food and paid for rent and concert tickets from her income as a model for girdles.

"Things change," he said, philosophically. "So it is."

Mr. Bary was short and soft-spoken, whereas his wife was a woman who took up space in the room, both physically and in her demeanor.

"There are Communists here too," she warned. "They have power. We must be careful. But such good people exist in this country also." Her voice turned rich with emotion. "I love this country. Mr. Sudduth, he is so kind. He helps so many people."

ONLY MUCH LATER would I get an idea of the extent of my benefactor's unique generosity. What he did for me, and for my sister, was part of the passionate mission he had undertaken to help students rendered homeless by the war. In the years from 1947 to 1950 he enabled more than four hundred DPs to study on scholarships in American universities and schools, including some, such as myself, at prestigious private secondary schools. He did it personally and almost single-handedly. Yet he was not a wealthy man.

William H. Sudduth was born and raised in Starkville, Mississippi, and had moved to New York as a young man. As the war ended he was living with his wife and two daughters in Greenwich, Connecticut, and working for American Express in Manhattan at a job he enjoyed. Then he took a year's leave and volunteered to serve with

UNRRA. I don't know what motivated him to do that. It could be that his marriage fell apart at about this time. He talked a great deal about his two daughters, but not about his wife. I had a sense that he was burdened by a need to keep some kind of tragic personal secret. Years after he entered my life as an angel, I set out to write a book about him, but soon realized I would not be able to do that. He would have been glad to tell me many great stories about other people, but would not share much about his inner life.

While working with UNRRA in Germany, he was moved by the plight of the refugees, especially young people and children separated from their parents. One day, he said, while walking down a corridor in a DP camp building, he heard a child crying, followed the sound, and found a boy, little older than a toddler, lying alone in a crib in an empty room. Nothing was known about him, not even his name, as Mr. Sudduth told the story. The boy had two club feet. His parents couldn't be found. Mr. Sudduth arranged for corrective surgery. He and the surgeon chose a birth date for him, and a name: Peter. Then he decided that since he was now, in effect, Peter's godfather, he had to bring him to the United States and find adoptive parents for him. This would prove to be difficult because of various bureaucratic procedures, but he succeeded.

Sometime after taking responsibility for Peter, he heard someone playing Mozart, beautifully, on a piano. In a recreation room down the hall from his office he discovered a nine-year-old girl, also alone; she had been accidentally separated from her father. He helped to locate the father in another camp, and to celebrate the reunion. As with Peter, he wanted to do more. He promised to make it possible for this talented girl to study at an American conservatory of music, and he did. She would become the first of his "daughters."

DPs from Eastern Europe tended to be well-educated people. While waiting to relocate, they tried to live as normally as possible, forming communities, engaging in cultural activities, and organizing schools in the camps. Some of the young people were studying at German universities. The Western Military Command required the universities to reserve 10 percent of their student admissions for qualified DPs. Most of those admitted attended classes while continuing to live in camps, but for those at Heidelberg University, UNRRA established a hostel because no camp existed nearby. Mr. Sudduth and volunteer social worker Ruth Praeger were appointed to be house parents at this hostel.

In 1947, when UNRRA was dissolved and replaced by the International Refugee Organization, the hostel was closed and Mr. Sudduth was dismissed. Before leaving, he made a pledge: he would bring all who had been in his charge at the hostel to the United States to continue their studies.

His work at American Express had included shepherding special clients on cruises and other luxury travels. Being fun-loving, naturally charming, genteel, and gregarious, he had made many friends.

With William H. Sudduth, many years later,
at the Guggenheim Museum in New York

When he returned from Heidelberg he extended his leave from American Express for another year, rented the apartment on East 87th Street, equipped it with secondhand furniture, and began calling prominent people he knew, asking them to sponsor DP students and establish scholarships for some of them at universities of which they were alumni. Ruth Praeger soon joined the endeavor.

The operation was very much ad hoc. There were no forms to fill out, no applications to file. People arrived at the apartment, Mr. Sudduth talked with them, then sat down at the telephone with his Rolodex. At this time, while the U.S. was chary about opening the doors more widely to refugees, many Americans were sympathetic and willing to help. The country also had a labor shortage. Scholarships and offers of employment and housing materialized. Sudduth also helped the students' families, as well as other refugees who found their way to him, usually by word of mouth. Among them, thanks to his friend and ally Mrs. Bary, were my sister Jūratė and myself. How Mrs. Bary found us I have no idea.

WHEN IT CAME time to apply to colleges, many of my Dana Hall classmates who had good academic records looked to Smith, Vassar, and Wellesley. I, however, didn't want to go to a women's college. At Dana Hall, as at home, I had lived among women and girls. I knew no boys (except for that boring one at Exeter) and the only adult male presence in my life was the mysterious Mr. Sudduth. I asked Miss Glazer for advice.

"What kind of college would you like to go to?"

"Co-ed," I said. "No fraternities or sororities. Students from different countries. And I will need a scholarship."

"Oberlin," she said immediately. "It was the first college in the country to admit both women and men. It was also the first to admit Negroes. In fact, have you heard of the Underground Railroad?" I had not. "Slaves fleeing from the South traveled a route that had stops where people would hide them and protect them. Oberlin was one."

"What else?"

"It's a very good liberal arts college, with an excellent conservatory of music. No fraternities or sororities, but lots of great activities. A tradition of social service. It's in Ohio. Students can't have cars. I don't know about scholarships, but I'd be glad to recommend you."

The following autumn, 1952, I would enter Oberlin with a full scholarship: tuition plus room and board.

The summer after graduating from Dana Hall, however, turned out to be another turning point in my education. I got a job as a waitress in Waterville, New Hampshire, at the Waterville Inn, a resort hotel, where all the dining room crew were college students. Among them was Peter Gardner, a young man with an infectious laugh who sang folksongs while playing the guitar and was light on his feet when he danced. We became close friends, talking about life, religion, and philosophy. We also danced, and swam, and climbed nearby Mount Osceola with others in the dining hall crew, and camped next to the fire lookout tower atop the mountain. We'd set out after finishing our after-dinner chores and returned in time to serve breakfast.

Peter had come to Waterville with his girlfriend Bobbie. They had been together for years, so I thought that nothing more than friendship was possible between us. Still, it often happened that when groups of us went for a hike along the creek he and I walked together, ahead of the others, and that I just happened to do my best swan dives at the pool when he was nearby.

One evening he and I were washing silverware together in a deep kitchen sink and our hands met in the water. The following Friday, Bobbie didn't come to the weekly square dance because she had a headache. The next morning she looked like she had been crying. Then she left. For the remainder of our time in Waterville, Peter and I were a couple, openly in love.

Peter was a Quaker and would be starting his senior year at Haverford College in September. He gave me some of Alexander Tolstoy's work on pacifism to read, and told me about Gandhi and nonviolent resistance.

I was skeptical.

"Maybe in India, against the British," I argued. "The British were not monsters. But Hitler and Stalin? How could you refuse to fight? It's cowardice to be passive in the face of such evil."

"The choice is not between fighting and refusing to fight. It's not a matter of being passive, of doing nothing. The choice is between violent and nonviolent means. You can't defeat violence by responding violently. That only brings more violence."

"Easy to say, easy to talk," I said. "Nobody has invaded this country. The partisans who went into the woods in Lithuania, Poland, France—they are my heroes. They only had rifles, but they did not give up."

"They were brave," Peter responded. "Many died, and they killed soldiers who were victims just as the partisans were, who only wanted to be at home with their families. What was gained by all that killing?"

I told him I was sorry that I wasn't old enough to join the underground before our family fled. I didn't tell him that I was not sure I would have had the courage.

I did consider that my father, who was a general and certainly brave, did not go into the forest. He had even told the Russians that he would be willing to work for them, if he could do so in his own country. He was a military man; he surely could not have agreed with Peter, yet I found these new ideas beautiful.

Peter knew that if he was ordered to become a soldier, he would refuse and declare himself a conscientious objector, no matter what the consequences. As a woman, I would face no such challenge because women were not drafted. Still, a time could come, one way or another, when I might have to make a choice.

That actually happened at the end of that very summer. I had turned eighteen and become eligible to apply for citizenship. The application form included a question with boxes to check for one of three possible answers.

Would I be willing to serve in the armed forces? Would I be willing to perform nonmilitary service in the armed forces? Would I perform alternative service at a nonmilitary organization? I wavered between the last two, then realized I had only one choice as a Christian. I checked the third box, and as I did so I felt brave, and also a bit frightened, for my becoming a citizen hinged on this form's official acceptance. Making that check mark to perform alternative service and then signing the application was a commitment, even if the question was only theoretical.

More important lessons about war, peace, and struggles for justice would follow at a retreat in Oberlin. A special guest had been invited: Pete Seeger. I already knew some of his songs because Peter had taught them to me, but about Pete himself I knew almost nothing.

That week I learned that he was believed to have supported Communism, but that in this country during the 1930s, people joined the Communist Party to fight for better wages and working conditions, oblivious of the tyranny in the Soviet Union. Americans seemed to have been deluded by the ideals of Communism because they had not experienced Communist reality. Puzzled, but drawn to Pete Seeger, I hung around, listening to the stories he told and sang about people who were oppressed and rose up for justice. He would give concerts at Oberlin more than once while I was a student there, and I went to all of them. It was on the way to one of them that he wrote "Where Have All the Flowers Gone?" And, of course, he was also a pacifist.

I majored in government. Although I was much more interested in literature, I thought it would have been self-indulgent to choose that major. The only literature classes I allowed myself to take were those in French or German, because they had the practical value of improving my language skills—yet Professor Heinz Politzer's seminar in German literature turned out to be one of the most eye-opening classes I had the good fortune to participate in, and not because he taught in German. He introduced me to Hermann Hesse, Thomas Mann, and Rainer Maria Rilke, who remains my favorite among all poets.

By this time I was no longer going to church. Jūratė had been no help. When I finally asked her my big questions, before leaving for college, her answer was only this: "If you can't believe, then you must pray for faith."

That made no sense to me. At Oberlin, I set out to find another church I might join. But Presbyterians and Methodists were too austere. Episcopalian Mass was beautiful and resembled the Catholic one, and in some ways I liked it better. At the one I attended, people didn't slip away after Communion, as many did in the Catholic Masses I had attended in Brooklyn; they all stayed till the end, and stayed in the pews as the priest walked down the center aisle and stopped just outside the door to speak to worshippers as they poured out. But Episcopalian Mass was so similar to the Catholic Mass that, as an ex-Catholic, I felt it was somehow fake.

The most appealing form of Christianity was that of the Quakers, the Friends—my friend Peter's faith. They came together in a meeting house rather than a church and mostly sat silently together. There was no priest, no sermon. Anyone who wanted to say something could break the silence with a few words. Then there was silence again. It was the kind of gathering Jesus would have favored, I thought, but in the end it was simply too plain for me. I missed the incense and the Gregorian chants, the candles and the flowers. So I passed through Oberlin searching for a spiritual home without finding one. Eventually I would find my path through Eastern philosophy, especially Buddhism.

Oberlin was a place that generated many questions, but not necessarily the answers. During late-night "bull sessions," I joined fellow students exploring thoughts that were emerging with our personal identities. In myriad ways, we were prompted to ask ourselves, Who am I? Where am I going? Where do I belong?

Some of my fellow students couldn't understand why my family had fled from the Russians to Austria if we were not Nazi sympathizers. When I mentioned Stalin's terror, someone would say, "It was wartime. The Russians couldn't afford internal enemies."

I would point out that Stalin's regime killed people because they were intellectuals, free spirits, successful farmers, because they hid food and seeds to keep from starving, or were seen as potential threats to the government because they were community leaders. Ukrainians, Poles, Lithuanians, Chechen people were considered unsubmissive, therefore threatening. So were some of Russia's great artists and writers and military leaders, so they were imprisoned and killed. Some small nations, such as the Buddhist Kalmyks, were almost entirely exterminated.

These discussions had me on the defensive and fighting off a feeling of guilt or shame. Should we have stayed in Lithuania? Would that have been more honorable than fleeing? My fellow students' experience, growing up in this country, was so different from mine that they couldn't understand choices that had to be made in wartime. But in truth, I didn't know much about the war either. I hadn't explored beyond my personal experience as a child. Still, there was no point, really, in arguing about who was more evil, Hitler or Stalin. The job at hand was to understand what could be done to change the course of human history, in which tyrants and mass slaughter have kept occurring.

But right then I would not dwell in the sorrowful past. There was so much more to discover.

Jūratė made me gloriously happy by driving down from Michigan for my Oberlin graduation. It was June 1956. She was now twenty-seven years old and the mother of two boys and a girl. In the next five years, two more girls would be born. I never saw her anymore except in a family context, at her home or at Mama's. During the past several years, she had been raising children with her husband, who at this time was an executive at the Buick Corporation. She no longer planned to become a doctor researching tuberculosis. She also had stopped playing the piano. There was a piano in the house, but only Jack played it. My older sister was no longer the wild, defiant girl I had so admired. But she had come.

It was not so much that she attended the graduation ceremony that thrilled me; it was the fact that she came alone and unencumbered. I couldn't recall being alone with her for more than a few moments since she went off to the University of Michigan—actually, not since the night we spent in the same room at Schloss Goldenstein before our First Communion, ten years ago.

I rode back to Flint with Jūratė. Boxes of books and papers, the slim Olivetti typewriter Mama had bought for me, a couple of suit-cases stuffed with clothing and shoes—everything fit easily into the capacious, luxurious Buick sedan. It was late afternoon when we got on the road through the flat Ohio countryside. The sun set, dusk came, and then the night. The beams our headlights cast on the road in front of us obliterated the shapes of trees and rocks and houses, intensifying the darkness around us, the warmth within the car. I don't remember what we talked about, but I know we both felt light and free.

11

WANDERING

After some days visiting first Jūratė and then the rest of the family, who had moved to Chicago in 1954, I started looking for a job. Contrary to my expectations, nothing exciting materialized. A friend who was a reporter for the *Chicago Sun-Times* got me an interview with his city editor, but he made it clear he had no interest in a girl with no newspaper experience. Nothing else beckoned. I felt obliged to spend at least some time living in Chicago for Mama's sake, after years of being far away.

So I took a job in the office of the League of Women Voters of Illinois. My work was basically clerical, but at least it would serve a good cause. I could bear it for a while, I thought—long enough to save enough money for a trip to Europe, to try to find a sense of direction.

I rented an apartment with a former Oberlin roommate, Martha, in Hyde Park, near the University of Chicago—a lively neighborhood where many young people lived. A graduate student in physics from Italy, Domenico, came over once or twice a week with his friend Romano. They cooked dinner for all of us, then Martha visited with Romano while Domenico and I exchanged language lessons. I worked with him on his English. Then we listened to some music. Then we worked on *Italian Through Pictures*.

One evening, Romano, somewhat embarrassed, asked if we could put his fiancée up for a couple of weeks. She was coming to visit. This was a surprise. Romano had not mentioned that he was engaged, but we welcomed Anna. She knew no English whatsoever, so that helped me in learning Italian. We learned eventually that she had been wondering why Romano's letters had cooled off and had decided she'd better come find out—which turned out to be a good move. The wedding happened shortly after. When I eventually took my planned trip to Europe, Anna's family welcomed me at their home in Tuscany.

It was an in-between time, a good time. And it was a perfect time to go see more of this world.

IN JUNE 1958, I found myself aboard a Holland-America Line ship in New York Harbor, ready to cross the Atlantic again. My intention had been to ramble through Europe with my childhood best friend, Ugnė, who lived in Paris but had come to visit me in Chicago. She had changed her mind about our plan at the last minute, however, so despite some trepidations, I was embarking alone. Or so I thought, until, as I was leaning over the railing watching the gangplank being pulled away, I heard shouts from the dock: "Rasa! Rasa!"

Two fellow Oberlin graduates were waving to me. When I waved back, they pointed to my right: "Look! Mike. Over there."

I turned and there, indeed, was their friend Mike, looking at me through oversized dark glasses. He, too, was traveling solo. Although at Oberlin our paths had seldom crossed, here among strangers and on the threshold of the unknown we were delighted to see each other. He would be entering Yale Law School in September and was headed for Europe with no specific destination, just to wander for a couple of months. I was to stop in London, where friends of my parents were expecting me for a weeklong visit, but had not decided where to go after that. Mike and I agreed to meet in Paris and then travel through France and Spain together.

The crossing from New York to Portsmouth took ten days, longer than most ocean liner crossings because we stopped at Reykjavik. Many of the passengers were young and, like us, traveling with backpacks. We had plenty of time for talk, dancing, and sipping brandy at the bar to stave off seasickness.

The day before we landed in England, a steward handed me a telegram: "MEET AT LONDON STATION STOP WILL WEAR RED ROSE." Even though the sender was my mother's friend, an elderly gentleman, I was charmed by the message. During the two-hour train ride from Portsmouth to Paddington Station I noticed that the landscape seemed tidily stitched together, like a handmade quilt. I saw no neglected patches of land of the sort you see along tracks and highways in America. Houses and vehicles seemed smaller than they were in the United States. Hedges ran alongside roads and divided fields.

I spotted him before our train had come to a full stop in London—a tall, dignified gentleman with a rose in a lapel of his charcoal gray coat, carrying a bouquet of red roses, and accompanied by a small white dog with a red rose pinned to the collar.

"Well, hello, hello. Welcome."

We shook hands.

Mr. and Mrs. Brazdžionis lived in Warwick Gardens, in an old two-story house that was still elegant, although the need to economize had taken its toll. Mr. Brazdžionis had been serving as Lithuania's ambassador to Great Britain when the Soviets invaded in 1941, and had remained in London as a shadow diplomat, representing a government that no longer existed yet was still recognized by Britain, the United States, and some other countries that had refused to accept the Soviet Union's absorption of the Baltic States. I felt I was visiting a place forgotten by time.

Mornings, after breakfast, I was sent off to explore historical and cultural sights of London. I would return for the big midday meal, we would go to our rooms to rest, and then, in late afternoon, Mr. Brazdžionis would drive the black sedan to some more distant site, sometimes outside the city. We might follow narrow hedge-lined roads to an old village, stopping at a house with a low-slung thatched roof and a threshold that had been worn down by footsteps during the past five hundred years. One gray day we visited the seashore, and my sandaled feet nearly froze. But we were always back home for tea.

Both my hosts suffered from a strange ailment: much of their hair had fallen out, and Mrs. Brazdžionis had bouts of vertigo. They said the doctors were puzzled but they themselves were convinced that they were being poisoned by lead in the wallpaper. People they told this to thought they were daft, Mrs. Brazdžionis said, but their troubles had started, months before, when paper was ripped off one wall to repair a leak in a water pipe. Only much later would we all learn that the toxicity of some old wallpaper and paint was hardly imaginary.

IN PARIS, I made my way to the American Express office, where Mike was to meet me. We proceeded in the manner customary with post-college wanderers: hitching rides, staying in youth hostels and cheap hotels. We met others like ourselves from various countries, laughed at the way, in France, whenever you asked someone how far something was, the answer was almost invariably *vingt minutes* (twenty minutes).

Gradually, I began to be annoyed with my travel companion, and he with me. Small things about him bugged me and that may well have been mutual. One evening we sat in a small restaurant in a town near the Spanish border waiting for our meals silently because we had just had one of our increasingly frequent tiffs and were cooling down.

I avoided Mike's eyes and focused, instead, on the young French couple at the next table. She was eating a strange geometrically patterned globular vegetable that looked like a thistle head. I asked the waiter for another look at the menu and, by a process of elimination, figured it must be *artichaut* (artichoke). The woman was picking off the leaves one by one, dipping them in a little bowl of melted butter, scraping them between her teeth to extract the soft fleshy part, and dropping the leavings into a bowl. I resolved to order *artichaut* next time I saw it on a menu.

Mike's pasta Alfredo arrived, together with my veal carbonara and asparagus. He fell to and was soon finished, while I chewed listlessly on a meal I would have enjoyed in a more pleasant mood. Finally I put down my knife and fork while my plate was still half full.

The French couple looked harmonious. She was wearing a flower-patterned pastel dress and blue shoes with small heels that reminded me of my mother's advice: Make sure you have nice shoes and you can look elegant no matter what you put on the rest of you. I was wearing simple black sandals with small heels that took up almost no space in my backpack, and a well-fitting sleeveless black cotton dress, the only dress I had packed. But Mike loomed across the table from me in the wrinkled checked shirt he usually wore on the road. His hair was unkempt, and he hadn't shaved for days.

It's a horrendous habit among young American men, I thought, to let the stubble grow on their chins while they are traveling abroad, not caring what they looked like because they were outside their country. Never mind that it's someone else's country.

"Why aren't you eating?" Mike demanded, in a too-loud voice.

"Not hungry. If you're done, let's go."

He banged his butter knife against the stem of his wine glass, apparently having read somewhere that this was a custom in southern Europe, though other diners had simply signaled their readiness of the bill with a small hand gesture. The scrupulous way he examined the bill embarrassed me. He was acting like the stereotypical bourgeois American abroad, I thought, always worried that the local people are out to cheat him. It was time to part with Mike. Fortunately, he was due to leave for home shortly.

ONCE I WAS on my own again, my travel map had four more specific destinations: an international volunteer work camp in a French village high in the Alps, near the Italian border; another work camp in Sardinia, run by the American Friends Service Committee; a visit with my mother's friends in Rome; then Paris. Beyond these stops I had no plans or time limits except those determined by what was in my wallet.

In the first camp I spent two weeks shoveling mud out of farmers' stables, mud that had washed down mountainsides during winter floods two years before. I was the only volunteer from the United States on this project; the others were mostly French, English, and German. I sometimes found myself translating among all three languages, which I enjoyed.

We loaded the mud into buckets, hauled it out of the barns, and piled it up outside. It was hard work, but I was glad to be doing something useful after weeks of sightseeing. We slept in a hayloft, washed at the village pump, and on Sundays, sore and tired, hiked to a glacier lake and even swam in it—briefly.

The second camp, in Sardinia, was a refugee resettlement project, organized by the AFSC with funding donated by a Hollywood actor, Don Murray. The AFSC and its local partners were starting a farm where some DPs still in refugee camps in Italy could relocate. Although World War II had ended in Europe thirteen years before, some people were still waiting to be resettled. They may have been found undesirable for political reasons or because of poor health.

We volunteers, many of us from the United States, hoed stony fields to prepare them for planting yellow tomatoes. Nobody was growing yellow tomatoes in Sardinia, so they presented a market opportunity. I never followed up to learn how this project turned out.

IN ROME, MR. and Mrs. Lozoraitis were expecting me in the villa that was the official headquarters of the prewar Lithuanian government. Stasys Lozoraitis was Free Lithuania's chief representative. I arrived grubby and tired. Waking up in a bed with smooth white sheets in a sunny room was heaven.

As Mr. and Mrs. Brazdžionis had done in London, my hosts in Rome left me to wander mornings and took me around in the afternoons. Eating formally at a dining room table, served by a man wearing white gloves, was most delightful after the past weeks' experience. The same man also served as chauffeur for our excursions. Lithuanian communities in the United States and elsewhere had stepped in with funds to sustain Lithuania's diplomatic presence here in Rome.

My hosts and I shared the news—or rather, the rumors—we had heard suggesting that my father might still be alive. The most promising had been a footnote in a book by a Pole who had been imprisoned in Russia. He noted that he had been in a cell with some engineers, including an aeronautical engineer from Lithuania. All had been sentenced to death, but their sentences had been commuted to hard labor. Mama had tried to find out more, with no success. The Lozoraitises had also tried, in vain.

Later I would realize that I had wasted an opportunity to learn about my native country and my family during this visit. We did not talk about what I felt was the impossible dream, that Lithuania could again be free. I thought that was geopolitically unrealistic, and that there was therefore no point in sustaining this vain hope. Perhaps I was afraid that such views would be considered a betrayal. But later

I regretted my cowardice in not voicing my thoughts. I might have learned something about the power of hope to defeat oppression.

IN LATE OCTOBER I was back in Paris to meet my friend Martha, who had been traveling too. My money was running out, the weather was cold and rainy, and I was tired of wandering. Either I had to find a way to survive here or I would have to go back home.

Should I try to get a job at the Paris office of the *New York Herald Tribune?* Though I could not expect to be hired as a reporter, having no experience, perhaps I could run copy or start in some other lowly position and work my way up? But as I considered such a possibility, it began to lose its appeal, for various reasons.

The American young people Martha and I met in the cafés had come to Paris to be artists or writers, but they seemed to be spending most of their time and energy searching for cheap rooms and cheap meals, and catch-as-catch-can income opportunities. At the same time, talking with my French contemporaries I found that many were highly opinionated about the United States, though they actually knew very little about the country. Their conviction of the superiority of French culture was irritating—far more irritating than any flaws in Mike's appearance and behavior had been. They thought they were very cosmopolitan, but their arrogance, I thought, made them provincial. One day I found myself defending America—the same America that Mike and I and others had so often fiercely criticized.

It was time to go home, home to America.

But first Martha and I explored Paris together for a few days. Each of us had an agenda: She wanted to meet artists. I wanted to talk with French Communists, to ask them how, living in the world capital of democracy, they could support the Soviet Union, especially now, after the Hungarian revolution of 1956. By now I understood, thanks to Pete Seeger and others, that in the United States during the 1930s

Communism meant primarily a struggle for labor rights, racial justice, and economic fairness. The brutalities of the Soviet Union were not widely known in America at the time, and during the war they were ignored because the Soviet Union was a key ally. But now, how could any thinking person be a Communist?

In our quest, Martha and I spent quite a bit of time at the Café des Artistes et Intellectuels on the lookout for artists and Communists. She was beautiful and self-confident, and men flocked to her; among them were artists.

Communists took longer to locate, but eventually someone introduced me to Kostya. He was not very communicative, so hoping to get a chance to talk with him openly, I accepted his invitation to his room one night. Martha and an artist friend of Kostya's came along, and while my Communist and I took the bed, they settled down on a mattress. We were amorously entangled when Kostya suddenly sat up and switched on the radio on the shelf above the bed. It was midnight, time for Radio Moscow news. After the broadcast ended, all of us fell asleep. Another educational opportunity had been lost.

IN MANY CULTURES, the Year of Wandering is enshrined in folklore. The young person—young man, usually—goes off to see the world. His character is tested and shaped by adventures and experiences. He comes back with a new sense of himself and a new understanding of the place where he started and where he belongs. By traveling in Europe, I found that America had become my home. I had become an American.

This didn't mean, however, that I knew where I belonged or what I should do with my life, as I had hoped my travels would help me discover. I was still tormented by guilt. I couldn't just turn my back on my native country, on my father, who had perished or was living in some prison camp deep in the Soviet Union. I didn't feel like an

American, but neither did I feel any strong kinship with the young Lithuanians I had come to know in Chicago.

Mama had moved the family there from Flint partly because Chicago had the largest Lithuanian community in the country, and she hoped that I would meet and marry a Lithuanian. I had made an effort to participate in the various social functions that brought young people together. The biggest youth organization was Catholic, but there was another, based not on religion but on a liberal point of view. Both had dances, picnics, parties, and trips to the Indiana dunes, which were known among Lithuanians as Palanga—and yes, Lake Michigan did resemble the Baltic Sea somewhat. I made some good friends but felt that this community was too limited—it was almost like a colony. I yearned for a wider world.

I didn't belong fully anywhere.

12

NEWSPAPER YEARS

I returned from Europe in November 1958, with no specific plans. In New York, I found Ugnė, who had been studying international relations at Columbia University while I was traveling. She invited me out to dinner with her friend, the Algerian delegate at the United Nations. Algeria was still fighting for independence, so his title was Observer. He asked me what I planned to do. Without thinking even a moment, I said I would like to write for a newspaper and might apply to the Graduate School of Journalism at Columbia University. He said he might be able to help. And he did, in an interesting way.

A couple of days after the dinner, Ugnė called to tell me that her friend had suggested to the correspondent of a large North African newspaper that he persuade the Moroccan delegate to the UN that he needed a press officer, and to tell him he knew a person he could highly recommend. This Moroccan delegate spoke elegant French, but no English. My French was not perfect, but it was pretty good. He hired me. My job was primarily to read stories that might be of interest to him in the American press and to provide him with a daily briefing in French. Consequently, when I was filling out my application to the journalism school, in which I was asked to list periodicals I read, I had a stunningly long and diverse list. The school accepted me, with financial aid.

Instructors at the school included reporters from the *New York Times* and the *New York Herald Tribune*. They sent us out into the city to cover real stories beside real reporters. I loved what we did, and knew I was now on a path that was right for me.

After completing the master's program, I expected to have to start at some small-town newspaper, but instead—another stroke of luck—the *Washington Post* hired me. Many of us who were graduating had sent applications to several news organizations, including the *Post*, not really expecting a response. Two of us, George Watson and I, were invited to come to Washington for an interview. The newspaper that congressmen read at breakfast took on both of us.

George was very sharp and a fast writer. But what made the managing editor, Alfred Friendly, choose me? Perhaps because I spoke French and German? Perhaps—as for my mother, so for me—speaking other languages served as a key. So many Americans spoke nothing but English.

Whatever the explanation, I happily moved to Washington, where I was assigned a gray metal desk just outside the women's restroom.

I watched President John F. Kennedy's inauguration on TV in the newsroom, and was stirred by his call to "Ask not what your country can do for you, ask what you can do for your country." And I stood among the hundreds of reporters covering his funeral. When I reached into my pocket for a pencil, I distinctly felt the eyes of a Secret Service agent upon me. During the days after the assassination, TV melted time, blurring the past and the present. At Dulles International Airport, arriving heads of state stopped for a photograph before the assembled press, while behind us film footage of John F. Kennedy's murder in Dallas was repeated endlessly on a screen.

Many events of momentous significance took place during my five years at the *Post*. The Reverend Martin Luther King Jr. spoke from the steps of the Lincoln Memorial to the multitude who had marched to the nation's capital for jobs and freedom and had gathered around the Reflecting Pool. What made the biggest impression on me that day, however, was not Dr. King but Stokely Carmichael and the other proud young Black men from the Student Nonviolent Coordinating Committee, SNCC, in their crisp white shirts and blue overalls. They were the future.

As a novice reporter, I was first assigned to write obituaries, usually on the evening shift, then was moved to general assignment on the day shift. Eventually I unearthed a story of corruption in the District of Columbia housing department. It took months to develop. As the story grew, the editors assigned a second reporter, Leslie H. Whitten, to it also. Les was an excellent newsman who had been covering the municipal court and relished a good story. We enjoyed working together, and became good friends. On the day our piece was published, the two of us walked unannounced into the conference room at the housing department to find the top people huddled around the table with the newspaper in front of them. That was a satisfying moment.

The way the paper handled our story, however, dismayed us. Before it saw print, the attorneys went over it so thoroughly and demanded so many modifications that it read more like a legal brief than an exposé. All the life and color had been wrung out of it. And in the long run, nothing changed. Months later, even some of the specific housing code violations we had pointed out had not been corrected.

Les left the paper to become an associate of syndicated columnist Jack Anderson. He later told me that while at the *Post* he hadn't been able to write some of the juicy stories he found—at this time, the erotic adventures of people in Congress or the White House were not considered to be publishable material—with Anderson he was free to write everything, but wasn't always believed. Eventually he left the news business to write detective stories and novels, often set in Washington.

I APPLIED TO the *New York Herald Tribune*, which had been my dream paper since journalism school because of its excellent writers. By this time I also had a reason other than my disappointment in the *Post* and admiration for the *Trib* to want to move to New York.

Soon after my arrival at the *Post* I had met a reporter who had just come back from Haiti. I met him in the elevator going down from the newsroom, on my way home. His name was Tom Wolfe, and he was tall and graceful, with eyelids that looked violet in a certain kind of light. As we were stepping out into the street he invited me to dinner. We proceeded to an Arabic restaurant, the Iron Gate Inn, and sat down in a booth that had once been a horse's stall.

In his story from Haiti on that morning's front page, Tom had reported that because of a semantic misunderstanding, many children had gone uncounted in the Haitian census. The census workers had been told to count "*hommes*," but children were commonly called *ti hommes,* so a great many of them were left out. It was a barely believable story, both funny and upsetting, written in a wholly original voice, with not a trace of newspaper jargon.

By the time I met Tom in the elevator, I was already enraptured by his writing.

The proprietor of the Iron Gate Inn came by and Tom asked about his family—he came there often—then ordered kibbeh. I did too, because I didn't know what it was and wanted to try something new. Kibbeh turned out to be baked ground lamb with pine nuts and was delicious.

The following week Tom was off to the Dominican Republic.

"Come with me," he urged. I could not, of course. Later a letter arrived: "Come, I have orchids growing out of my armpits."

Ugnė would have gone, but I was not sufficiently daring.

Tom and I both had apartments near Dupont Circle. Mine was a studio (one room with kitchen) on the way to Georgetown, on the top floor of a two-story wooden house with a floor that sloped so much that if you dropped a pencil on the high side it would roll all the way down to the opposite wall.

A plaque beside the front door noted that Martha Washington had once stayed in this house.

Tom's place was a loft with a high sloping ceiling above a restaurant called Mama Margarita's. For a good Italian dinner all we had to do was go downstairs.

Across the street was a movie theater where *Never on Sunday*, starring Melina Mercouri, seemed to be playing forever.

Tom suggested I move in with him, since we were spending just about all our nights together anyway and his place was bigger. But I wouldn't do it, for fear that my mother might come to visit and be shocked.

THE EDITORS OF the *Washington Post* didn't know what to do with Tom. His writing was too unconventional for them. So they sent him out to the suburbs. Even there he came up with surprises. Once the executive editor, J. Russell Wiggins, accused him of making up an exceptionally hilarious tale. Tom phoned his source, a policeman, and asked him to call Wiggins and confirm it. The policeman did. Tom would become famous as a brilliant writer, but he was also an excellent reporter, passionate about staying true to the facts. The *Post* was too stodgy to handle him. So eventually he moved on to the *Herald Tribune*, which was delighted to take him on.

After he left, Tom and I took turns traveling to visit each other on our days off. And in 1965 my dream paper hired me, as well. I had put in an application some months before. Whether an opening simply materialized or Tom put in a good word for me I don't know.

The newsroom of the *New York Herald Tribune* looked like a set for an old movie. Reporters sat in rows at oak desks with antique telephones attached to them. You flipped a switch on the leg of the desk to speak or listen. A friend who was a longtime editor at the *New York Times* came to pick me up for dinner once and could not believe his eyes.

"It's something out of the nineteenth century," he said.

My dream paper was slowly losing a long battle for survival. It lacked sufficient resources to compete with the *New York Times* in the breadth of its coverage. Indeed, it could barely cover the local news. In several efforts to save the paper, a series of brilliant editors had brought in sets of brilliant writers, and so the *Trib* became a writer's paper. Tom fit right in—and then he outraged the literary establishment with some hilarious and devastating stories about the *New Yorker* magazine and the *New York Review of Books*. He was an enfant terrible, enjoying himself while poking at flaws of high-status cultural icons. He particularly enjoyed needling the liberal establishment.

While the *Washington Post* was bogged down by its sense of self-importance, the *Herald Tribune* valued a good story well told. It did not necessarily have to be a world-shaking story. I was sent out to check out a police report that a cat had fallen down a chimney of a multistory apartment house on the West Side of Manhattan. Such a report might have been news in a little town, but not normally in the world's biggest city. But it was one of those slow days. I was waiting for an assignment, so the city editor, Dave Laventhol, sent me out. I found several firemen on the roof of the apartment house trying to figure out how to rescue the cat, or make sure it was dead. There was no way to reach it from above, the building was too high, and the chimney went all the way down to the basement. The firemen, after extensive discussion, eventually knocked out some bricks in the basement and pulled out the cat, who showed no sign of injury.

Laventhol was so delighted he slotted the story into the bottom of the front page, and then he went down into the press room to read it in type, taking me with him. Union rules prohibited us from touching the linotype. If we had, the printers could have stopped work immediately. I was thrilled, as though I had been admitted to an inner sanctum.

"And you know," Laventhol said, shaking his head as we made our way back upstairs, marveling at the absurdity of giving so much attention to the incident, "there isn't even such a crime as leaving the scene of a dead cat."

Some of the people I worked with in that newsroom later became famous authors. Others I could not imagine surviving anywhere but here: Inky Blackman, for instance, a rewrite man who wore suspenders to hold up trousers too wide for him—he had been a much wider man before a serious illness led to an enormous weight loss. Inky became a hero in our newsroom for a memo he wrote castigating a reporter for using the word *treasure* unnecessarily in front of *trove*. The use of needless words was severely frowned upon. Inky's rebuke was both eloquent and very funny. I wish I still had a copy.

Protests against the Vietnam War were growing at this time, and were often led by veterans. I covered numerous demonstrations. Most participants were young, but some grand old rebels stood out: the pacifist A. J. Muste of the Fellowship of Reconciliation; Norman Thomas, who ran for U.S. president six times as the Socialist candidate; A. Phillip Randolph, leader of the Brotherhood of Sleeping Car Porters, the first predominantly African American labor union. Grace Paley was among writers who took part, and the wonderful Bread and Puppet Theater was almost always present, carrying giant puppets. One of the marches was scheduled to cross Manhattan on 42nd Street during the evening rush hour and end at the United Nations. Only a few people showed up for it, but I will always remember Muste and Thomas striding along the crowded sidewalk through rain and darkness, ignored by passersby, visionaries undaunted and undeterred.

I loved the *Trib*. Less than a year after I arrived, however, it folded. I was heartbroken. Someone told me that the city editor of the *New York Times*, Abe Rosenthal, had a spot for a general assignment reporter and would be interested in talking with me. I made an appointment for early one morning. We sat down in a cubicle with a view of the huge newsroom filled with gray metal desks, much like the newsroom of the *Washington Post*. One of the first questions Rosenthal put to me was "Why do you want to work for the *New York Times*?"

Wasn't the answer obvious?

"Because I can no longer work for the *Trib*. The *Times* is my second choice," I answered, knowing that was the wrong answer if I wanted the job.

Rosenthal was visibly taken aback. He told me he wanted reporters for whom the *Times* was the first choice. I have never regretted my reply.

THE *HERALD TRIBUNE* expired at a time that my personal life had also taken a downward turn. Tom and I had parted. We had split up before, more than once, always for the same reason. I wanted to marry and have a family. He said he didn't want children. So I'd say goodbye, start dating other men, but then I'd miss him terribly, and call him. He'd come right back, and the cycle would repeat. I just couldn't let go and move on.

One evening, out on a date with one of the assistant city editors, I chose a Middle Eastern restaurant I had been to with Tom. And there he was, with his friend Clay Felker, the editor of *New York Magazine*. I stopped at their table to say hello, and melted. The next day Tom and I were back together. It had become a self-destructive relationship for me, but did not seem to cause much pain for him.

I began freelancing, writing for various magazines. Clay gave me some of my best assignments. But I felt unmoored and miserable, so I decided to leave the city for a while, called an editor I knew at Macmillan, and proposed a book on something I had heard about: a place in California called the Esalen Institute, where a new kind of psychology was being practiced and taught. Instead of focusing on neurosis, it nurtured a person's potential for personal growth. I had written an article about one of the psychologists in what had become known as the Human Potential Movement. I proposed to explore it in some depth in a book.

The editor, Alan Rinzler, liked my idea, and I soon had a contract for a book to be called *Turning On Without Drugs*. Published in 1969 as *Turning On*, it went beyond what I found in Esalen, delving into the cultural and social shift then under way on the West Coast, influenced by psychedelic experiences and Eastern mysticism. I've met quite a few people who, after reading this book, had moved from the East Coast to Northern California.

I had never yearned to live on the West Coast myself, but while in San Francisco I met a recently divorced sculptor named Melvin Moss, who had grown up in New York and moved west to go to art school. At this time he was teaching at the California College of Arts and Crafts in Oakland. His father, Leon Moss, had immigrated from the Ukraine when he was eighteen years old, sent by his family to prevent his being drafted into the czar's military service.

A relative living in Brooklyn had been expected to help the boy get an education, but instead sent him to work in the garment district, where he learned to cut coats. Mel's mother, who was a cousin of his father, was born in New York. She worked as a bookkeeper, played ragtime piano and the accordion, and cooked delicious, abundant meals for her husband, son, and daughter.

They argued, interrupted each other, and laughed a lot.

They were wonderful.

Mel was, in some ways, the opposite of Tom: his life was an open book, and he welcomed me into it with no reservations. He had a four-year-old daughter, Tara. One evening, as the three of us were eating spaghetti together at the house of a friend of his, I fell in love with both of them at once. I returned to New York to write the book, but told Mel I would be back by the time the lupine bloomed again in Big Sur.

THE SPRING OF 1968 was a fine time to arrive in San Francisco. Creative spirits and original thinkers had gathered here from far and wide, bringing hopeful new ideas for a world without war.

Mel and I married and had a daughter whom we named Usha. That's an Indian name—Usha is the Goddess of Dawn. We were listening to a lot of music from India, and we also liked the sound of the name in both Lithuanian and Yiddish. In Lithuanian, dawn is *aušra*.

Our home was often a lively scene. Most of our friends were artists.

Mel built musical instruments: slit drums and mbiras. During the 1970s and '80s, musicians gathered in his studio every week to play new music that drew on sounds from many parts of the world. Occasionally they performed in art galleries as Moiré Pulse.

I continued to write articles for magazines and other publications. For several years I was on the staff of the Pacific News Service, a small news organization that brought to light issues of social justice that received only scant attention in the mainstream press. My next book, *Wholly Round*, focused on the ecology movement of the 1970s.

The third, *A Time to Be Born, A Time to Die—Conflicts and Ethics in an Intensive Care Nursery,* explored dilemmas raised by advanced medical technology. In both the books, the subtext was the effect of technology on perception.

In 1986 an opportunity came along to take charge of a quarterly magazine about the California coast published by the State Coastal Conservancy, an agency dedicated to coastal protection for the benefit of people and wildlife. I found much pleasure and satisfaction as the editor of *California Coast & Ocean* over the next twenty-five years.

Mel and I lived together until he died in 2005.

We married and had a family.

13

························

RETURN TO LITHUANIA

In the spring of 1989, I heard the birds of Lithuania calling: *Come home, come home.* I heard the chirps of the little sparrow I had learned to know as *žvirblis*.

Something unbelievable was happening. The Soviet Union was falling apart. Rebellion had erupted among nations along the edges of the empire. In San Francisco we read news reports of thousands of Lithuanians marching through the streets of Vilnius, carrying the yellow, green, and red flag, singing. Similar events were taking place in the other two Baltic States.

Protests had earlier focused on environmental destruction. More than three thousand people had encircled the Chernobyl-style nuclear power plant at Ignalina, protesting plans to expand it. More recently, demands for political autonomy had surfaced, even the dream of independence. Mama sat on the couch in my living room, watching the news. A middle-aged man in a rumpled jacket was being interviewed: Vytautas Landsbergis.

"Imagine that," she said. "And he looks pretty good for his age."

"Mama, that is not the Landsbergis you're thinking of, the one who was such a good friend of Tėtė's. That's his son, he's a composer and music professor—and the leader of Sąjudis, Lithuania's liberation movement."

"Ach, so."

Mama was ninety-three years old. For the very old, the past and the present sometimes melt into each other. She had continued to work as a nurse in Chicago hospitals until she was nearly eighty, then had moved west to be close to two of her daughters and their families. She lived with Elena, helping to raise her granddaughter Antonia, until she became so forgetful that it was no longer safe for her to stay at home alone. Then she moved to an assisted living residence for elderly women near my office in Oakland. It was easy for me to visit her there, and to take her out for walks and to my house.

As she had done as far back as I could remember, Mama kept a framed portrait of my father on her dresser, but she seldom talked about him now. We had finally received official word about his death. For years we had been writing to various agencies, including the Red Cross, in vain. Before leaving New York for California I had sent one more inquiry. A reply dated January 26, 1968, arrived from the New York chapter of the Red Cross: "The International Committee of the Red Cross undertook a search for your father and learned that he died on October 16, 1941. No other information was made available to us." He had lived only eight more months after his arrest.

Families of people who have disappeared can never assume the missing person is dead. My mother stayed loyal to my father all those many years; she never had another relationship with any man. After she read the letter, it seemed to me that a burden was lifted from her heart. He was gone. There was nothing more she could do. She actually flirted a bit with a Lithuanian artist about her age and bought a small painting of his. In Lithuania, a large seascape had hung in our living room. It depicted a boundless ocean. My sisters and I had, over the years, tried in vain to find something that might replace it for Mama. The painting she bought from the artist in Chicago, however, was not at all like the one she had lost. It was a sunny pastel image of surf and sand, and included a rainbow.

I HAD WRITTEN to my cousin Danutė in Kaunas, giving her the date of my expected arrival, a few days before solstice, but my visa had been delayed, so I was a day late leaving Helsinki. On the train from Tallinn I shared a compartment with two other passengers: a Ukrainian woman who wore a countrywoman's headscarf and looked to be in her late thirties, and a boyish-looking blond Russian soldier. Jack London's *Call of the Wild* lay on the seat next to the soldier. He was learning English, he said. He told me he had had been stationed in Estonia for many years and liked living there. If the Baltics succeeded in their goal of breaking away from the Soviet Union, he said, he hoped to stay. When I asked if he spoke Estonian he replied that he did not because there was no need to: all Estonians spoke Russian.

The typical attitude of the colonizer, I thought.

After a while the Ukrainian woman pulled some food out of a bag she carried—bread, cheese, and an apple—and shared them with me. Although we had no common language, I think she understood that I was coming home after a long absence. Before getting off in Riga, she handed me a small medallion with an enamel image of the Virgin Mary, saying something the soldier translated as, "For your protection."

Was the Russian soldier also here for my protection? It was rather odd that of only two other passengers in this compartment, one should be a Soviet military man, and that he should happen to be reading an American novel, in English. But I was not the frightened child on a train that I had been in 1941 and 1944. He was just a Russian kid in a uniform, and I was old enough to be his grandmother. World War II had ended many years before he was born.

‣ ‣ ‣

MY EXCITEMENT MOUNTED as we approached my native land. I was standing in the corridor, looking out the window at the trees—pines, just as I remembered them—when as we stopped at a small station I heard an announcement over the loudspeaker in Lithuanian. My own private language, spoken within my family and with a few friends, was sounding out in public, amplified. Unreal.

The soldier was standing next to me, studying my face.

"You are happy?"

"Yes, very happy."

Speechless with joy, in fact.

When we arrived in Vilnius in late afternoon, my eyes were drawn to two people standing together in the mostly empty plaza beside the train platform: a tiny, gray-haired woman and a tall, much younger man, his right arm around her shoulders. She was holding a huge bouquet of gladiolas. I felt drawn to them, so I approached them to ask where I could catch a taxi.

"Raselė?" the elderly lady said tentatively, and then, with confidence, "Raselė!"

That's the affectionate diminutive for "Rasa."

"Danutė?"

How did my cousin know I would be on this train? I had wired from Helsinki that I would get in touch as soon as I arrived, and had intended to do so from the hotel where I was booked. But I had not given her the date and time of my arrival.

"A journalist called me," she said. "He is eager to interview you."

And how did the journalist know?

The tall young man with Danutė was Jonas, the youngest of her sister Aldona's sons. He had a car and drove us to the high-rise Soviet-built Hotel Lietuva. The desk clerk took my passport and gave me a key. A slow elevator released us into a hallway with stained carpeting.

My room was furnished with a single bed, a bedside table, a small wooden desk, and a mini-refrigerator into which Jonas piled the several bottles of mineral water he had brought with him.

"Don't drink the water from the tap," he warned.

Danutė checked the lamps. The one on the desk did not work; the one next to the bed was missing a bulb.

"We will ask the hotel to replace it," she said. For now, the globe light in the ceiling would suffice. It was a light one might find in a train station, glaring above our heads.

"Best not to talk too much in here," my cousin said, looking up toward the ceiling fixture. She knew about walls and ceilings with ears. "We'll go now. You rest, and see you tomorrow. The journalist, Edmundas Ganusauskas, will meet you in the lobby after breakfast and take you where you want to go, and afterward we'll pick you up by the cathedral."

I wasn't particularly interested in meeting with any journalist, not right then. I wanted to see people in Sąjūdis. But Danutė seemed to think this man was owed some gratitude for having notified her of the time of my arrival, so I didn't object.

When we met in the morning, Ganusauskas insisted on taking me immediately to the nearby Gediminas Castle, on the rocky hill behind Vilnius Cathedral, to show me something he said I had to see. I didn't like the assertive manner in which he took me by my elbow— though I am sure he merely wanted to be polite—or how he began to question me en route.

"Do you remember, did you and your mother spend your last night in Kaunas in your own apartment or somewhere else?"

The question struck me as strange, and as rude. I had just arrived, hadn't had time yet to get my bearings, and, without preamble, he wanted me to tell him details about a night forty-nine years ago, when I was six years old. I also didn't like his tone. It made me feel that I was under interrogation.

"I don't remember, sorry."

I did appreciate, however, what Ganusauskas wanted me to see in the castle. It was an exhibition of personal items and letters from prisoners in Siberian labor camps. At the entrance was a wall map with pins stuck in locations to which Lithuanians had been shipped—hundreds of distant places, some above the Arctic Circle, around Lake Baikal, in Kazakhstan, and also in the Ural Mountains, the continental divide between Europe and Asia.

Inside, among old photographs, rosaries, and other treasures, were letters written on birch bark, inked on tiny scraps of paper. Most were to family members, informing them that life was good, there was plenty of food, there was no reason to complain.

As I looked at these letters, tears came to my eyes, tears I did not want this journalist to see. I had avoided delving into the history witnessed in this exhibition. My mother and her friends, and younger Lithuanians in the United States as well, talked about the evil deeds Stalin had committed on our people, but they seemed to overlook the suffering of other people: the Native Americans, for instance, the Armenians driven into the sea by the Turks, or the Vietnamese during the American war. Although it's natural for humans to identify most closely with those who are most like them, the narrowness of the national focus had caused me to turn away. But now, in the castle of Gediminas, I grieved for my people.

Ganusauskas next escorted me to the office of Sąjūdis, on Gediminas Street, in a building that faced the cathedral. It was bustling with people coming and going on urgent errands. Landsbergis was at a meeting in Moscow, someone told me.

Wanting to talk with some other Sąjūdis people, I thanked Ganusauskas and made it clear, I thought, that he should leave me now. But he stayed close by my side—too close, looking over my shoulder at what I was writing in my notebook. It was only when I met my relatives again that I shed him.

▶ ▶ ▶

AFTER LUNCH IN a restaurant on Gediminas Street, Jonas drove me to the home of Vytautas Landsbergis-Žemkalnis, who was my godfather and one of my father's best friends, as well as the father of the leader of Sąjūdis.

He had also fled during the war, to search (successfully) for his younger son, Gabrielius, whom the Nazis had seized and imprisoned in a concentration camp, while his wife and their elder son, Vytautas, had remained in Lithuania. After the war's end, father and son were admitted to Australia as DPs, but in 1959, after Stalin's death, the elder Landsbergis had returned. He was allowed to reclaim the family's prewar home and to resume his practice of architecture, although not to teach. Gabrielius also came back, later.

We sat on the veranda, at the long table where my father had played chess with the boy who was now the leader of Lithuania's struggle for freedom. "He sat right there," his father said, pointing to the spot. "And sometimes he let Vytukas win."

I took a seat next to the place where my father had liked to sit. Across a time gap of forty-nine years, the past touched the present, evoking both sorrow and joy.

I HAD COME back to Lithuania at a period in its history that would be remembered as the Days of Mourning and Hope. My six-day visit was dreamlike. I felt I had somehow been transported to a place that was both familiar and completely new to me. And almost every day offered more evidence that the memory of my father's life and work was cherished and protected.

All the airplanes he had designed had been destroyed by the occupying military forces—except for one, his first. When the Russians invaded in 1940, the ANBO I was already a relic from the early days of aviation, on exhibit at the Vytautas the Great War Museum in Kaunas. Someone, perhaps some of his fellow aviators, had dismantled it, put it into a large box, and stored it in the museum basement, hidden behind seemingly useless stuff. For nearly a half century it remained there. Then, not long before my visit, some of the surviving veteran aviators had decided it was safe to bring it out into the light again. Two of them, Jonas Balčiūnas and Viktoras Ašmenskas, took me to see it, in a Kaunas building serving temporarily as the aviation museum.

We had a photograph of this first ANBO in our family album. But here, unbelievably, I stood in front of that actual airplane. Hanging from the ceiling, it looked like a large toy. Could it really have flown? I stretched to touch the wooden propeller, a wheel, a canvas-covered silver wing; I was barely able to believe my senses.

"We will soon have it back in the museum," said Mr. Balčiūnas.

All too soon, the aviators rushed us outside again, to another appointment. Everything was moving too fast for me to take in. Would I be able to remember what I had just seen?

SEVERAL OF MY relatives took turns escorting me around and introducing me to three generations of family. My cousins Danutė, Aldona, and Antanas were all older than me. All the others had been born after we had left Lithuania. In 1940, when the Red Army arrived, Danutė had just begun her first year at the University of Vilnius.

"What happened to you after the Russians took over?" I asked her over coffee and apple cake in the tiny apartment in Kaunas where she lived with her daughter, Vida.

"It was cold. We kept our coats on in the classrooms. The auditorium was frozen. Every day someone else was missing."

One morning as she was walking to class, she remembered, a fellow student waved to her from the back of a truck.

"We never saw him again."

Danutė's mother, my Aunt Antanina, had had a dream in which my mother sat on a chair, dressed in black.

"Something must be wrong with Antanas," she'd told her daughter. Soon after, on March 6, 1941, as Danutė was walking past a cluster of people on her way to the university, she heard someone say, "They have arrested General Gustaitis."

Danutė's brother, also named Antanas, had also been arrested, for carrying a letter to someone deemed to be subversive, and spent a year in a prison camp in the Ural Mountains, where he worked on building a railroad. "He used to say, 'Each rail cost a man's life,'" Danutė remembered. After he came home, close to death from starvation, he was forbidden to complete his studies in Lithuania, but managed to do so in Moscow. He became a hydrological engineer.

Danutė married a fellow student, and soon they had a little girl. "But it was short, our married life," she said. Her husband was arrested for possessing forbidden literature. He caught a fever and died in prison camp. She succeeded in graduating from the university, and after the war ended, she started to teach at the girls' gymnasium in Marijampolė, where her sister Aldona was a student in her last year. They shared a rented room in town.

In 1949, during another wave of mass deportations—this time focused on farmers to prepare the way for collectivization—Danutė's parents and sister were shipped to Siberia. On the Sunday they were seized, Aldona was at the farm for the weekend, while Danutė had stayed in town with her little daughter. Yet she also was visited.

"When I heard the pounding on the door," Danutė said, "the first thing I thought was, How shall I dress the child? But they didn't arrest me. They took our landlord, a widower with two half-grown boys. Later three men came back to inventory his belongings. I asked that these be assigned to me, so I could sell them and send the money to our landlord and his sons, but they would not do that."

The leader of the three-man inventory team, a Georgian physician, told her, "I am not a Marxist, but you Lithuanians don't know how to live in the Soviet Union. You must own no more than you can carry."

Left alone with her child, Danutė continued to teach in Marijampolė. One day not long after her family's deportation, she was summoned by the school's security officer—a secret police functionary. He asked her to sign a cooperation agreement. She refused. She would not spy on others.

"He kept me for three hours," Danutė said. "We both got tired. On the table in front of him lay many photographs. He picked one up and showed it to me.

"'Do you know this woman?' he asked. 'Yes,' I said. 'Avoid dealing with her,' he said. That woman was cooperating. I understood that they don't respect those who agree to work with them."

She moved to Kaunas and found clerical work that paid enough to cover rent and food.

"The man who hired me told me, 'I know nothing about you.' That meant he did not want to know," my cousin said.

I wanted to hear from her sister, Aldona, about her nine years in Siberia, but she told me that "living through that time once was enough." I did not press her.

When I visited Danutė again, she had something to give me: my father's personal photo album, which she had kept safe during the past half century of military occupation. I had not known it existed. I took it into my hands and lifted the brown cardboard cover.

The photographs affixed to the black pages were all from the early years of Lithuania's aviation history, 1919 and 1920. Images of wrecked airplanes and funeral rites predominated.

Inside a giant zeppelin hangar, a coffin rests on a bier bedecked with pine branches, illuminated by a sunbeam streaming down through a skylight. Inside the coffin, I would later learn, lies the body of the first graduate of the aviation school to die in battle. Two propeller blades form a cross at his head. A soldier stands to his right, rifle at rest; to his left a woman leans on the closed box, head bent in sorrow *(see p. 50)*.

Behind the coffin, against the back wall, two small pine trees stand between two windows. A garland of pine branches loops from above and links to the noses of two airplanes that flank the coffin. As I gaze at this beautifully photographed image, from the vantage point of a theatergoer facing the stage, I can almost smell the aroma of Lithuania's beloved pines and feel the silence.

On the opposite page in the album, a portrait of this unlucky aviator shows him as a lad with quiet eyes and full lips, his heavy military jacket belted at the waist and across the chest, his cap tilted jauntily to the right.

So young.

His funeral procession follows, seen from an aerial perspective, and then there is a photo of the crumpled aircraft, surrounded by a cluster of young men and a small boy. Then more photos of wrecks. Why did my father choose these tragic images for his personal album, I wondered. Why didn't he include pictures showing the good times he and his friends had while learning to fly? Perhaps he wanted to be sure to remember these classmates and the accidents that killed them. When he built his own aircraft, safety would be paramount in his mind.

I lingered over a haunting image of a biplane standing in the snow outside the zeppelin hangar. Also seen from an aerial perspective, it seems far away, though I'm not sure. Tiny dark figures are swarming around the aircraft, blots of black against the white ground. The image was mysterious; it made me think of the great Russian filmmaker Andrei Tarkovsky, whose work lives on the border between shared reality and dream. The longer I looked, the more the photograph drew me in. I studied it, trying to read more into it than it could reveal, longing for something that is no more and perhaps never was. This winter moment in my father's album spoke to me of the transience of life and of eternity.

Brave cousin Danutė, she took a risk in saving this book, considering that my father was officially a criminal, a traitor to the Soviet Union. I placed it on the table in front of her.

"Take it," she said, handing it to me again.

"It belongs in Lithuania," I replied.

My father's album now resides in the photo archives of Lithuania's Aviation Museum, at the airfield where he spent most of his creative life.

TIME SPUN BACKWARD during my visit, and the present collided again and again with the past. This happened most dramatically at Rumšiškės Ethnographic Museum, near Kaunas, where several typical country villages and farms from different regions have been reconstructed and restored amid fields, forests, and ponds. The museum extends over nearly two hundred hectares, an area four times as large as the Vatican. Among its 140 buildings is the old wooden church from Sasnava, predecessor of the brick church standing there now, and a farmhouse very much like the one where my father was born.

As Jonas and I walked toward the first of the villages, I took off my shoes to feel the soft grass on my feet, pushing out of my mind the knowledge that we were visiting an exhibition of historical relics. What I saw here was much more like what I remembered of Lithuania than what existed today. As we were leaving, I spotted a photograph mounted on a board by the gate: the distraught face of an elderly farmer. No caption was needed.

Little or nothing remained of what I had most longed to see again. When I asked my relatives if I could visit Raišupis, they took me to an expanse of empty fields. Uncle Jonas and Aunt Antanina's farm had been completely leveled. The farmhouse and other structures were gone. The little stream that ran through the property had been channelized and dammed. Some of the family were now living in the nearby village, Sasnava, where they had built two concrete houses and were constructing a larger building, intending to turn it into an inn.

Although the family would later scatter, this would be the place where it often gathered on holidays and special occasions. The church was just down the road, and across from it the old cemetery where they all expected to be laid to rest in the family plot, easy to visit.

My paternal grandparents' farm, in Obelinė, had also been destroyed, but the trees that had surrounded the farmyard still stood. Part of the land had been divided into small garden plots, where nearby residents, including teachers at the Marijampolė Gymnasium, grew vegetables and flowers. A marker similar to a tombstone had recently been erected near the pond in honor of my father's memory.

The military building near the airfield, where we had lived before the war, looked shabby. Our apartment had been subdivided. The back door to the building was broken. Two little blond girls with braids were jumping rope outside. For a moment I wanted to tell them I lived here when I was a child, but I didn't. The brick building before me seemed to be only a clumsy copy of the childhood home I remembered. What I remembered no longer existed.

Far more cheerful was the scene at our old orchard down the road, where I remembered living in the gardener's cottage during the Nazi occupation. It was now home to a couple and their two boys. When I came to the gate and introduced myself, the man seemed both excited and frightened. He was proud that the orchard had belonged to General Antanas Gustaitis, but worried about my presence: Lithuanians living abroad had been reclaiming their lost properties.

He asked if that was why I had come, and when I assured him that was not my intention, he was clearly relieved. He and his wife worked in a radio factory in Kaunas, he said, and had traded their apartment in the city for this place. They would soon be building a white brick house. Would I tell him where my father had planned to build a house? I told him my father had no plans for a house in

Cover of the invitation to the celebration in Obelinė

the orchard. He was satisfied with the apartment we had lived in. I recalled that someone had told me that his air force colleagues used to tease him about his lack of interest in personal wealth.

"My mother planted a variety of cherries, plums, and apples here," I told the couple.

"We gave cuttings of the plums to several neighbors," the woman said. "So now your mother's plums are everywhere."

Before we left, the man picked a bag of cherries for us. My mother's cherries. I wished the family a good life in their home.

ON THE SUNDAY before my departure from Lithuania, a celebration took place at my father's birthplace, commemorating the ANBO IV tour of Europe he led in 1934. The event had been scheduled for an earlier date, but after Danutė learned I was coming, she managed to get it postponed so I could attend.

The festivities had already begun by the time I arrived with most of my relatives. Several dozen people had gathered in a field beyond the trees that surrounded the former farmstead. The sky was pale blue, the particular, inimitable pale blue of my childhood. Skydivers dropped from little airplanes, landing on hay that had been spread on the ground. Pilots performed acrobatic maneuvers, much the way the early airmen, my father among them, had done three-quarters of a century ago.

Then the speeches began. Vytautas Landsbergis-Žemkalnis talked at great length and I lost his thread. The day was hot. People were sweating in the sun. Somebody held up an umbrella to shade the old man. Surely he talked too long, yet nobody showed any sign of restlessness.

Only a little while before, it had been dangerous to mention my father's name in public. Now I was hearing him praised as a national hero.

After the speeches—I too was obliged to say a few words—everyone gathered at long wooden tables in the shade to partake of food prepared by teachers at the school from which my father had graduated. As his daughter, I was treated as a celebrity. The teachers had a gift for me: a horseshoe they had found here while preparing the site for this celebration. I have kept it ever since on the windowsill of my study.

An elderly beekeeper with a kind, weathered face came to our table, with honeycombs in his hands dripping liquid gold. Women and men wearing traditional Lithuanian costumes rose to dance, the women's long handwoven multicolor skirts swirling as they moved in circles and in squares, meeting, passing, changing partners, spooling and unspooling to the sounds of an accordion.

I felt I was under a spell. Was all this real? Was I truly here, in my native land? The trees, the grasses, and the sky answered: Yes, you have come home.

14

LITHUANIA BREAKS FREE

ater that summer, on August 23, 1989, some two million Estonians, Latvians, and Lithuanians linked hands in a six-hundred-kilometer human chain connecting their three countries. This massive peaceful demonstration, called the Baltic Way, marked the fiftieth anniversary of the Stalin-Hitler Pact, which divided the Baltic States between the Soviet Union and Hitler. This astonishing event made news worldwide. In a coffeehouse in Berkeley, California, I eavesdropped on two men worrying that it might undermine Gorbachev's Perestroika policy of reform. But in the Baltics, what people were seeking was not reform but the restoration of self-government.

According to Landsbergis, Gorbachev's promises, including greater economic freedom, turned out to be mostly illusory. They wouldn't actually release the grip of Moscow's control.

That grip, however, was slipping. The Soviet Union was coming apart at its edges, as liberation movements spread though nations forcibly seized since the beginning of World War II. In Georgia, brutal military force was applied to crush the rebellion. But in Lithuania and the other Baltic States, careful strategic steps, supported by non-violent popular demonstrations, continued to gain ground.

The leaders of Lithuania's liberation movement, Sąjūdis, sought to outwit the occupying power. In March 1990, they proposed a slate of candidates for delegates to the convention of the Supreme Soviet Council of Deputies in Moscow. Such elections had up to then featured only a single slate, chosen by the Kremlin; those named to represent individual republics did not have to live in those republics but could be from anyplace in the USSR. The preselected candidates were elected unanimously in Moscow.

The Sąjūdis slate won six to one against the preselected slate, claiming thirty-six of the forty-two seats in the Supreme Soviet Council of Deputies assigned to the Lithuanian Soviet Republic. When this elected slate was ignored at the convention, Landsbergis objected to the seating of the preselected slate. In his book *Lūžis prie Baltijos, Politinė Autobiografija* (*Break on the Baltic, a Political Autobiography*), published in 1997 in Lithuania, he recalled saying, "We don't want to vote for the Tajiks, Kazaks, and others whom we don't know, nor to have others vote for us."

Landsbergis heard someone shout, "You don't trust us?" But he also noticed that among the Tajik delegates, seated near the Lithuanians, "the younger ones supported us; the older, bemedaled ones were angry."

LITHUANIA WAS THE first of the Baltic States to formally break away from the Soviet Union. The situation of Estonia and Latvia was complicated by the presence of a larger number of Russian residents and by political divisions, but within the following several months, both also declared independence.

On the evening of March 11, 1990, in Vilnius, the Lithuanian

Socialist Republic's Supreme Council, now dominated by Sąjūdis, voted to delete *Socialist* from its name, thus becoming the Supreme Council of the Lithuanian Republic. Behind the podium, the tricolor Lithuanian flag rose on pulleys, covering the Soviet five-pointed red star, hammer, and sickle. The council voted to restore preoccupation Lithuania's official emblem, a galloping horseman with his sword raised to strike. Applause erupted in the hall.

In its first legislative action, the council, Lithuania's new parliament, declared the same night that "the sovereign powers of the State of Lithuania are restored, and henceforth, Lithuania is again an independent state."

This declaration was passed with 124 delegates voting yes, 6 abstaining, and none opposed. The 6 abstainers were Poles loyal to the Communist Party, Landsbergis wrote.

"They explained that the declaration was a surprise to them and that, not knowing their constituents' views, they did not know how to vote."

It was early morning when the new parliament adjourned. People were waiting outside bearing flowers. The news traveled out into the world.

Czechoslovakia's president Václav Havel promptly suggested that his country could serve as neutral ground for negotiations with Moscow. Iceland also offered to serve as an intermediary. Canada's parliament voted to support the declaration of independence. The Scandinavian nations and Poland came out in support. The reaction of the United States, however, was evasive.

How would Gorbachev react?

"A war of nerves began," Landsbergis wrote. Top Soviet military officers stationed in Lithuania visited his office with threats, and various military maneuvers were staged in the country. Provocateurs tried to start fights in crowds, but Sąjūdis leaders cautioned that any violence would benefit only the Soviets.

The day before Easter, Gorbachev issued an ultimatum to the Lithuanian rebels, warning that extraordinary measures would be taken unless they returned to the situation existing on March 10, the day before the declaration of independence. He demanded a response within three days. When Western journalists asked Landsbergis for comment, he told them that "in our state we celebrate a religious holiday unknown to the Kremlin called Easter. . . . We will reply to the ultimatum after the holiday."

On April 18, Moscow cut off all oil deliveries, 80 percent of the natural gas, and transport to Lithuania of various important raw materials and products. The Lithuanians toughed it out, although they worried about the upcoming autumn harvest without fuel for farm machinery and trucks.

The stress of the blockade created fertile ground for unrest, but people muddled through, as they had in the early years of their independence after the First World War, when fuel and other necessities were similarly scarce. Entrepreneurs brought gasoline from Byelorussia, at prices considerably higher than the price of Soviet fuel. Soviet soldiers also sold gasoline on the black market. The KGB tried in vain to stop them.

Lithuania's representatives tried repeatedly to meet with Gorbachev, seeking to establish friendly relations as neighbors, but he refused, ruling out any possibility of negotiations. Eventually, however, the blockade failed to achieve the intended purpose of causing the breakaway state's economic collapse, and he invited the leaders of the three Baltic nations to discuss a compromise. During talks at a dacha outside of Moscow, he no longer demanded that Lithuania's declaration of independence be revoked, but did suggest a moratorium on its implementation. The Lithuanians agreed to the freeze, with a variety of limitations and escape clauses, to last for a hundred days, beginning with the formal start of negotiations. The Soviets lifted the blockade.

Throughout the stalemate, the Baltic leaders were showered with advice from Western countries telling them that they were acting foolishly and endangering Gorbachev's attempted reforms. Landsbergis, the music professor who was leading his nation to freedom, replied that they had been charged with carrying out their people's will and were not empowered to act otherwise.

The specter of Soviet military might loomed behind the struggle, and on Sunday, January 13, 1991, it struck. Soviet tanks rolled into Lithuania's capital. *New York Times* correspondent Bill Keller reported from Vilnius:

> *A column of Soviet Army tanks, plowing through a street crowd of civilians and a cordon of parked cars, seized the television broadcast center of Lithuania in the early-morning darkness today in a fusillade of cannon and gunfire. At least 11 civilians were killed and 100 or more were wounded. . . . The raid signaled that the Kremlin is fully resorting to force to back President Mikhail S. Gorbachev's demands that the independence movement yield from its defiance of central authority. . . . The raid stunned a crowd of thousands gathered outside the center who had been singing and dancing through the night in playful protection of the broadcast center. . . . The first eight bodies taken to one hospital included an old man shot in the head and a young boy.*

The official death count was fifteen. Hundreds were wounded. Four days later, Keller reported that hundreds of thousands of mourners had walked in a funeral procession to Vilnius Cathedral carrying candles and flowers, bearing the open coffins of nine of the victims as church bells rang. Contingents of Poles, Ukrainians, Byelorussians, and Russians walked with the Lithuanians. Britain and Sweden were represented by senior diplomats. The United States had sent a low-level official from its consulate in Saint Petersburg. As an American citizen, I found that shameful.

Landsbergis did not walk in the procession, persuaded not to by his supporters, who were concerned for his safety. Instead, early on the morning of the funeral he emerged from the parliament building for the first time since the Soviet assault to visit the sports stadium where the dead were laid out, and stood with each for a while as part of the honor guard. He then returned to the parliament building, where many deputies remained, wearing coats against the winter cold. Expecting an assault on parliament, volunteers for its defense had been pouring gasoline into bottles for use as bombs. Windows had to be left open to allow the fumes to escape.

Meanwhile, Moscow's propaganda machine was in full swing. A popular TV journalist relayed the "news" that, upon closer examination, it turned out that all the dead either had been victims of traffic accidents or had suffered heart attacks. He praised the Soviet troops that had "saved" Lithuania from pogroms against Russians and other ethnic populations supposedly planned by the Landsbergis government.

"The city was calm," Keller reported.

The Landsbergis government remained inside the parliament building, where the volunteer defenders stacked furniture against windows and doors; meanwhile, outside, a massive crowd remained assembled, and more concrete blocks were added to the barricades that had been raised around the building. Landsbergis had tried to reach Gorbachev as the tanks were moving in but was told he was not available.

The January 13 attack had been a blow to Gorbachev's reputation in the West as a liberal reformer and raised international support for Lithuania. Among the steps Sąjūdis took to strengthen that support was a plebiscite. On February 9, 1991, voters were asked to confirm the declaration in its constitution that "Lithuania is an independent democratic republic." Of those voting, 90 percent answered yes. Although the Soviets argued that the vote was merely an opinion poll, it was a victory for the Lithuanians.

Soviet military moves continued. Lithuanians viewed them as rehearsals for further violent actions. In June 1991, troops briefly surrounded the parliament, and later they took over the telephone exchange. At several Lithuanian border control stations, agents on duty—under orders not to resist uniformed Soviet officers—were severely beaten by assailants in the night. On July 31, seven guards at a checkpoint on the Byelorussian border were found dead, hunched facedown on the ground, with bullets through their heads. These murders, as well as other violent assaults on Lithuanian government officials, were attributed by many to a special military detachment allied with the Soviet secret police. Calls for the ouster of the Soviet military grew louder.

DEMAND FOR DEMOCRACY seemed to be bursting out around the world during the late 1980s and early 1990s. A moving photograph of a man standing alone in front of a tank in Beijing's Tiananmen Square on June 5, 1989, spread across the globe. In San Francisco, I joined a demonstration for Baltic freedom, sharing space with supporters of the vast student-led protest in Beijing demanding freedom of speech and democracy.

Mikhail Gorbachev was briefly ousted in August 1991 by hard-line Communists who opposed his reforms. Boris Yeltsin and other pro-democracy leaders foiled the attempted coup. Gorbachev returned to office, but he had been weakened.

One by one, other nations reestablished diplomatic relations that had been interrupted when the Soviet Army occupied Lithuania in 1941. The first was Iceland. Denmark and Norway quickly followed.

The United States lagged behind many others, acting only two days before the Soviet Union.

On September 17, 1991, Lithuania, Latvia, and Estonia were admitted to membership in the United Nations. On December 25, Mikhail Gorbachev resigned. That same day, the Union of Soviet Socialist Republics ceased to exist. The Russian Federation, headed by Yeltsin, took over as the successor, promising democracy.

Lithuanians who had settled in other countries since World War II, including several friends from my days in Chicago, began to return to their native land, and found important work to do there, helping to rebuild shattered institutions and solve current problems. My feeling of guilt revived. Had I strayed too far from my heritage?

15

CHASING GHOSTS

I'm sitting on the living room couch in my home in San Francisco with my step-grandson Sandor, watching a videotape someone has brought from Lithuania. Somber processions move across the screen. Coffins are being loaded onto an airplane. The remains of Lithuanians who died in Siberia and were buried there are being brought back for reburial in home ground.

Tears stream down my face as I watch. Why? My father was buried, surely, in some mass grave near the Moscow prison where he was executed with a shot to the back of his head. His body will not be found, will not be returned to be laid in the peaceful little cemetery in Sasnava, with others of his family. Someday I will tell my grandchildren the story. It was war. Millions were killed. My father was among them.

The mourning continues, but these are also days of hope. Another videotape, brought to our house by the Japanese poet Nanao Sakaki, shows scenes from his visit with the poet Allen Ginsberg to Prague, where they were welcomed by the playwright Václav Havel, president of Czechoslovakia. Poetry has triumphed over oppression, I tell myself. Surely a new era of peace and cooperation has begun. We must not bury the future under the sorrows of the past.

But there is more to learn. One day a thick envelope arrives from Lithuania containing a newspaper clipping with two photographs: mugshots of my father. I stuff it back into the envelope. Who sent these to me, and where were they found? I was so horrified I did not even take note of the return address on the envelope. And then I lost it, probably threw it out with junk mail by mistake, without ever reading the story.

A dark moment during the marvelous celebration in Obelinė kept coming back to mind. Before the feasting ended, Ganusauskas, the persistent journalist, had approached me. He and one of the aviation veterans had something to tell me.

"We found Pribulis, the scout who was supposed to take your father safely across the border," Ganusauskas had said. "He lives not far from here. We told him you are here and asked if he would talk to you. But he is afraid. He said it's too soon, that the Russians broke all his fingers, one by one."

I would, indeed, have wanted to see this man who allegedly betrayed my father, and to ask him a few questions. He might lie, but perhaps not. Any fact that could be added to what was known was surely worth going after. As a journalist as well as a daughter, I felt an obligation. But even if he had been willing to meet me, I had no more time then. My visit was ending.

"Too soon," Pribulis had said.

So he expected to be able to speak sometime later? Now, perhaps?

THREE YEARS AFTER my first return to Lithuania, I was there again with one specific goal: to talk with the man who was believed to have betrayed my father.

My cousin Antanas had learned his home address and drove me

to the town of Alytus. I asked that he wait in his car, a block away, climbed the apartment house stairway alone, and knocked on a door. It was opened by a woman whose age was hard to guess because her face seemed ravaged by life experiences. She may have been about my age, or much older.

"I am looking for Jonas Pribulis," I said.

"Who is looking?"

"I am a daughter of Antanas Gustaitis."

"You came too late. He died six months ago."

She closed the door.

We returned to Kaunas. Mr. Balčiūnas joined us for lunch at Danutė's.

"So now we can roll the stone onto the grave of General Antanas Gustaitis," he said.

After I got back to San Francisco, I wrote a letter addressed to "Daughter of Jonas Pribulis." I was sure that the woman who opened the door to me at that apartment was his daughter. What a miserable life she must have had. Whatever her father did, it was not her fault.

"If ever you remember anything at all that your father told you about Antanas Gustaitis, please write to me," I wrote. Not surprisingly, there was no reply.

BY THIS TIME, the jubilance of liberation had settled down and yielded to the struggle to rebuild the state and—perhaps the most difficult task—free the citizens' minds from the legacy of fear and mistrust left by the years of Soviet rule.

Many people who had held positions of political and economic power still maintained it. Some were now genuinely loyal to the new government; others pretended to be. Some used their Russian contacts to build wealth for themselves by, for example, becoming middlemen in the sale of Russia's natural resources, especially lumber and steel, to Western corporations. Thieves were stripping brass and copper off plaques and monuments to sell as scrap metal. In Palanga, a beloved statue of Birutė disappeared one night; after widespread outrage ensued, however, it was anonymously returned.

Russian troops were still stationed in the country, but many had been withdrawn. Two of the veteran aviators I had met on my first visit took me up in a small plane with newly painted Lithuanian insignia on a flight from Kaunas to the airfield in Počiūnai, gleefully passing over a decommissioned Soviet army base. As we landed we were greeted by a group of young men who had been practicing skydiving. We walked to a hangar where Lithuanians were constructing gliders for customers in the West.

The transition to a market economy had opened new opportunities for people who were young and energetic. Older people living on pensions and those having to rely on government salaries had to struggle to make ends meet if they did not get support from their families. Everyone, however, seemed to delight in some of the newly available luxuries—melons from the republic of Abkhzia, bananas.

My relatives were tight knit, worked hard, and supported one another. Danutė and Antanas, the oldest two of my three cousins, whose parents were the aunt and uncle I so fondly remembered from my childhood, were living in Kaunas, both retired. The family of Aldona and her husband, Juozas, was mostly in the Vilnius region. All but one of their seven children were doing all right. The exception was their firstborn, Viktoras, who was mentally ill. He lived with his parents, under the loving care of his mother. Lina, their second child, was a cardiologist. She supplemented her tiny government salary by taking private patients on her own time.

Rasa, whom I call Raselė, the youngest and also a physician, had a job with an international pharmaceutical corporation, while her husband, Armindas, likewise a doctor, worked for the national health service. Jonas, who had wanted to study microbiology but was not permitted to because he refused to join the Communist Party, now had a nursery business. His brother Vitas worked with him. Their sister Rūta and her family lived in the village of Sasnava, next door to Aldona's parents, and worked in agricultural enterprises. Stasys, the husband of Aldona's daughter Vida, supplemented his teacher's salary by driving to Germany and Denmark to buy used plumbing fixtures to sell in Lithuania. This was a dangerous occupation: he was robbed more than once in Poland.

Once the links with my relatives were established, they multiplied. My older sister, Jūratė, returned several times, bringing her husband and children. In June of 2001, when I was sixty-seven years old, I went back again with Elena, who remembered nothing of her childhood before we left Lithuania in 1944. I had hoped that the visit would awaken some memories for her, but it did not. Elena's daughter, Antonia, a student about to begin her final year at Antioch College, had preceded us to Vilnius, having taken a volunteer summer job in an after-school center. Her grandmother had lived with her and Elena for Antonia's entire childhood, so she spoke Lithuanian. She also intended to do some research in the ancestral land for a senior project.

During our week together, my sister, my niece, and I made the rounds of relatives, visited some of the major historical sites, and enjoyed traditional cheese, potato pancakes, and *cepelinai* (zeppelins)—dumplings made of grated potatoes stuffed with meat, cheese, or mushrooms—which every restaurant seemed to have on the menu.

Much had changed since my previous visit. Numerous new eateries had opened, and the servers were no longer sullen, the way they had tended to be in Soviet Lithuania. Supermarket-style groceries offered wide selections of products from Western Europe, and retail businesses of various sorts seemed to be thriving. With financial aid from the European Union, water and sanitation systems had been modernized, rivers had been cleaned up, and vegetation had been restored to riverbanks that had been lined with concrete. Books were being published reclaiming history that had been suppressed for half a century, linking it to the present or trying to correct dogma.

I saw a sticker inside a book warning that it had been published during the "time of stagnation," meaning Soviet times. History that had been rewritten during the Soviet occupation was now being corrected from the current perspective. Cell phones were ubiquitous. Our younger relatives called each other so often that they always knew where the others were.

Our visit coincided with solstice, which in Lithuania is St. John's Day, dedicated to the celebration of everyone named for the saint, with festivities that feature rituals from pagan times. Lithuanians are as proud to be good Catholics as they are to have been among the last people in Europe to be Christianized. St. John's Day embodies that dichotomy. People dance around a bonfire, couples jump over it together when the flames go down, and young people venture into the woods, alone, to search for the fern blossom that, according to folklore, can only be found on that night. Anyone who finds it, according to the old belief, becomes a seer, with the ability to read others' thoughts and understand the language of birds.

Jonas, wearing an oak-leaf crown because he was one of those being celebrated, hosted a big party on a hillside beside his nursery. He was doing well, growing plants from seeds and seedlings imported from Scandinavian countries and Israel, providing landscaping services to clients that included Catholic institutions and private businesses. His family, his several employees, neighbors, and friends danced and feasted. My sister, my niece, and I stayed until the bonfire had died down to embers.

While celebrating their ancient traditions, many young Lithuanians were now also eagerly traveling to places beyond the borders of the former Soviet Union, learning about distant lands such as India and Tibet, and about Eastern philosophy.

It so happened that the Dalai Lama came to Vilnius during our visit. We had seen posters at the airport when we arrived, announcing that he was to give two lectures. We very much wanted to attend, but the first one was sold out and the second, to be given in a park, and open to all, was scheduled for the day of our departure, too late for us.

We decided to try our luck, to show up for the first talk—an hour early, in hopes that someone might have turned in some tickets. And behold, somebody had—three tickets. The spiritual leader of the oppressed nation of Tibet, who had supported the Lithuanians' struggle for freedom, spoke in Tibetan, which a translator conveyed into English and a second translator then rendered into Lithuanian. His talk touched on questions that had troubled me long ago and had resurfaced when I found my way back to Lithuania. What is my duty? Where do I belong?

The Dalai Lama began by saying that although many people had been turning to Buddhism, he recommended that in seeking a path one first search within one's own religion and tradition, because there are many paths and the faith we are born into might well suit us best. But some people may choose the Buddhist path, and that's all right too, he said. My sister had been a practicing Buddhist for years. I felt at home in the Buddhist philosophy but had not studied or practiced deeply. Although I grasped only some of what the Dalai Lama said, he somehow laid my questions to rest, transmitting peace and joy, simply by his presence.

16

ALDONA'S STORY

Eventually, at the request of her daughter Raselė, my cousin Aldona agreed to have her story recorded for the family. She talked with a journalist, Irma Laužikaite, and Raselė sent the resulting manuscript to me in San Francisco by email. I immediately printed it out and sat down to read it at my kitchen table.

How many blinks of an eye fit into eighty-eight years? And how many moments implant themselves into memory so firmly that they seem to have happened yesterday? Kicking off my clogs, leaving them with the other children's clogs in the corridor of the elementary school. Snowdrifts so huge that if you fell into them it was hard to scramble out. In wartime, stockings mended over and over—everyone in the classroom has the same kind. The pounding on the door before morning. Stribai have forced themselves inside. . . .

I COULD ALMOST hear Aldona's voice as I read, her slow reflective way of speaking.

In the winter of 1949, she was seventeen years old, in her final year of the gymnasium in Marijampolė, sharing a room in town with her sister Danutė, who was teaching at the same school.

"Everyone was anxious," she said. "One after another, my classmates were disappearing—missing from class."

During this time the Soviet regime was collectivizing agriculture by force in the Baltic States. It was quashing resistance by deporting independent farmers to Siberia and confiscating their land. On June 22, 1948, and March 25–28, 1949, the regime forcibly removed 90,000 people in two massive operations.

In carrying out these population removals, the Soviets used local Communist volunteers to hunt down and round up the targeted "enemies of the people" and transport them to trains. These goons, who were rewarded by being exempt from service in the army, were known as *stribai*, a name derived from the Russian *istrebiteli* (to destroy). Their official name was Destroyer Battalion, later changed to Defenders of the People, and their headquarters was in Moscow.

"It was at dawn on a Sunday that the stribai woke us up," Aldona recalled. She heard the dog bark, then a horse and wagon approaching, then a banging on the door. As her father rose to open, she lay frozen in her bed. Several men entered, pointing rifles.

"They ordered us to gather our things."

As I read these words, fear cramped my gut. Something on the fringes of memory stirred, perhaps a childhood nightmare.

Many of the more substantial farmers in the Marijampolė region had already been deported, and Aldona's father had been fairly sure that their family's turn would come soon. That probability had become a near-certainty after July 6, 1948, when stribai raided a neighbor's farm and found five partisans hiding there. A shootout followed. The farm was burned to the ground, its owners taken away. All five partisans were killed. Aldona's father saw the flames while riding home from Marijampolė and, unaware of the cause, stopped to help. He was ordered to load the corpses into his wagon and haul them to the nearest village, Sasnava, where they were put on display. Everyone who had been in the vicinity that day was arrested and interrogated.

After that, Aldona's parents had hurried to get ready. They sold much of the livestock, to have some cash. They stored some grain with neighbors who were less likely to be seized because their farm was smaller. Knowing that deportees would only be allowed to take with them what they could carry, they prepared two packages of food that could be kept a long time: smoked bacon, potatoes, garlic, onions, dried beets, turnips, apples. One package they dispatched to their daughters' lodgings in Marijampolė; the other they hid at home, within easy reach.

In the early years of World War II, Aldona had carried packages like these to the post office, addressed to her brother, Antanas, and to Danutė's husband, Jonas, both imprisoned in distant labor camps. Jonas died of a lung infection on the European side of the Ural Mountains, near the Arctic Circle, leaving Danutė a widow at age twenty-one, with a nine-month-old daughter. Antanas had returned after a year of forced labor.

"Mama was so terrified she could not do anything," Aldona continued. "My father tied our bedding up into bundles, with the food. My hands shook so violently, it was hard to dress."

Aldona had no clothing to pack, for she was only home for the weekend and had intended to go back to Marijampolė after the midday Sunday meal with her parents.

Before closing the garden gate behind him, her father unchained the dog and poured milk into a bowl for the cat.

AT THIS POINT I had to stop reading. During all those years I'd taken shelter in memories of happiness in Raišupis, my fantasy paradise, I never imagined this moment when my aunt, uncle, and cousin were driven out. Almost seventy years have passed since they stepped into the cold early light under the guns of the *stribai*. Or maybe the sky was still dark. Snow crunched under the rubber soles of their felt boots.

When Aldona was recalling these moments, she was in Vilnius, where she was living with her oldest daughter, Lina, on the fourth floor of a modern apartment house. She and her interviewer, Irma, sat facing each other across the round kitchen table covered with a linen cloth. On the table I pictured two teacups, a teapot, and a plate with sliced cheese arranged in overlapping layers, a basket of rye bread, and a small plate of cucumber pickles. Maybe some sweet buns too. It must have been easier for my cousin to talk to Irma than it would have been to talk to me, because Irma, too, knew what life had been like in Soviet times.

The driver of the horse-drawn wagon waiting outside Aldona's home was a neighbor who had been ordered to deliver the family to the Marijampolė railway station. The wagon swayed as the wheels slid into ruts and mud puddles along the dirt road Aldona had walked hundreds of times, two kilometers to elementary school, then later, twelve kilometers to the secondary school in Marijampolė. She used to pace her progress "pole to pole," counting roadside utility line poles. She knew every tree along this road. She knew nothing now of what lay ahead.

"The railway station reminded me of market day—a crowd of people sitting on bundles," Aldona recalled. "More wagons kept arriving; the guards recorded them, counted, marked them on their lists. They called no names, asked for no documents." Those who arrived in the wagons were only numbers now and would be numbers for many years, people without identity papers or passports.

They were ordered to board the train, about fifty into each red-and-green cattle car. Aldona took note of some elevated platforms inside, but her parents piled their bundles into a corner, where they would sit and sleep the entire journey.

When she learned that the train would not be leaving anytime soon, Aldona asked for permission to retrieve some clothing and bedding from her rented room, nearby. Two guards escorted her there and back. Meanwhile, a crowd had gathered at the station, behind a line of soldiers who kept people from coming close to the train. Aldona dropped her bundle with her parents, then squeezed into a spot at a small, high window and peeked out through the iron bars. She heard her sister's voice: "Aldutė, Aldutė! I'm here!"

Danutė threaded her way through the crowd until she stood directly opposite the window, close enough to talk. She and her little girl, too, had been awakened in the predawn by a banging. She had wrapped a blanket around little Vida and held her tight while the landlord opened the door and two men had entered. They demanded documents and scrutinized them, then returned hers but kept the landlord's.

"They took him and his two boys," Danutė told her sister. "They're also on the train."

"Move back!" a guard yelled. As Danutė slowly followed the order, she heard her sister call out:

"How I'd love to have a loaf of bread!"

"I'll get it!" Danutė shouted.

She ran to the bakery and quickly returned with a loaf, but when she tried to hand it to Aldona, a guard lowered his rifle across her path.

Immediately, one of her students was at her side.

"Teacher, give it to me," she said, snatching the bread and, before the guard could stop her, pushing past him and handing it up to Aldona. Then, just as quickly, the girl was gone.

The train stood at the station throughout the day and most of the night.

"When it finally started to move toward the unknown, people wept. I was also anxious, but afterward . . . somehow, for young people it was not quite the same. We were traveling into the unknown, but we were preparing ourselves to live."

After two stops in Lithuania, during which more freight cars were attached, the train moved east, for three weeks.

"Even though it was many years ago," said Aldona, "even now when I'm in a car that stops at the tracks to let a freight train pass, such a heavy memory crosses my heart. And at the Kaunas tunnel, I remember the feeling I had then, as though we were in that train again."

Through the tiny high windows, she watched the light in the sky changing from day to night. Now and then she put her face close to the window to see a flat monochromatic landscape. The train was moving through vast expanses of snow-covered fields, marshlands, dark forests. When it curved around a bend, she tried to count the cars, but there were too many.

The deportees sat in silence most of the time. To relieve the monotony and forget the cold, hunger, and sadness, Aldona and some of the other young people sometimes perched on one of the sleeping platforms and sang. The familiar Lithuanian songs lifted their spirits, but made others cry. Her mother wept every day.

Nobody in her car died during the three-week journey, Aldona said, and she believes that nobody starved. Whenever the train stopped at a station, the men would go out and find something to buy from the locals. Everyone had some rubles. And everyone had brought food from home. Many had baked extra bread, or slaughtered a pig, not knowing but sensing what would happen. The Lithuanians had endured chaos and hardship many times under occupying armies—they knew how to survive.

The deportees also found ways to express their anger and defy their captors, even though they were aware that resistance would have been futile. After every stop, when the train began to move again, somebody would grab the bucket that served as the common toilet and fling its contents out, trying to hit a guard.

"What did that accomplish?" Aldona reflected. "When you think of it, what were they guilty of, these guards?"

Finally, the train arrived in Irkutsk, north of Mongolia and Lake Baikal, in the land of the indigenous Buriat people, over five thousand kilometers from home.

Filthy, on unsteady legs, blinking after weeks in dim light, men, women, and children spilled out of the fetid cars into the cold fresh air. Their railroad journey ended here, in one of the largest cities in eastern Siberia. From here they would travel by truck, two families per truck, to their final destination.

The vehicle Aldona and her parents boarded was part of a convoy that would continue north another five hundred kilometers for another two days through the immense Siberian forest, the taiga. It was a rough journey. As they bounced on roads deeply pitted with potholes, her mother moaned, "*Va-jeʒau, va-jeʒau,*" invoking the name of Jesus. They stopped for the night at a Russian Orthodox church that had been converted into a warehouse, and then continued north into the Zhigalov region, and pulled in at the New Life Collective Farm.

A single street was lined with simple small wooden houses. Beyond these, Aldona saw brown fields of stubble, enclosed by the forest. It was almost the end of March; snow had begun to melt, and women and children were gleaning wheat. They must be hungry to be doing that, Aldona thought. What nourishment might possibly remain in the scattered ears after months under rain and snow?

Everyone—mostly women and children—came running to see what the trucks had brought. Russians, Aldona thought. Hungry Russians. How would they receive the Lithuanians? But she was soon relieved.

"We felt no hostility," she said. This *kolkhoʒ* (collective farm) needed more labor. That's why we were brought here."

The Lithuanians were dispersed among the many derelict houses, which, vacant for a long time, had been stripped of everything except for tile stoves and plank beds. The previous residents had been deported to some other place after the Russian revolution.

Right away the newcomers went out to gather firewood.

"As soon as the houses warmed up, the bedbugs revived."

Aldona had never experienced bedbugs at home. They would prove to be a relentless plague in Siberia.

"The Russian women were clean, they worked hard, they whitened their walls with chalk, but the bedbugs laid their eggs under the chalk," she said. "They pushed their beds away from the walls, into the middle of the room, but the bedbugs dropped from the ceiling. When my first baby was born, I couldn't understand why he couldn't sleep. I turned on the light—his head was covered with bedbugs."

Just reading this made me shudder. What a horror for this young mother, not to be able to protect her baby son from these loathsome parasites, crawling slowly over his tender scalp, bloated with his blood, emanating a disgusting smell.

At the New Life kolkhoz, women did most of the work. The few men who had returned from the front drove tractors and trucks, worked as farm machinery mechanics and on construction jobs. Aldona and her father felled trees, chopped wood, shoveled snow, spread manure, plowed and planted. Each morning all the workers lined up; the komandant counted them, then assigned the work for the day. Whatever Aldona's task, she did not complain. She knew how to do almost every kind of farm work, having helped her parents since she was a child.

One of the jobs she was assigned to was highly desirable: accountant in the office. But it came with a condition: she would have to sign an agreement to be an informer.

"I wouldn't sign, so they threw me out," she said.

It took time to get used to the climate. In the summer they were plagued by biting flies.

"At first our hands swelled terribly, and they tried to get into our eyes—even though we tried to hide them and wore long sleeves, they tried get into our eyes. We wore netting over our heads, like beekeepers. When I surveyed the fields I ran to escape them. But eventually we got used to these flies and our hands stopped swelling."

Winters were so cold that the walls crackled. Fortunately, there was no wind until March, when the cold begins to withdraw.

"Had there been winds in winter, we would not have survived. We all walked in felt boots with thick soles, made locally. The ones from Lithuania, with rubber soles, were insufficient."

What helped was knowing that, at the end of the day, her mother would be waiting in a warm house, with warm water for washing and a meal she had prepared. For some reason, Aldona said, her mother was allowed to stay home, so she kept house, as she had done all her life.

"I remember how hard it was for a Lithuanian boy who was alone—he had been deported alone. He would come home and have to cook. We Lithuanians did help him."

Many children who had been deported without parents, or whose parents had died, did not survive.

Workers were compensated with flour, which alone would not have sufficed to sustain life, "but Lithuanians know how to live. They had all brought some money and immediately began to look for livestock. We bought a goat and a piglet, which we kept in a little shed, and in our room, behind the stove, we kept chickens. They clucked at night, the rooster crowed."

The deportees had also brought seeds with them, and they started gardens beside their houses. The Russians did not garden as much, Aldona said, but everyone went to the forest with buckets to gather cranberries, red and black currants, and mushrooms.

Lithuanians and Russians did not mingle much socially, but they were friendly and had things to learn from each other. Russian women showed the Lithuanians how to grow cucumbers in the cold climate by starting them in rows of manure, and Lithuanians, surprised to see Russians digging for potatoes with a spade, taught them how to make a wooden plow.

"And how wonderful the soil is there," said Aldona. "Plow it twice and the wheat rises like a wall."

Reading these words of Aldona's I remembered something she had said during one of my earlier visits to Lithuania.

"Nature is beautiful there too, and the earth is very rich."

"There were about fifty of us Lithuanians in the kolkhoz," she told her interviewer. "Life did not stop. After all, the eyes that cry also laugh," so the whole community joined in both funerals and celebrations. "We had a black and white funeral flag, and made the coffins and accompanied the dead to burial with hymns. And we celebrated holidays together, and put on dances. Young people would gather in someone's house—often it was ours—someone would bring an accordion or a harmonica." Some young people came, secretly, from nearby collective farms, even though they knew that they would be jailed if caught outside the area to which they were confined.

Among them was the tall, good-looking Juozas Deltuva, who had arrived on the same train as Aldona but in a different car. They had met in the church where their convoy stopped overnight en route from Irkutsk to the New Life farm.

"There was no place to sleep, so we young people walked around and talked," she said.

Their courtship was brief. They applied for permission to marry. "Because we had no documents, we were given 'passports': our photos were pasted on a piece of paper and permission was granted," said Aldona.

On January 31, 1951, almost two years after arriving in Siberia, Aldona Kedytė and Juozas Deltuva put on their best clean work clothes and walked, together, through the snow-laden forest to an office in a nearby village to sign a paper that stated they were now husband and wife. They had no rings to exchange or priest to hear their vows. Then they walked to the New Life kolkhoz and sat for a while with Aldona's parents and neighbors. That was the beginning of their sixty-two years together.

In the next six and a half years, Aldona gave birth to five of their seven children. Their first son's birth was extremely difficult, and so was his infancy. Her father came with a horse-drawn flatbed wagon to collect her and the baby from the village clinic where she had delivered. It was April, still cold. She held little Viktoras in her arms, tucked into a pillow, while letting her feet dangle over the wagon's edge. When they came to the river they had to cross, they saw water atop the ice. The thaw had begun. There was no bridge.

"I held the child tightly, lifted my feet, and we drove across. My feet got wet. On the other side of the river, a Lithuanian family lived. They let me in so I could change my shoes and stockings. I was wary of catching cold, with the baby."

The infant cried a lot. He would nurse and cry, still hungry. Aldona also cried, for she had almost no breast milk. She managed to buy some hard-to-find cow's milk and rice from a neighbor, and made a paste. That was not enough, but it was the best she could do. And then the bedbugs attacked.

Life improved somewhat after Stalin died, in 1952. "After he kicked the bucket we felt more free," said Aldona. "We were, at last, given personal documents, and the children received birth certificates." They were no longer only numbers; they were people again, with names, and were permitted to move beyond the assigned collective farm.

Aldona with her family transferred to another kolkhoz, then to a town on the Lena River, where she and Juozas found jobs, paid for in rubles. She cleaned rooms in a hotel—"so many bedbugs!"—and her husband worked as machinist in a lumber mill. "We brought our cow, on a barge. The children went to nursery school. In winter we took them there by sled. But when I heard that they were speaking to each other in Russian, I almost had a stroke."

One day Aldona heard that some children's sailor suits were to arrive at a shop the next day. "I stood in line almost all night," she said. "I simply had to get one for Viktorėlis."

Life had become easier; the deportees' hopes began to stir. They had signed papers stating that they were banished from their homeland for life, but had never doubted that one day they would return. As the bonds of their confinement loosened, Aldona's longing to go home grew. Memories began to haunt her, painfully.

After the children had gone to sleep, and she was preparing food and clothing for the next day, she would hear her father's bees in the sunny orchard, see the apple trees dressed in clouds of white blossoms. She allowed herself to be a child again, kicking off her clogs inside the door of the schoolhouse, dancing in patched stockings on the wooden classroom floor. She remembered walking through the woods from Raišupis to her grandparents' house in Obelinė. Her grandmother, surprised, stood in her doorway, clapping her hands, chanting, "Aniutė, Aniutė dropped down from the sky!"

One person actually did come from the sky, and that was her Uncle Antanas. When they heard the clatter of the ANBO, someone would run out of the house and spread a sheet on the grass. He would circle the house and wave, then drop a small bag filled with sand onto the sheet. In it was a letter, announcing when he would visit. And he would swing by Obelinė too, to say hello to his parents. All Aldona's mother's brothers loved her very much, so it was at her house they would gather to await Antanas on the appointed day. Aldona would be dispatched to the hill overlooking the road to watch for the cloud of dust signaling the approach of her uncle's black Mercedes.

Like the storks who winter thousands of miles away from their nests on the rooftops in Lithuania, Aldona heard the call. She knew it was time to go home.

Permission to leave came from the authorities in the autumn of 1957, and Aldona's parents left soon after, but Juozas still had a year to go on his sentence, so Aldona decided to stay with him and the children. And then, by the time he was free to go, nature intervened.

Aldona was pregnant with her fifth child, due at Christmastime. The family had to cross the Lena River immediately, before it froze over. Any delay might mean that they would have to wait until the ice was solid enough for sleighs and trucks. But by then the baby's due date would be too close to undertake the arduous journey. And if they waited until after the birth, they would have to stay until the infant was strong enough to travel. Months—at least until spring. That was too long! They decided to leave right away, while the boats were still running.

Packing was easy. They did not have much more than their bedding and a change of clothing—just about as much as they had come with nine years before.

"Not so many children's clothes, either," said Aldona. "As the saying goes, one set on your skin, the other on the fence."

But that year the Lena froze earlier than usual. All navigation stopped. When Aldona realized she would be spending another winter in Siberia, she thought she could not bear it. That was when she cried, inconsolably.

They decided not to wait for spring. On March 4, 1958, the family set out for home, on the ice. The baby, Jonas—Jonukas—was two and a half months old, and Aldona had enough breast milk for him. The eldest was going on seven. They crossed the frozen Lena in a truck, Aldona sitting next to the driver with the infant in her arms, her husband and the other four children in back, wrapped in coats and scarves and bedding. As the truck bounced along the road for two days, retracing their route to the kolkhoz, Aldona remembered how her mother had pleaded with Holy Mary when the wheels hit potholes and hoped her journey home would not be so difficult.

"Two military men were also riding in the truck with us," she recalled. "One of them remarked, 'It must be hard, with so many children.' The other answered, 'Not hard for them; they're going home.'"

Yes. going home. They boarded a train in Irkutsk—a passenger train, not a cattle train—and arrived in Kaunas in the midst of a snowstorm. Danutė and some of her husband's in-laws were at the station to meet them. Because nobody had room for such a large family, two of the children and Juozas went to his relatives; two others, Aldona, and the baby went with Aldona's sister to the minuscule apartment overlooking the Nemunas River, where Danutė lived with her daughter Vida.

I imagine the little flock stepping down the snow-covered steps of the railroad station and making their way along the silent street, in deepening snow—two women, one carrying an infant, the other lugging bags, with two small children alongside, muffled in wool and felt.

"A taxi stopped," Aldona remembered. "The driver said: 'What kind of company is this?' and he gave us a ride."

The snowdrifts were still high a few days later when Aldona, Juozas, and the children arrived by train in Marijampolė. Her father met them with a horse-drawn sleigh. The farm in Raišupis was now a kolkhoz. Her parents had been permitted to move into two rooms of their old home, and now they gave up one of those rooms to Aldona and her family. So for a time, nine people shared those two rooms.

The farm was generally in poor shape. Fences had been used for firewood, roofs were torn. The apple trees were broken and damaged. Calves had been tied up in the orchard.

"What can you do? Such were the times," Aldona said.

The family continued to live and work on the farm that had been their family's for generations. Aldona's father tended the bees and other animals. Everyone brought him sick animals—he was good at understanding what ailed them and what they needed. Aldona worked hard, as she had her entire life.

Her mother was disabled by Parkinson's disease, confined to bed for her last ten years. Aldona took care of her, as well as the children—two more were born in Lithuania, so she soon had seven. She helped them with schoolwork. "I would stir a pot and recite at the same time," she recalled, as her mother had helped her. She assumed ever greater responsibilities at the kolkhoz because everyone trusted her.

"There wasn't a day when I didn't see the sun rise," she reflected.

Many of the former independent farms that had been turned into collective farms or state farms were later demolished, among them the family homestead in Raišupis. The family moved into the village and, over time, scattered to other towns and countries.

No one was left behind in Siberia. All will be buried in the little family plot across the road from the church in Sasnava. Aldona already has the black dress and black shoes she wants to wear in her coffin. She is ready, but not in a hurry. She lives, warm and comfortable, with her daughter Lina in a small apartment on the top floor of a four-story building in Vilnius. Jonas brings flowers from his nursery and blueberries from his farm. Raselė and her brother Vitas often drop by. She listens to the news on the radio.

"If you want to know anything, just ask Mama," Raselė told me.

Aldona is at peace here, still ready to laugh at anything she can see as amusing, surrounded by love, generating love around her while keeping the dark shadows at bay.

Lina has a little house by a lake, in the forest, Aldona told me during one of my visits, but "when she took me there I saw the tall pines and they reminded me of Siberia so much that I told her I won't go there anymore."

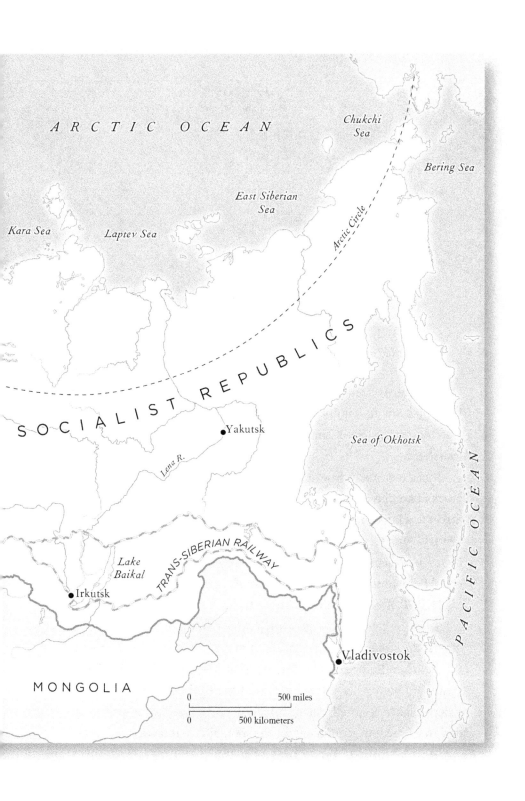

THE DARKEST PLACE

W ord reached me in San Francisco that the Soviet secret police record of my father's interrogation in prison had been brought from Moscow to Vilnius and was now accessible to the public. I felt I had to read it. So in summer 2014, I returned to Lithuania for the fourth time.

Jonas met me in front of Vilnius Cathedral and we walked a few blocks past the fashionable shops and restaurants along Gediminas Street to a building fronting Lūkiškių Aikštė, a square with a notable history. During the 1863–64 uprising against the Russian Empire, it was an execution site. Twenty-one alleged rebel leaders were executed here, nine of them shot and twelve hanged.

In 1920, a stone commemorating the executed rebellion leader was placed in the center of the square. In 1936, while Vilnius was in Polish hands, the stone was moved aside to make room for a monument to the Polish military commander, Marshal Josef Pilsudsky. In 1952, a statue of Lenin replaced that of Pilsudsky. By 1991, with Lithuania's independence restored, the government announced a competition to design a Freedom Monument for the spot. No clear favorite emerged, so the contest was repeated, again with unsatisfactory results. Some of the younger Lithuanians wanted no monument, only recreational space. A decision was postponed.

Fronting on the square, on Gediminas Street, was the massive building that was our goal. It had been constructed in 1890 and housed a courthouse when Lithuania was part of the Russian Empire. From 1940 to 1990 it was headquarters for occupying forces' secret police—the Nazis' Gestapo, the Soviet NKVD, and its successor, the KGB. Some of the cells where prisoners were confined and interrogated could now be visited as part of a Museum of Occupations and Freedom Fights. Upstairs are courtrooms. A stairway leads from the lobby to the Special Archive, where formerly secret files on Soviet political prisoners are available to the public for viewing.

I had made an appointment and my father's file was waiting for me. From behind a desk just outside the door to the reading room, a young woman handed me a sheaf of old papers, roughly bound. My breath caught in my throat. Written in ink on the scuffed and dog-eared paper cover was "Byla 1066. A Gustaitis."

I carried the file into the spacious, empty reading room, placed it on one of the tables, and could not bring myself to open it.

Leaf shadows cast by maple trees outside the tall windows danced on the sunlit table, across the dingy gray paper cover. Such an unlikely object it was, brought into the light from the darkest place at the darkest time of my father's life. In these pages I would find whatever my father said, or was alleged to have said, to interrogators in the Butyrka prison between early March 1941 and the following October, when he was killed.

Jonas had kindly come with me to translate, for we knew that the documents were almost all in Russian. He sat down next to me. I would look at a page, then he would read and render it into Lithuanian, and I would take notes. During the several months that followed, *Plieno Sparnai* (*Steel Wings*), an online publication dedicated to Lithuania's aviation history, would translate the document into Lithuanian and post it on the internet.

The first items we saw in the file were forms on which basic biographical information was recorded, and an inventory of items taken from the prisoner after he was arrested. Among these were a few family photographs, including one of Jūratė and me with our father, the last photo of us together. We have a near-identical one in our family album, except in that one Tėtė is looking straight ahead, while in this one, the one he took with him, he is gazing protectively down at me.

When I saw that I felt a flash of joy. His gaze was so tender. There were also mugshots, direct and in profile, of a gaunt man with sunken eyes—the originals of the photos in the newspaper clipping I had received in the mail after my first trip to Lithuania. I barely recognized my father. What had been done to him?

Also among the items listed as having been in his possession were "a yellow metal ring" (surely his wedding ring), a "yellow metal

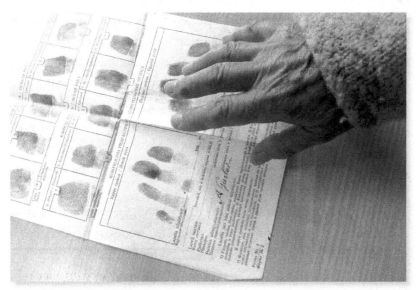

My father's fingerprints

watch," and some foreign currency: 60 British pounds sterling, 22 German marks, 149 American dollars. Also glasses with horn and metal frames, a flashlight, an address book, a map of Lithuania, a passport, woolen socks, underwear, a tie.

On turning a page, I came upon a set of fingerprints, each fingertip in its own little box and, below these, a print of both palms spread. I placed my fingers on the hand prints, closed my eyes, and tried to imagine that I was touching my father's palm. Then I drew back. These were the prints of a dead man. What am I doing here? I asked myself.

I found no drawings of my father's ANBO designs. My mother had told me he had taken some with him, but they were not in this file. The bulk of the file contained records of interrogations, thirteen of them between March 5 and June 25–26. The time each session began and ended was noted. They lasted between three and fifteen hours. Nine of the thirteen took place at night.

I had expected to find questions about his expertise, airplane design and construction, but found none. The single goal of these interrogations seems to have been to make a case that my father was a traitor to the Soviet Union. The same questions related to his attempted escape were asked repeatedly. The wording in some of the answers suggests strongly that they were altered. My mother would have known. I was grateful that she was spared having to read this grim document.

"Tell under what circumstances you were apprehended," the interrogator asked on March 5, during the first session, in the prison in Kaunas.

"I was apprehended on March 4, at about 19:30 hours (7:30 p.m.) after I had gotten off the train at the Šeštokai station and was trying to cross illegally into Germany."

"With what purpose did you try to cross the USSR border illegally?"

"My only intention was to travel through Germany and Portugal to North America. Toward that end I had been registered on July 12, 1940, at the American consulate as a candidate for emigration."

A handwritten "Voluntary Statement by the Accused," dated March 7, three days after his capture, records my father as stating,

The thought of crossing the border illegally came to me in the beginning of 1940, when I withdrew from military service. At first I avoided this thought because I did not want to leave my country. But gradually more reasons and considerations emerged, which led me to act. . . . The basic reason is that I was dismissed from my profession as military aviator, to which I have dedicated the last twenty-two years of my life. . . . I hoped that in North America, where commercial aviation is thriving, I would find an interesting job in my specialty and have opportunities to fly, at least in sports aviation. . . . I decided to cross the German border to accomplish my goal of moving to North America. My wife, as daughter of a German, had a right to German citizenship [as did a German citizen's entire family] but I did not want to use this option. I wanted to be free to move on . . . and therefore, having given permission to my wife to repatriate, I decided to leave by crossing the border illegally.

In saying that my mother's father was German, my father was clearly trying to protect her. She had falsely claimed German roots so as to be able to leave the country with the ethnic German residents of Lithuania. The goal was to get the family across the border, reunite on the other side, and travel together out of Germany, if not to North America, then to South America. The Argentinian consul in Kaunas had arranged for visas for our whole family, to be picked up in Berlin. All we had to do was get there.

In a later interrogation, my father acknowledged that he had obtained a false document to support the claim of my mother's German origins. But right then, having no way to know whether his family had succeeded in escaping, he repeated the fabrication created for our protection.

On the night of March 10–11, pressed for further reasons for his attempt to leave the country, he was outspoken: "I was never an advocate of Sovietization, so I was displeased when the Soviet Army took over Lithuania. My displeasure grew stronger in October 1940, when the military air force, which I headed, was disbanded."

"If you applied for a visa to emigrate to North America, why did you try to cross illegally?" the interrogator asked.

My father replied that he knew that a visa to emigrate was almost impossible to get and that he feared that if one was denied, he would be sent to work in the depths of Russia and then would not be able to realize his intention of moving to America.

JONAS AND I pored over the scuffed, discolored pages. Hours passed. The interrogators returned again and again to specifics of the attempted escape.

"Who was helping you to cross the border illegally?"

My father responded that he had asked a former aide of his, Lieutenant Tandžiulis, to find trustworthy people who occupied themselves with border crossings, and that Tandžiulis had introduced him to a man whose last name was Kosmanas, who had been the head of the German Cultural Society. Kosmanas took charge of making the arrangements.

On March 2, he met with my father and his allies and set March 4 as the date of departure. He said he would send an experienced guide who had never failed, and assured my father that he would have no trouble entering Germany or moving on from Germany. He told him that the guide, who would identify himself as Adomas, would expect to be paid three thousand rubles.

"What assignment did Kosmanas give you?" asked the interrogator.

"No assignment."

"Why was he interested in helping you in your illegal border crossing?"

"I know nothing about that because he said nothing about that."

On the day of departure, Adomas was to meet with my father and Tandžiulis at eleven a.m., but he appeared only at 1:50 p.m., an hour before the train's scheduled departure. My father paid him the three thousand rubles, as he had agreed to do. The guide then told him that the train tickets had to be bought in town, at a travel bureau, rather than at the station. Then he said he would see them on the train and left. Tandžiulis went for the tickets, accompanied by an ally, while my father proceeded to the station alone, intending to meet Tandžiulis there. But he was worried that somebody might recognize him if he waited in the station, so he boarded the train without a ticket and bought one from the conductor en route, paying a fine.

Tandžiulis did not appear on the train. Adomas did, but after making his presence known to my father, he kept his distance.

"I am guessing that Tandžiulis was late," my father wrote in his "Voluntary Statement," as recorded on the day after his arrest. Or did he perhaps, at the last minute, change his mind about fleeing? What is known is that he later joined the anti-Soviet resistance in Lithuania, and was killed in 1949.

On March 5, in the Kaunas prison, my father was brought face to face with the two men who were to have guided his escape. Pribulis (aka Adomas) denied ever seeing him before, while the second man, identified as Anza, gave a straightforward account:

"Gustaitis asked me to give him a ride. I invited him to get up into the wagon, and we met in this way, and soon the border guards stopped us all. . . . As the border guards were checking our documents, Gustaitis jumped out of the wagon and started to run. They began to shoot with their pistols, and only because of that he stopped."

"Yes, I was stopped as he described," my father confirmed.

All the subsequent interrogations recorded in my father's file took place in Moscow, in the Butyrka prison to which he was taken by special convoy, by train, on the following day. The NKVD file consists mostly of reports of these interrogation sessions, ten in March, one each in April, May, and June. The three of longest duration began late in the evening, paused for a few hours in the morning, then continued. One can only guess what means of persuasion might have been employed between or during the interrogations. Sometimes, before a pause, the interrogator accuses my father of not telling all he knows and tells him that he will need to elaborate.

"In earlier interrogations, about your anti-Soviet connections . . . you have named only those who prepared your illegal crossing," the

The Soviet secret police file on Antanas Gustaitis compiled in a Moscow prison is now available for viewing at Lithuania's Special Archive in Vilnius

questioner is recorded as saying on March 17. "Point out your col-
laborators in anti-Soviet actions in the Lithuanian Soviet Socialist
Republic."

My father denied having undertaken anti-Soviet activities in
Lithuania, as he had done several times before.

"I understood very well the power of Soviet intelligence, and
therefore thought that such opposition was too risky and that it could
require unnecessary sacrifices."

"You are holding on to your nationalistic anti-Soviet positions
and trying to mislead the interrogation."

"Without denying my nationalistic convictions," my father
answered, "I still don't intend to mislead the interrogations. Please
believe that I am telling the truth."

"Your assurances and attempts to hide your anti-Soviet activities
and ties are worthless. You will have to give us detailed testimony
when we return to this."

What followed this obvious threat?

In his introduction to his Lithuanian translation of the file,
posted on the internet, Gintautas Kačergis notes that breaks during
long interrogations tended to be followed by "amplifications" that
"revealed" one or more additional examples of Antanas Gustaitis's
"activities." He allegedly stated that he was trying to flee so that he
could continue anti-Soviet actions from abroad, and that he passed
strategic information about the location of Soviet airfields to the Germans, and he is recorded as confessing that he was a participant in a
plan to organize a Lithuania Freedom Committee with the ultimate
goal of establishing a "bourgeois-democratic government" in Lithuania when an opportunity to do so arose.

SOME OF THE reports were handwritten, some were typed. Each was
signed A. Gustaitis. Toward the end of the record, the signature was

hard to decipher, and it was not at all clear that it was in his hand. Certainly the language in some of the reports and the "confession" was not his.

The secret trial was held on July 7, 1941. Neither the defendant nor legal counsel was present. A certificate in the NKVD file states that the death sentence was carried out on October 16, 1941. On that day, the Wehrmacht was approaching Moscow.

Byla 1066, the A Gustaitis file in the Special Archive in Vilnius, translated from Russian to Lithuanian by Gintautas Kačergis, has been posted at www.plienosparnai.it. The Soviet secret police record of my father's 1941 interrogation in Moscow during one of the grimmest war years in Russia is now available, in Lithuanian and Russian, on the internet. Those who study the history of that time may find it useful. What I have quoted here is my translation from Lithuanian into English.

I think I have now learned all that is possible to learn about my father's last months of life.

THE MORNING AFTER visiting the Special Archive, I was in Marijampolė, exploring further the dark history of the war years. A small museum in the center of the town is dedicated to the resistance. It contains documents, photographs, and various relics of partisans who hid in the forests and fought the Soviet occupation well into the 1950s, and of Lithuanians who had been banished to "the cold lands."

The elderly volunteer guide showed me a photograph of himself as a child, with his mother, and the sewing machine that helped them both to survive. He sang a haunting song his mother had taught him, and gave me a small book he had written. Also on exhibit was a photograph of the teacher who had betrayed a young relative of mine and other students who were putting out a clandestine newspaper, and that teacher's later apology. The students had been shot.

With Aldona's daughter Rūta as my guide for the day, I next visited the art museum, housed in a former synagogue. A stained-glass window depicting Mary, the mother of Jesus, dominated the central space. I looked for a plaque or other acknowledgment of the building's history and found none. The museum employee I spoke with said that she and other staff had wanted to install a plaque, but had been denied permission by government officials. When I asked what the current Jewish population of the town was, she said she wasn't sure, but it was very small. Another synagogue, nearby, had been restored and was open.

My sister Jūratė had told me that she had visited a massacre site on the Šešupė River at the edge of Marijampolė. At my request, Rūta took me to it, first stopping at a school to pick up her six-year-old granddaughter. The three of us followed a footpath down the riverbank to a wide meadow where a black granite monument stood, flanked by fresh flowers in vases. In front of it, on the ground, lay a row of river pebbles on which names had been written in colored chalk. Jewish names. Rūta's granddaughter picked up one of the stones and asked, "What are these?"

"These are names of some of the children buried here," her grandmother answered. "Put it back."

I lingered in the sunny meadow, trying to grasp what I was looking at. Here beside the wide Šešupė River, men with guns had driven eight thousand people to slaughter on September 1, 1941. Seven thousand of them were Jews. Here lay nearly all of the missing Jewish population of the Marijampolė region. A soft breeze was blowing. Wildflowers were in bloom. Yesterday or perhaps this morning, someone had come here and remembered some of the dead by writing their names on little stones.

In his book *Bloodlands*, historian Timothy Snyder wrote,

In the middle of Europe in the middle of the twentieth century, the Nazi and Soviet regimes murdered some 14 million people. The place where all of the victims died, the bloodlands, extends from central Poland to western Russia, through Ukraine, Belarus and the Baltic States. Not one of the 14 million was a soldier. Most were women, children, and the aged.

The mass grave at the edge of Marijampolė is one of hundreds throughout Lithuania. More than 95 percent of Lithuania's Jewish population was murdered by the Nazis. Mostly, as here, they were shot near their homes, their bodies dumped into pits.

In Kaunas, the Ninth Fort was a killing ground. It is now a museum. Remains continue to be found at more sites. As I was about to leave Lithuania after this visit, I picked up the daily *Lietuvos Rytas* at the Vilnius airport and read that authorities were in a quandary about some bags filled with human bones found in the Fourth Fort while it was being cleaned up in preparation for its repurposing. No decision had been made on the proper way to lay these bones to rest, the article stated, because it was not possible to know whether the remains included those of people of other faiths as well as Jews and therefore, what religious leaders other than rabbis should be asked to conduct ceremonies. A committee had suspended deliberations.

Oh my beautiful, blood-soaked land!

18

ECHOES, GHOSTS, AND SPIRITS

Today as I write this, on March 4, 2015, it's exactly seventy-four years since my father was captured by Soviet guards as he was walking from the train station in the little town of Šeštokai on his way to meet the man who was to escort him secretly across the border of German-occupied Poland.

Here in San Francisco this early morning, the sky is cloudless, the weather unseasonably warm. I walk through a small forest in McLaren Park to the blue water tower atop a hill, with California mountain lilac and jasmine in bloom along the path, then gaze past the city's high-rise towers to the hills across the bay.

Tonight a full moon will rise. In Lithuania, night has already fallen. As of today, seventy-four years ago, my father would never again smell jasmine, or the lilacs he loved, or gaze at the open sky. What remained of his life—eight more months—would pass in dank prison cells.

Last night I opened an email from my cousin Jonas, with three photographs attached. He had traveled to Šeštokai to take them for me.

"Not much has changed here," he wrote. "I found the place where it happened."

The first photo showed the train station, a one-story red brick building. A round blue clock mounted on the side facing the tracks reads 4:30. The second showed a muddy unpaved road.

"This is where they stopped him."

The third was of a black iron cross, with the inscription "Remember those who departed on the roads of suffering 1941–1952."

This station was one of the collection points for people being deported to the cold lands. In June 1941, thousands of people were hauled by rail to the Soviet gulag, and, after the Nazis invaded, to Hitler's forced-labor factories and concentration camps. Deportations continued for the next eleven years.

I stared at the photographs on my computer screen, imagining the wheeze of the train's steam engine, the wheels clanging and grinding to a stop. On March 4, 1941, my father stepped off the train on the side opposite the station. He saw a boy waiting to show him the way, as promised. Without looking at my father, this boy started walking alongside the tracks, in the direction the train had been traveling. My father followed some distance behind him; Adomas followed my father. It was dusk. Rainy. The ground was wet.

Here in San Francisco today, I watch my father walk behind the boy for about two hundred meters, to the road that crosses the tracks. The train is still at the station. A horse-drawn wagon approaches. My father speaks to the driver. In his email note, Jonas imagines the brief conversation:

> *"Hello Uncle. Good-looking horse."*
> *"They're taking our horses from us."*
> *"Can you give me a ride up the road?"*
> *"Sure, step up. With two of us, the road will be shorter."*

As my father is stepping up into the wagon, uniformed Russians appear and ask for documents. Looking at those of the driver, one of them exclaims, "Aha. Anza! We have been looking for you."

My father runs toward the forest. He has to cross an open field to reach it and knows he probably won't, but sees no other choice.

"*Stoy!*" (Stop!) Then a shot.

ON THIS SPRING morning in San Francisco, yellow oxalis—the gardener's bane—is dazzlingly lovely among the green grasses in McLaren Park. Looking across downtown from the hill on which the blue water tower stands, I see that on the other side of the bay, a brown haze cloaks the East Bay hills.

No rain this past winter. We're in the worst drought in the 120 years that rainfall has been measured, or perhaps in 1,200 years, because of the unprecedented warm weather, a scientist said on the news this morning. Not enough snow in the Sierra. Also very little in Lithuania—the blueberries Jonas has invested in planting might yield a poor harvest again.

In California, we say to each other, "What a beautiful day!" but feel uncomfortable saying it.

I am reminded of newspaper stories telling how, just before World War II broke out or some other disaster obliterated life as people knew it, in the great cities of the world, from Paris to Buenos Aires, the boulevards were brightly lit and the cafés full of people who pretended they did not see the darkness ahead.

Descending from the hilltop with the blue tower, I come upon the Philosopher's Way, a trail with markers designed for rest and contemplation. On the first of these, a bench, a black granite slate is imprinted with the words of the Japanese philosopher Kitaro Nishida:

Thinking has its own laws. It functions of its own accord and does not follow our will. To merge with the object of thought—that is, to direct one's attention to it—is voluntary, but I think perception is the same in this respect: we are able to see what we want to see by freely turning our attention toward it.

Today, by choice, I turn my attention to my father's last traces. It's almost embarrassing to say, but I am overcome with grief. I'm eighty years old. He was forty-three that day in Šeštokai. But it's true. For many years his loss was an absence, a longing. I felt grief when I went back to Lithuania the first time, in 1989, and again when I watched a film of the returning of the remains of the dead from Siberia. What I felt when my father vanished from my life, I don't know. Confusion, I think, certainly. But I did not think he was lost forever.

Grief arises in waves, stirred by events and experiences, as ocean waves are stirred by winds and earthquakes on the ocean floor.

When I found out that the traitor guide was dead I felt grief because that meant nothing more could be gleaned about my father. Or so I thought then, before I had read the NKVD file. But now that I have seen the last traces of his passage—his fingerprints, his signatures, and now these photographs taken by Jonas in Šeštokai, I also feel something different.

I feel I was summoned to bear witness to his lonely suffering. To be with him, strange as that may seem.

A FEW NIGHTS ago I consorted with shadows again. I searched the internet for the name "Ugnė Karvelis" and clicked on a link. The effect was that of a rock crashing through river ice, tearing a ragged hole in its glassy surface. The ice was surprisingly thin. The rock plunged into the water below, opening a black hole. The white winter silence shattered.

Ugnė has stepped out of the doorway of the centuries-old building where she has lived for decades on the top floor, above other ancient rooftops. She looks strong and vigorous. I'm surprised to see that her hair is not gray, like mine, though it's lighter than it used to be. She glances to the right and left, about to cross the street, then turns to the camera and I hear her familiar smoked-away gravelly voice say, in Lithuanian, "This is my neighborhood. I will show you."

A strange brew of emotions overwhelms me. Ugnė has been dead for more than eleven years, yet there she is.

She's unreachable, as all ghosts are unreachable to us on this side of the threshold. I see and hear her as through one-way glass; she can't see me. The camera tilts up to her windows, then follows her along the street, to a tree on the left bank of the Seine.

"It's very old," I hear her say as she touches the rough bark tenderly. "We chat."

Her shrug and self-deprecating smile—that's the Ugnė I have loved. My dearest childhood friend, I still have the little scrap of white cloth with the brown stain of our blood comingled in eternal friendship. Do you remember how we pricked our fingers with a sewing needle as we sat in a tree before I left for America?

Now I see Ugnė at a poetry reading in someone's living room. Young people mostly. She's at the back of the room; I see the smoke from her cigarette rising from behind a man in the foreground. Then she's dancing with another man; I'm happy to see her laughing. The last time I saw you, Ugnė, the last night we spent in Paris together, you took me to a bar and there flirted endlessly with a man you had no interest in—that was so stupid. And you were so drunk. I was, of course, hurt—you were wasting the little time that we had left together. We ended up with the old onion soup at dawn at Les Halles, which has disappeared, too. And here I am, looking at a screen, whining to a ghost beyond the one-way mirror. No meeting of the eyes is possible. No message can get through.

I click. No more. Click again. The screen goes dark.

I went to bed disturbed by the conflicting emotions that had characterized my friendship with Ugnė in its latter phases. Now, surely, those emotions were irrelevant, and certainly embarrassing to admit. Part of the mix was jealousy. I could not help comparing her accomplishments to mine. She translated some of the great Latin American poets into French and saw their books through publication: work by Julio Cortázar, Gabriel García Márquez, also by some Lithuanian poets. After our homeland regained independence, she became Lithuania's representative to the United Nations Educational Social and Cultural Organization. She is credited with the designation of Old Vilnius as a UNESCO World Heritage Site. An academic secondary school has been named after her near her birthplace. And what had I accomplished during my long life? I remind myself again that Ugnė's name means *flame* and mine means *dew*. Morning dew refreshes, but leaves no trace.

The following morning I wanted to see the film of Ugnė again, to be seduced again by the illusion that she was still alive. But I reminded myself of Andrej Tarkovsky's film *Solaris*, which shows how dangerous it is to hang out with ghosts. They can seduce and consume you.

ANOTHER MORNING, IN December. The sky is wondrous after two days of longed-for rain. It's periwinkle blue, with wisps of gray fog and brilliantly white sunlit clouds. More rain is promised. We all hope it comes. On my walk to Twin Peaks, a parkland near my home, I stop to look out over the city and watch the light show.

Sunlight is pouring onto undulating rows of identical little white houses in the southeastern hills, turning their monotony into a necklace of white seashells laid at the foot of San Bruno Mountain. Sunbeams spotlight individual buildings here and there, light up clusters of houses, then move on. Passing clouds, heavenly artists, keep changing the effects. Silver light bounces off the surface of the Bay; I reach for my sunglasses against the glare. On the eastern shore, fog banks hover above the Oakland hills. To the west, the ocean is hulled in gray.

I plop down on the rock at the summit, facing east. A runner in red shorts and black shirt bounces up, plugs in his ears with wires hanging down toward some kind of apparatus attached to his shirt pocket. Without stopping or even raising his head to take in the view, he continues down the opposite side of the peak.

Just then two ravens streak through the air in front of me, swoop toward downtown, and turn in a grand loop, side by side in elegant harmony. Their gleaming wingtips curl gently upward as they shift direction, then they carve a spiral, soar upward and away. In their wake I fill with quiet happiness.

Those ravens slipped through the air the way a dolphin slips through water; they coasted by on currents I can't even see. I'm a bottom-dweller in our ocean of air. Yet for a moment, just an evanescent moment, I also flew.

When I see birds in formation, I am reminded of my father. He must have watched ravens, crows—and probably owls and storks—and studied their flight dynamics while he was a boy. Anyone who hopes to fly surely does that, and even more so anyone who hopes to build airplanes. Did he or anyone ever try to design a craft that flowed within the air the way these ravens do, I wonder. I know that later, when he was training young aviators, my father encouraged them to learn gliding. Flying without a powerful motor, or with no motor at all, requires an understanding of wind and air currents.

My father's first ANBO was lightweight, its wood-framed wings covered with canvas. It certainly had more in common with a bird than with the U.S. Navy Blue Angels' aircraft, for example, which roar across our city once a year and inspire today's children who dream of flying.

The Blue Angels come as conquerors. They blaze through the air. Their roar sets dogs to howling, and in their wake a stinking trail of fuel exhaust drifts down on city and bay. I have to admit that they also thrill me with their power and daring. I do admire their precise maneuvers. But it seems to me that progress in aviation could have taken a different course, one more in tune with the birds, were it not for a human preference for brute force over harmony with the elements. The most valuable advances in aviation came in developing aircraft for war. Although perhaps this is not at the end of our story. Some brilliant dreamer may one day build a plane with a flexible body and wings, an aircraft that moves like a heron or pelican, falcon or stork. Why not?

I know nothing of aeronautics; it's brash to fantasize in ignorance. But like most of us, probably, I dream of flying. Sometimes I watch hang gliders take to the air over the ocean, here in the city, off the sea bluffs of old Fort Funston. Harnessed to the glider, legs tucked into a pod, they jump off the bluff and morph into human dragonflies with giant wings. Hands on a horizontal bar in front of them, they steer by moving it and shifting their tails. What joy that must bring, to be airborne, with only the sound of wind and surf flowing past your ears. One day I saw a wheelchair at the top of the takeoff bluff. Someone was left paraplegic after a crash, but he still flies.

Hang gliders have a limited range, of course, and they depend on the wind. And you can't make war with dragonflies, human or otherwise; they're only good for experiencing unity with natural forces. For killing, what's now popular is the drone—not the drone that tends to the queen bee so all in the hive can have honey, no, the kind that is controlled by a stick from as far away as across a continent and an ocean. No sentient being is aboard such a craft as it rains death on command.

Time to descend. I turn in the four directions and say a silent thank-you for the morning.

➤ ➤ ➤

YET ANOTHER DAY, at 3:30 p.m., the wind atop Twin Peaks is so powerful it scares me—I'm all alone and so exposed up here.

Down below, in the city, power drills are tearing up streets to repair long-neglected gas pipes. Excavators are digging under hoisted-up Victorian houses to make new rooms and garages. The harsh sounds drown out birdsong.

This wind, it's huge. It shoots out spirits, the way a forest fire shoots out flames. I can almost see them coming at me; their shapes are familiar from my childhood fairy-tale books. Their voices—there are several—are almost human. I can't make out any words, but they are kvetching. Annoyed, impatient. I'm glad to leave the peaks and return to the sunny urban valley. I'll brew some lavender mint tea when I get home.

19

THE ANBO SQUADRON

I n July 2016, I took my daughter and grandson to Lithuania, to introduce them to the country and people they knew only from what I had told them and what they had seen in photographs. I had wanted to do that for years, but the time had never seemed right. My previous trips had been driven by my mission to learn all I could about my father and his fate. I did not want to take them to any of the dark places I had to visit. But now it was high time. I was eighty-two years old.

Jaden was eleven, a year older than I was when we fled in 1944, old enough to observe and retain strong impressions. His great-grandfather would have been pleased with him, for he was a thoughtful, kind, and perceptive boy who enjoyed mathematics and liked to build things that moved. As for Usha, my daughter, I knew she had been waiting to be asked to come.

I worried a bit as we prepared for the journey. We would have to speak English. It was shameful that I, a daughter of Antanas Gustaitis, had not taught them Lithuanian, but too late now to do anything about that. They would get by. I did not know how many of the relatives spoke English, but surely the younger ones did; they were learning it in school. They would probably be glad to practice by talking with Usha and Jaden.

Still, knowing even a few words in a foreign country you're visiting will ease the traveler's way almost anywhere. So I made a few flash cards and corralled Usha and Jaden at my dining room table for some elementary lessons.

"*Labas* . . . hello." I held up a card.

"*Labas,*" in unison.

"*Malonu*. That means it's pleasant, or it's a pleasure. You say that when you meet someone. You shake hands and say *Malonu*."

"*Malonu*." I was thrilled, hearing them speak the Lithuanian words.

"*Gerą dieną* . . . good day. . . .

"*Gerą vakarą* . . . good evening. . . .

"*Gerai* . . . good. . . .

"*Prašau* . . .

"*Ačiū* . . .

"Jaden, your pronunciation is perfect!"

"I like the sounds," he said. Pure delight for his grandmother's ears!

"Enough for today. *Iki*. That's *ciao*, or see you later. Oh, one more:

"*Puiku* . . . wonderful."

"*Malonu*," Usha replied.

I COULDN'T SLEEP the night before our early-morning departure. I was excited but also fearful. Lying in bed in the dark, listening to the old grandfather clock ticking away the hours left before the alarm went off, I let my mind ramble, trying to understand. It seemed that something fragile and dear to me was threatened. I realized that by bringing my American daughter and grandson to the land from which I came, I was giving up a secret place that on some level I wanted to keep to myself, the Lietuva that would never be Lithuania, the untranslatable home of my nostalgia for a place lost in childhood. Each time I had returned to the land of my birth, where I spoke the language, memory rushed into me and became part of who I had become. I was both restored to wholeness and once more divided. We who have been uprooted, so many millions of us around the world, are all this way, I suspect.

For some reason, I thought of Laura's collection in Tennessee Williams's *The Glass Menagerie*. But why? Many decades had passed since I saw that play. At the time, I had felt a kinship with Laura, the fragile, lonely child-woman who escaped from her miserable life into an imagined world by means of glass figurines. What had brought Laura's menagerie to mind now?

I too had treasured some glass animals, the ones I carried with me into exile in 1944. What happened to most of them I had no idea; somehow they were lost along the way. Only the translucent polar bear remained. I had given it to Usha some years back and had forgotten about it until one day, as I was beginning to write this family story, she put it in front of me on my desk.

"Here, Mom," she said, "maybe this will help you."

As I remembered that moment, lying in my bed in the dark, love for my beautiful daughter swept away my anxiety.

It was almost dawn, almost time to get up. The ghosts had disappeared with the night and excitement took over. I was about to share my Lithuania with Usha and Jaden—the real, living Lithuania, which the three of us would explore together.

And after this journey is over and the story is told, I thought, I would return that little glass bear to her.

ARMINDAS AND VIDA met us at the airport in Palanga. We drove through the little resort town, past gabled houses painted in blue and green and warm hues of ochre, gold, and brown; then through the business district, where shop windows displayed stylish clothing and local craftsmen sat in sidewalk booths draped with amber necklaces for sale. We passed a square, a church, and then turned into a wide street shaded by tall maple trees, along which the houses were set back behind trees and lawns. Armindas turned left at the edge of a pine forest and pulled up in front of a modern three-story apartment house built of earth-toned bricks, with balconies and large windows.

"Look, Jaden, your great-grandfather's airplane!" Usha called out.

She had spotted the sign on the wall beside the entry: a little plane, carved into a plaque, and next to it the words "Vila ANBO."

The villa fronted on the pine forest, a city park. It was surrounded by a lawn and ringed by pines and maples that screened it from other buildings. To the right of the entry a brilliant red canna flower caught my eye. We have a cluster of them in our garden in San Francisco, but I was surprised to see it here, so much farther north. No doubt it came from the nursery of Vida's brother Jonas, I thought.

The door opened. Vida's husband, Stasys, and their son Povilas emerged to welcome us with handshakes and warm embraces. Jaden said, "*Labai malonu.*"

The men took our bags and led us inside. The family lived on the first floor, renting apartments on the upper floors to vacationers during the summer season.

As we took off our shoes and entered the apartment where we would be staying, on the second floor, I saw Usha's face light up. Whatever she might have expected on her first trip to her mother's "old country," it was not this airy light-filled space, which could well have been featured in a glossy magazine as a model of contemporary

Nordic design. Several windows framed in light natural wood looked out at pines on three sides. On the fourth side, a spiral staircase led to a loft.

"Povilas built that," said Vida. "This is his place, except when it's rented out during the summer. Maybe Jaden would like to sleep up there."

Povilas, the younger of Vida and Stasys's two sons, managed the vacation rental business with his parents. Seeing him now, I was startled by his physical resemblance to my father, with his deep-set blue eyes, high forehead, and roundish face. I first met him in 1989, when he was a little boy. He would be in his midthirties now.

"Rest a while—come down when you want to," said Stasys.

"Perhaps you'd like to eat something? Or some tea?" Vida offered. "Or would you like to take a swim first? It's only a five-minute walk to the beach."

I translated for Jaden and Usha. The beach, of course.

"Povilas will go with you," said Vida. "Raselė is also by the sea, with the two boys. She's also vacationing here this week with her family. I'll phone her and she'll find you. They usually go farther up the shore, where there aren't so many people."

Raselė was the only relative Usha and Jaden had already met, although only briefly. Several months before, she had come to San Francisco to attend a medical conference. She and Armindas spoke English, as did their two teenage sons, Tomas and Paulius. We would be spending quite a bit of time together later.

Vida and Stasys left us so we could get ready. Before putting on our bathing suits we took a closer look at our elegant lodgings. Jaden climbed up into the loft, considered sleeping up there, under the skylight, so he could see the stars, but decided that it would be cozier down below, nearer to his mom.

Usha loved the light gray parquet floor—its soft gleam that didn't shine, the way it felt under her feet.

"Warm," she said.

The wood, ash, had been oiled and polished but not varnished. As a yoga teacher, Usha spent a lot of time on floors, and she knew when one felt good.

Like Goldilocks in the kitchen of the Three Bears, we peeked into cupboards, and found them well stocked.

Coffee, cookies, and crackers, a charming hexagonal cardboard box containing six kinds of herbal tea, each with a romantic name in Lithuanian: "Strawberry Dawn, Raising the Sun from the Dew," "Lazy Cinnamon Afternoon in the Apple Orchard," "Raspberry Evening, Drenching the Heart with Honey."

In the refrigerator we found milk, several single-portion containers of yogurt topped with granola—just what a health-conscious young person would look for in the United States. All the food items were produced in Lithuania and labeled "*biologique,*" which is the European Union equivalent of the American "organic" label. In the bathroom, too, the shampoo and conditioner, soap, face cream, and toothpaste were all attractively packaged, organic, and Lithuanian. And these were not the miniature cosmetics one gets in good hotels; they were the size you'd buy for your own home.

Long ago, our ancestors used to greet guests at the door with bread and salt. But these gifts went beyond the requirements of traditional hospitality. They reflected Vida's warmth and generosity.

I was continuously astonished and delighted at the wide variety of organic items now being produced in my native country. During my first return to Lithuania, in 1989, I had visited a pharmacy where all the shelves were bare. The pharmacist, a woman in a white coat, told me she had only one product for sale: a small tin of Tiger Balm from North Vietnam. I bought it. Now there seemed to be a well-stocked pharmacy on every street corner, carrying a wide variety of medicines, health products, and cosmetics.

When we came downstairs, wearing bathing suits under shirts and pants, Povilas was waiting. From Vila ANBO, the pathway to the beach took us past the adjacent multistory hotel to Love's Lane, a pedestrian and bicycle pathway that ran behind the willow and pine thickets of the dunes, parallel to the shore. From the other side of Love's Lane, a narrow boardwalk led across the dunes to the beach. I stopped and let the young people go ahead, for I wanted to take in everything slowly, with all my senses. This was my fifth trip to Lithuania, but being here continued to be wondrous. It would take a while to become real.

Walking along the boardwalk I noticed, with pleasure, that the dunes were far more carefully protected here than in any California beach town I had visited. Willows and pines held sand in place and captured fierce winds that blew in from the beach. Low fences made from loosely woven willow branches had been installed here and there, in addition, to catch blowing sand. This boardwalk, which connected to others, kept people from trampling the dunes, and helped vegetation to survive. Yet I saw no sign warning people not to stray from it. I was impressed.

When I reached the end of the boardwalk, at the beach, I was surprised to see it was rather crowded, for it was a weekday. But then it came to me: summer on the Baltic Sea is short—only about five weeks in July and August. Just about everyone goes on vacation then, and to a beach if possible.

I took off my shoes and was about to step down into the sand when my foot took me back in time. I could not have been older than five. It was a warm day, like today. I had defied my grandmother and, at this very spot or one just like it, had taken off my sandals. The sand was hot, really hot, it burned my soles. Today my soles were tough and I felt the warm sand seep between my toes pleasantly. Aging had its benefits.

Usha was sitting close to the waterline, looking out at the sea.

"Mom, let's just stay here," she said. "Let's not go anywhere else."

Jaden was in the water, swimming with Povilas, who also spoke good English, having studied in Ireland. When Raselė, Armindas, and their two sons joined us, Jaden and Usha no longer needed my translation services. The boys had learned English in school, and on the internet. Their parents were multilingual.

THE DAYS PASSED seamlessly, flowing hour to hour with no intrusion of clocks or appointments, no set times for anything, one delightful experience melting into the next, punctuated by leisurely conversations around the dining table.

We drifted from beach to town to places familiar to me from childhood that I wanted to share with my offspring. And we sat around Vida's table, talking and laughing.

Raselė took Usha and me to a fish dealer for smoked salmon and to the farmers market for wild mushrooms, honey, and hand-crafted gifts, while Jaden and his cousins tooled around on bicycles. The beach called to us in the morning, the woods in the afternoon, just as had been true when I was a child. The remembered past kept coming to mind, then dissolving in the sound of today's bright young voices. In this country, the past is never truly gone—it keeps slipping into the present through cracks in time.

JUST BEFORE SUNSET on our first day, drawn to the beach one more time, I seemed to see my parents walking arm in arm along the shore, toward the long pier, called the Bridge, where people used to stroll on summer evenings then—and continue to do so now. Mama was wearing a loose white summer dress, and a fringed, patterned scarf was wrapped around her head in the style of the 1920s. I could not see my father quite so clearly, but he was with her.

We meandered down Love's Lane to the National Amber Museum, in the restored palace of Count Tiškevičius, built in 1987 and surrounded by a formal garden that is now part of the Palanga Botanical Garden. In front of the grand staircase of the palace a bronze statue of Eglė, Queen of Serpents, stands in a pool, splashed by water.

During the summer season, every Thursday actors dressed as people from the late nineteenth century stroll about the grounds late in the afternoon. The second day of our visit in Palanga fell on a Thursday, so we went to look. As we approached the palace, a horse-drawn carriage filled with merrymakers passed at the edge of the woods beyond the formal lawn. Closer by, a couple strolled, arm in arm, across the grass, he in a tall hat and a formal jacket with tails, swinging a cane; she serenely erect in a long gray dress, a black cape over her shoulders. They were not performing anything; they were just here, among the vacationers flushed from their day in the sun, but apart, in their own time, making no contact with those of us here in the present.

Usha laughed and raised her camera at the sight of a nursemaid in starched white cap and white ruffled apron wheeling a baby in a perambulator, passing a woman in shorts with her child in a stroller. Boys from a century ago ran across the grass. A little girl in a starched white pinafore appeared, pursued by another nursemaid.

Lithuanians honor the past. They mourn it, they celebrate it, and play with it. They relive it. They love historical pageants and processions. In this country, the past is never separate from their present.

We moved on into the Amber Museum, where we admired a rich collection of jewelry and other items crafted from the fossilized resin found on the shores of the Baltic Sea. The museum collection of some twenty-eight thousand pieces includes ancient necklaces and elegantly designed contemporary jewelry. I doubt there is a single woman in the country who does not own something made of amber.

Around the table in the evening, the family talked about Lukas, one of Aldona's grandchildren, due back in a few days from an expedition known as Mission Siberia, which was visiting a former gulag site at Igarka, north of the Arctic Circle. Everyone was proud of Lukas—not only the family but the whole local community. Mission Siberia is an effort to make sure historical memory stays alive and to maintain a link between the present and the past.

Toward those ends, this was the sixteenth summer that groups of young men and women traveled to remote forced-labor sites in Siberia where Lithuanians endured or died during Stalin's time. The young volunteers mend cemetery fences, replace broken or rotten crosses on graves, and visit fellow countrymen who remained, by choice or necessity, after the others returned to their homeland after Stalin's demise. Candidates for this hard-labor expedition are selected for their capacity for endurance and other personal qualities, and must pass a challenging wilderness survival test. Lukas did well. He's an agronomy student and a farmer.

"This year there were eight hundred applications," Povilas said. "Lukas is one of only sixteen who got to go."

Vida left the table and returned a moment later with a clipping from the local *Farmer's Advisor*. A photo on the front page showed Lukas, the local boy, squatting behind a cluster of wheat stalks and inspecting them.

"We'll bring him here to Palanga for a couple of days to recover, then we're going on a trip the other way—Sweden, Copenhagen," said Armindas, who was to lead the four-day excursion, taking his sons, Povilas and Lukas. They also had tickets to a Kanye West concert in Warsaw. Talk about time travel!

➤ ➤ ➤

OUR THREE DAYS in Palanga were over all too soon. On our fourth morning in Lithuania, Raselė would take us to Kaunas, the city where I was born, where my ninety-six-year-old cousin, the oldest, was expecting our visit. I looked forward to seeing her and her daughter, but not so much to another, mandatory, stop in the city, at the Vytautas the Great War Museum, where my father's first ANBO was exhibited. Or rather, it would be more accurate to say that it was stored there, for it was impossible to actually see the whole plane, suspended as it was above a huge glass case that blocked a full view.

The glass case contained the wreck of the *Lituanica*, the aircraft flown in 1933 by Darius and Girėnas from New York across the Atlantic, crashing in a German forest just six hundred kilometers from their destination, Kaunas. The case had been manufactured in Czechoslovakia according to incorrect specifications, a museum official had explained. But there was no explanation for the placement of the ANBO above it, where it was only partly visible. I had been shocked and angry on a previous visit, when I saw my father's first aircraft so poorly installed, but nevertheless felt obliged to take Usha and Jaden to it.

"You may be interested in stopping at the airfield in Počiūnai," Povilas said before we left Palanga with Raselė. "There's a man there who has almost completed building a copy of the ANBO II. He will show it to you if you can get there before ten in the morning. After that he'll be busy with an international gliding competition, which starts at noon."

"I wish we could," I replied. "But there will be no time tomorrow."

"We will make time; it's not far from Kaunas," put in Stasys, who was to take charge of us the next day.

➤ ➤ ➤

OUR TIME IN Lithuania was almost over. Its purpose, to introduce Usha and Jaden to my native land and their relatives, had been accomplished. I know they wished they had learned a bit more of the language before coming, but they put to good use the few words they had: *Ačiū. Labai malonu buvo. Sudiev.* Thank you. It was lovely. Goodbye. The hugs and kisses needed no translation.

When Aldona and I said goodbye—both of us aware that it could well be for the last time—she put her hands on my shoulders, looked into my eyes, and said, "We will see each other again. If not here, then elsewhere."

The way she said it, almost laughing, lightened my heart. And yet her life had been so full of sorrow. I remembered what her tragically ill eldest son, Viktoras, had said when we parted after a previous visit: "Do not think of me. Think of the oak tree brought back from Siberia that took root here and flourished."

He had been the most gifted of Aldona's children, so cruelly struck down by illness, mercifully at rest now in the family plot. His room remains empty. His mother won't go in.

"Why should I? It's the room of suffering," she explains.

WHEN STASYS ARRIVED at the hotel where we were staying in Kaunas the next morning, the rain had stopped. He drove with us into the sunny countryside, past woodlands and pastures. Some newly mowed fields were strewn with bundles of hay wrapped in white plastic. The kind of harvesting I remembered, with scythes, pitchforks, and horse-drawn wagons, ended long ago, as did the kind practiced during Soviet times at collective farms, when huge mounds of cut grass were sometimes left to rot in the rain. Now here was the Lithuanian harvest, just as in other modern countries, bundled in plastic, ready for mechanized pickup.

At ten a.m., as scheduled, we arrived at Počiūnai Airfield, thirty-eight kilometers southeast of Kaunas, a grass field surrounded by forest, one of some thirty "green airfields" serving villages and towns throughout Lithuania. This one was well known as the site of international gliding competitions. One was being held today. Dozens of gliders stood on the grass, lined up, ready for takeoff at noon, weather permitting. I saw them as we parked next to a small hangar, but a moment later forgot them as my gaze was captured by what was immediately before me.

Inside the small white hangar, open in front, stood the second airplane my father had built, in 1927, while home for vacation from his studies of aeronautical engineering in Paris.

With Rolandas Kalinauskas and his nearly completed copy of the ANBO II.
Photo of my father with the original plane in the background.

For a moment I was disoriented. I had seen it only in black-and-white photographs. Here it was in full color and three dimensions, a two-seater monoplane, open cockpit, body silver and brown, a propeller of polished wood. Still unfinished, it lacked wings. Of course this was the reproduction we had come to see, but looking at it I felt caught in a twist of time somewhere between now and the past.

From the hangar, a man was coming to meet us. He was decades older than my father had been when he built this airplane, but seemed to be of about my father's height and had his compact build. It was Rolandas Kalinauskas, the retired aviation engineer and test pilot who was reconstructing this airplane. He had a hearty, energetic look about him. His weathered face suggested a good-natured disposition, and his handshake was warm.

As we entered the hangar we were met by another man, tall and slim, with a merry look in his eyes and a wide smile. He was wearing the dark blue uniform of a Lithuanian airman from my father's time, with a jaunty cap on his head, two rows of metal buttons across his chest, insignia on the lapels.

He took us up in a plane he had built, the Volungė.

"As long as we were going to build the airplane," he explained, "we decided to have uniforms made too."

Soon I too was smiling, in happy disbelief. But perhaps the proper attitude here would have been to suspend disbelief, as one does in theater. This hangar, built of canvas stretched over a metal frame, could be a stage, set for the performance of a play set in the 1920s. The legendary hero, a young man, never appears but somehow manifests or is channeled. We have come to watch, but learned that audience participation is required, so we too are part of this play.

I walked around the aircraft with Kalinauskas, Usha, and Jaden, sliding my hands over the wooden propeller, peering inside the open cockpit.

"It's almost ready," Kalinauskas said. "We have the wings— there, against the wall—and only need to attach them and finish a few more things. In a few weeks we will present it to the public at an air show. It's not a replica, because we had no drawings. We worked from photographs and had to improvise."

Two of the photographs, blown up to poster size, were tacked to the back wall of the hangar. I knew both of them. In one, which I've also seen in books, the ANBO is making a turn high above Kaunas and the river Nemunas. In the other, my father stands beside the plane, his round, smiling face framed by a leather aviator helmet, ear-flaps hanging down, his right hand tucked into his leather jacket at waist level, Napoleon-style. He is young, posing playfully.

This was my younger sister's favorite photograph of our father. She kept it atop the piano in her living room, framed in silver. It was kind of a shock to see here, blown up giant-size, tacked to a wall. But how marvelous, really. How refreshing. Liberating. The tall pilot tucked his right hand into his jacket, Gustaitis-style. We laughed.

"Once I photoshopped my own face into that picture," said Kalinauskas. "*Rolandas irgi nori būti ore.*" Rolandas also wants to be in the air.

▶ ▶ ▶

BUILDING THE REPRODUCTION was definitely fun, but at the same time also a serious endeavor. Kalinauskas and members of the ANBO Squadron, an informal group of engineers and aircraft builders, want to "bring her wings back to Lithuania."

The country's aviation history ended with the ANBO VIII. Since the beginning of World War II, no more airplanes have been built in Lithuania. Yet Lithuanians have continued to yearn to fly.

Kalinauskas said that he and his allies in the ANBO Squadron intend to rebuild as many as possible of my father's airplanes, fly them around the country, visit festivals, demonstrate them, offer flights in them. They hope to remind Lithuanians of their aviation history and stimulate its resumption. The ANBO II is a start. They realize that to reproduce all the ANBOs is probably an impossible dream. All but the very first of my father's planes were destroyed, by either the Soviets or the Germans. The ANBO I was a museum exhibit now, out of reach. Kalinauskas said a museum official had explained that it was being saved for the next generation.

"But we are the next generation," he had protested. "We need to touch the fuselage, feel it, examine it. . . . Just like those early aviators."

Kalinauskas had fallen in love with flight early in life. As a child, he said, he lived in the country, in a place where the sight of an airplane overhead was rare and exciting. When he grew older he decided he wanted to be a pilot, but his grandmother discouraged him, saying, "They won't let you fly because you're Lithuanian." And indeed, whether for that reason or another, when he applied to the Soviet air force, he was refused. So, as he tells the story, he decided to build his own airplane and eventually did build not just one but five. Access to the air opened after Lithuania regained independence.

The idea of rebuilding the ANBO II grew out of some discussions among pilots who habitually gathered at this airfield when they had free time. As they talked about Lithuania's aviation history and its abrupt end, someone suggested they rebuild Antanas Gustaitis's ANBOs.

The group launched the ANBO Squadron with a website and the slogan "Let's return her wings to Lithuania."

There had been a previous attempt by others to replicate one of my father's planes, in honor of his hundredth birthday. But, due to lack of funding, the government instead issued two postage stamps honoring him and named the aviation institute after him.

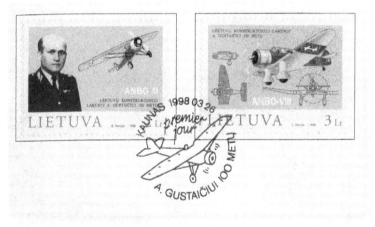

On the hundredth anniversary of the birth of Antanas Gustaitis,
Lithuania issued two postage stamps in his honor. The government also
named the nation's military aviation institute after him.

Kalinauskas and his allies dipped into their own pockets and gathered contributions from friends and sympathizers. They bought parts for the aircraft when the opportunity arose. Kalinauskas often flew to Kaunas to search for needed hardware at the flea market. As they started working on their project they found problems to solve, improvements to make, new requirements to meet.

"Now you need a radio," for example, Kalinauskas said.

The ANBO Squadron would like to build a replica of the ANBO IV, which flew around Europe in the celebrated tour in 1934, but that would take far more money than they could raise on their own.

"We already found a motor, in England," said Kalinauskas.

I turned to look for Jaden and saw that he was sitting in the pilot's seat of the ANBO, looking enormously pleased. The tall, uniformed aviator was handing him a helmet made of soft black leather.

"This one is Russian," he said. "A Lithuanian one is being made."

Jaden put it on his head. Cameras flashed, recording images of the great-grandson of Antanas Gustaitis in the pilot's seat. Then we all went outside and Kalinauskas asked, "Would you like to go up?"

"Yes!" Jaden called out.

"Yes!" echoed his mother.

Gen. Gustaitis's great-grandson getting ready to fly

Kalinauskas led us to one of the airplanes he had designed and built, the *Volungė,* a four-seater standing near the hangar, ready for flight. We climbed in, with Usha and Jaden in back, me in the co-pilot's seat. Moments later the propeller chugged and turned and we were rolling.

I had never flown with my father. Now I summoned all my senses and imagined it was he who was the pilot. I was seeing what he had seen, taking off from green fields not much different from this one. We lifted off, rose toward the sky, and soon were crossing the shining, slowly winding Nemunas River. The checkered green landscape of fields and forests was expanding below us.

"That's my home," said Kalinauskas, pointing down at a red house, with a barn next to it, at the edge of a woodland near the airfield.

"That's where I built the ANBO."

Later, Usha would tell me, "When we started rising above the green countryside—it was very emotional for me. I felt for the first time that something in me—that I belonged here."

After we touched ground again, Kalinauskas sighed.

"Ah," he said, "we have caught the aviation disease and we'll never be cured."

Back in the hangar, a journalist stood, with a video camera mounted on a tripod, waiting to interview me. The visit of a daughter, granddaughter, and great-grandson of Antanas Gustaitis to the ANBO reconstruction project was a news item. I was glad to be wearing an elegant skirt and blouse from a designer shop in Palanga. Mama would have approved.

When I stepped in front of the microphone I was intoxicated, giddy, and also aware that Jaden was seeing his grandmother, the one who sometimes made pancakes for breakfast, in another capacity. I said I was delighted to have met these heirs to Lithuania's extraordinary aviation history. I said I had dreaded taking my daughter and grandson to the War Museum to see the ANBO I because it was so poorly displayed that one could only partly see it, stuck high above a glass case enclosing the wreck of the *Lituanica*.

"But now I don't need to take them there," I said. "Let the ANBO I be a relic, preserved in the museum, inaccessible right now—but surely not forever. Today, here, we have the living legacy of my father's work among these aviators who, like him, have a passion for flying and for building the wings to get them up into the air."

JADEN CAME AWAY with an invitation. Before we left the ANBO aficionados, Kalinauskas had taken him aside, led him to a small glider, and gestured that he should get in.

"It's a bit beat up," he said, "because fifty children have learned to fly in it. They can start learning when they're nine."

"Maybe when you are nineteen, or sooner, you will come for a summer," added Stasys. "Spend one month in Palanga, one month in Sasnava, and one month in Vilnius with the family, and you'll learn Lithuanian."

"So we will expect you," said Kalinauskas, looking into Jaden's eyes. "Will you return?"

"I will," he answered solemnly as they shook hands.

An invitation to come back, learn to glide

I don't know. He might or he might not. Nobody should be held to such a declaration made at age eleven. But my heart fluttered nonetheless. I think, and hope, that this morning with the ANBO Squadron, and the visit to his great-grandparents' land, may have given him a new and wider sense of belonging, expanding his vision of himself and the world and helping him to find his rightful place in it.

As we made our way toward lunch with relatives in Sasnava village, the glider competition was getting under way, with 133 flyers from twenty-nine countries competing. Airplanes pulled them up into the air by a rope, then released them to continue north on their own all the way to Estonia, due back this same day. Some of these graceful, silent aircraft seemed to be accompanying us, while at least one was trailed by a stork.

IT'S DONE. I'M back home in San Francisco, swaying in a space between my familiar world and one of memory enhanced by new experiences. I know I belong where I am, here in Northern California. Yet like most, perhaps all, who have been forced to leave their native country, I will always retain a painful longing for my original homeland.

Those magical days in Lithuania are already drifting away, like an island detaching from the continent where I've been living most of my life. Now it's time for me to write in English again, even though the sound of my beloved first language still rings inside my head.

As I start to unpack my suitcase, I pick up the blouse I wore for the goodbye dinner at Raselė's house in Vilnius. I lift it to my face and inhale the fragrances of my Lithuania. For another few days the aromas of sea air, fresh grass, and apples will hold me here, between my two worlds.

EPILOGUE

My mother, Bronė Gustaitienė, passed from this world just before dawn on July 12, 1998. She had celebrated her hundredth birthday the previous November and had been praying to Holy Mary to come for her. I sat by her bed, looking out the window, and asking the Mother of God to take her. Through the window I saw a white cloud rolling toward us along the ground through the trees in the adjacent schoolyard. And I felt the joyous spirit of a young woman rise, like a wisp of white mist, right in front of me.

In a film made in Lithuania to celebrate the hundredth birthday of Antanas Gustaitis, there's a glimpse of my parents dancing at a ball. It's just a glimpse, but enough to bring the moment to life for me. They are both so full of love and pride in each other, enveloped in each other. He's firmly built, wide-chested, physical. He feels her breathing and her movements. She's in a white dress, slim and graceful, so happy to have his left arm around her waist, her right hand in his left. Her other hand, on his shoulder, feels rough cloth and protection, and she's glad to be led across the floor in a waltz. People are watching them, but they only see each other, navigating gracefully, strong and independent together. If lovers can be reunited in the afterlife, then surely these two deserve to be.

On the evening before our mother's death, my sister Elena had been walking at sunset on a beach in Oregon. She noticed a small airplane above the ocean, flying south.

The First Sun

The first Sun asked
The world's first Life:
"Who are you"
No answer.

Years passed.
The last Sun
asked
the last question from the western ocean
on a soundless evening:
"Who are you?"
No answer.

Calcutta
Morning / 27 July 1941
Rabindranath Tagore

ACKNOWLEDGMENTS

To write this story I drew on information published about Antanas Gustaitis in Lithuania and the Lithuanian press in the United
States. I had help from veteran aviators, especially Jonas Balčiūnas
and Viktoras Ašmenskas, whom I met in Lithuania, and from historians, journalists, and others who had studied my father's life and
achievements. The vivid memoirs of Leonardas Peseckas and Simas
Stanaitis brought the early days of aviation in Lithuania to life for me.

I'm grateful to Algirdas Gamziukas for his biography, *Antanas
Norėjo Būti Ore* (*Antanas Wanted to Be in the Air*), published by Lithuania's Technical Museum (now the Aviation Museum) in Kaunas
in 1997. For the account of events that climaxed on March 11, 1990,
in the Act of the Reestablishment of the State of Lithuania, I relied
on Vytautas Landsbergis's *Lūžis Prie Baltijos, Politinė Autobiografija*
(*Break on the Baltic, a Political Autobiography*) and news media. Timothy Snyder's book *Bloodlands* expanded my understanding of the
horrors of World War II.

Staff at Lithuania's Aviation Museum in Kaunas, and of Lithuania's Central State Archive in Vilnius, especially those in the pho-

tography department, were generous with their time and attention to my quest for documents and photographs. At the Gymnasium of Rygiškių Jonas in Marijampolė—the gymnasium my father attended, since renamed to honor the revered linguist Jonas Jablonskis, who was known as Rygiškių Jonas—the librarian, Snaiguolė Raguckienė, shared her knowledge of the school's history with me, and also her home.

Jonas Deltuva came with me to the Special Archive to translate the NKVD file on my father from Russian into Lithuanian. Gintautas Kačergis later translated the file for the online periodical *Plieno Sparnai* (*Steel Wings*), which is dedicated to Lithuania's aviation history. Aviation historian Mindaugas Sereičikas initiated that project for *Plieno Sparnai* and responded to many of my questions. My friend Danutė Janutienė provided much patient support, for years, especially with language. Milton Viorst helped me to travel to Lithuania in 1989 and encouraged me to write my father's story.

During each of my five journeys to my native land, my cousins and their children and grandchildren welcomed me into their homes and guided me through historical and contemporary Lithuania. My daughter, grandson, and I experienced lovely days in Palanga with Vida Daugelienė, her husband Stasys Daugela, and their son Povilas Daugela. Rasa (Raselė) Varkalienė and her family were generous hosts and guides, especially in Vilnius, as were Jonas Deltuva and Laima Deltuvienė. Lina Grigonienė shared her home. Rūta Paltanavičienė led me through today's Marijampolė. A visit with Rolandas Kalinauskas was an unexpected delight. Thanks also to photographer Petras Lozda for his generosity.

Throughout the years that I worked on this memoir, Mary Jo McConahay and Jean Molesky-Poz offered helpful commentary during weekly sessions in which we discussed the writing each of us was doing. Anne Canright, dear friend and outstanding editor, read and gently improved the manuscript. Alan Rinzler, editor of my first book, *Turning On*, has my appreciation for his work on this one. Thanks to Elina Cohen for designing the book, and to Laura Duffy for the cover. Leslie Tilley alerted me to errors, double-checked historical facts, and smoothed awkwardly worded sentences. Proofreader Amy J. Schneider captured errors in the edited text. Any that remain are the author's. My daughter Usha, my two sisters, Jūratė Moriartey and Elena Gustaitis, and Elena's daughter Antonia all helped in my efforts to reconstruct memories and experiences through words. Thanks to my grandson Jaden Korinthias for technical assistance.

I hope that *Flight* opens a small window into the history of the small country on the Baltic Sea from which I came, and that it resonates with others who arrived in the United States as refugees.

ABOUT THE AUTHOR

RASA GUSTAITIS has worked as a journalist for more than sixty years, starting as a cityside reporter at the *Washington Post* in 1960, after graduating from the Columbia University Graduate School of Journalism. She moved on to the *New York Herald Tribune*, a great paper that folded ten months after she arrived, in 1965. Since then she has been an editor and writer at the Pacific News Service, has taught journalism at San Francisco State University and the University of California, Berkeley, and has written for numerous magazines.

Her first book, *Turning On* (1968, Macmillan), explored changing lifestyles linked to psychedelic experiences and Eastern philosophies. It took her to San Francisco, where she settled in 1968. In *Wholly Round* (1973, Holt, Rinehart and Winston), she delved into the ecology movement of the late 1960s and early 1970s. *A Time to Be Born, A Time to Die: Conflicts and Ethics in an Intensive Care Nursery* (1986, Addison-Wesley), co-authored with Ernlé Young, took an intimate look at the effects of neonatal technology on the lives of extremely frail newborns. It grew out of a study Gustaitis undertook while she was a Professional Journalism Fellow at Stanford University in 1983–84. From 1986 through 2005, Gustaitis was the editor of *California Coast & Ocean*, a quarterly magazine dedicated to conservation issues along California's coast.

CPSIA information can be obtained
at www.ICGtesting.com
Printed in the USA
LVHW010426040822
725114LV00003B/212